EAST GERMAN DISSIDENTS
AND THE REVOLUTION OF 1989

East German Dissidents and the Revolution of 1989

Social Movement in a Leninist Regime

Christian Joppke

*Associate Professor
and Jean Monnet Fellow
Department of Political and Social Sciences
European University Institute, Florence*

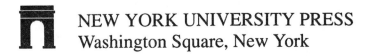 NEW YORK UNIVERSITY PRESS
Washington Square, New York

© Christian Joppke 1995

First published in the U.S.A. in 1995 by
NEW YORK UNIVERSITY PRESS
Washington Square
New York, N.Y. 10003

Library of Congress Cataloging-in-Publication Data
Joppke, Christian.
East German dissidents and the revolution of 1989 : social movement in a
Leninist regime / Christian Joppke.
p.   cm.
Includes bibliographical references and index.
ISBN 0–8147–4219–X — ISBN 0–8147–4220–3 (pbk.)
1. Opposition (Political science)—Germany—East—History.
2. Germany (East)—Politics and government—1989–1990.   3. German
reunification question (1949–1990)   4. Socialism—Germany (East)–
–History.   I. Title.
D289.J67   1995
843. 087—dc20
                                                             94–12762
                                                               CIP

Printed in Great Britain

Contents

Since he has chosen its side,
he is bound up with this fragile republic,
its prosperity is his,
but also its ruin.

Stefan Heym

Introduction

In 1976, Polish dissident Adam Michnik, in his short but influential essay *A New Evolutionism*, outlined a new program of opposition politics in communist regimes.[1] Reflecting on the failure of "revisionist" attempts to reform communism on its own grounds, Michnik opts for a new departure: "In my opinion, an unceasing struggle for ... an expansion of civil liberties and human rights is the only course East European dissidents can take" (Michnik, 1985:142). In his equally celebrated indictment of "real socialism," *The Alternative*, East German dissident Rudolf Bahro dismissed the new emphasis on rights and pluralism as "obsessions" of the intellectuals, and he pleaded instead for a reform of the ruling party and a return to the original goals of the communist revolution.[2]

These differing statements, issued almost simultaneously by two equally famous critics of communist rule, point to the puzzle that this book seeks to explore. Whereas Eastern European dissidents gradually abandoned the hope of a reformed communism and thus prepared and anticipated the revolutions of 1989, East German dissidents continued to lead a struggle for the reform, rather than the end, of communism. This book investigates the causes and implications of this anomaly. The normative assumption underlying this investigation is that the turn of Eastern European dissident movements to human rights dissidence represented an important advance over previous forms of opposition in communist systems. As a result of a long and arduous learning process, Eastern European dissidents learned to see communist regimes for what they were: Leninist dictatorships, irreformable in principle, and at odds with the pluralism of interests and the differentiation of spheres and functions in a modern society. In abrogating utopia and opting for what Poles called a "normal society" with the rule of law, pluralism, and a market economy, Eastern European dissidents laid the intellectual foundation for the revolutions of 1989, which were fought not on behalf of a grandiose new scheme but for a return to history and "normality."[3] If the insidious distinction between capitalism and socialism had haunted much of twentieth-century politics, the Eastern European revolutions reinstated Karl Popper's insight that the more fundamental distinction was the one between open and closed societies.

Put in simple terms, the story of this book is the story of an insight that failed to come in East Germany. To be sure, the notion of insight may appear risky in this context, because it conveys the existence of an unchanging objective "truth," and thus confounds the more appropriate view of historical reality as at any given time contingent and dependent on our interpretations of it. But could we imagine the existence of a second Germany today, democratic *and* socialist, pluralistic *and* committed to utopia, in a world that had meanwhile recognized that there is no alternative to a secular society where interest conflict is regulated rather than abolished? Absurd or unlikely as it seems in retrospect, such a second Germany, open yet socialist, is exactly what East German dissidents were trying to achieve, as we know, in vain.[4] Alone among the Eastern European dissident movements, whose leaders attained prominent roles in the post-communist reconstruction of their societies, the East German movement sees itself as the loser of 1989. The fall of communism was not welcomed here as, however fragile and precarious, a victory of liberty; instead, it was denounced as the imposition of capitalism and predatory colonization by the western part of the divided nation. Because this perception is still widely shared by East (and West) German intellectuals and continues to contaminate the political and intellectual life of Germany today, an examination of its roots is of more than academic interest.

What accounts for the stubborn commitment of East German dissidents to the "revisionist" reform of communism? To answer this question, one must first realize what political opposition in the communist half of the divided German nation could possibly mean. If one questioned, in Eastern European dissident manner, the constitutive principles and ideology of communism, one questioned the very existence of East Germany as a separate state. In divided Germany, the functional equivalent to "dissidence" proper was to exit to the West, where citizenship rights and a civil society were already in place. Exit, however, could be taken only individually, thus neutralizing the political articulation of the underlying disaffection with communism. Most importantly, because political opposition in East Germany was premised on rejecting the exit option, it had to imply a paradoxical loyalty to the opposed regime. As the following chapters will show, Albert Hirschman's (1970) theory of "exit" and "voice" as alternative modes of redressing grievances in organizations and states goes a long way toward explaining some peculiarities of the East German dissident movement.

The core argument of this book, however, is that East German exceptionalism has deeper roots in German history and culture, particularly the history of nationhood and nationalism. When Eastern European dissidents abandoned the premises of communism, they began to look at their societies as national collectivities that were denied the right of self-determination, thus reinventing the "French connection" between citizenship and nationhood.[5] In East-Central Europe, the invocation of national identities allowed communism to be seen as what it was in this region – imposition by a foreign power. Nationalism was a crucial resource in the exit from communism in that it allowed communism to be seen "from the outside." Such an outside view was foreclosed to East German dissidents. When the Hungarian dissident Miklos Haraszti (1987:160) looked back to the time before communism, he saw at least traces of a "democratic past." When East German dissidents looked back, they saw a nation wiped out in total moral and military defeat. In postwar Germany, the legacy of Nazism delegitimized any positive national identifications, let alone nationalism as societal mobilization on behalf of national self-determination. On the contrary, its "anti-fascist" foundation myth equipped the East German communist regime with a legitimacy that was exceptional in Eastern Europe. At least in the view of the intellectuals, who – as elsewhere in Eastern Europe – became the main carriers of dissent and opposition, communism never lost the aura of being the adequate response to Germany's dreadful past. Nationalism is certainly the single most ambiguous political phenomenon in the modern world, and nowhere has its darker side become more viciously expressed than in Germany. Though aware of its ambiguity, this study nevertheless stresses the positive function of nationalism in bundling the grievances of societies under communism and providing an effective counter-discourse to communist rule.

Though an account of East German exceptionalism will loom large in the following chapters, this book can also be read more generally as the study of a social movement in a Leninist regime.[6] Previous studies of opposition movements in communism were mostly written from the descriptive angle of historians or area specialists, but rarely from an explicit social movement perspective.[7] My own previous work focused on social movements in liberal democracies (see Joppke, 1993), and the initial interest in undertaking the present study was to shed light on the different forms and careers of social movements in communist regimes. As I will elaborate in detail, the logic of social movements in both regime types is fundamentally different. A *first* difference concerns the typical claims and goals of social movements. In liberal democracies, which are secular, pluralist, and based on complex institutionalized rules and procedures, social movements (especially the recent "new social movements") tackle the deficit of meaning, collective control and active history-making. By contrast, Leninist regimes are themselves couched in the language of social movements, with their stress on *virtuoso* activism, change in permanence, and "generalized beliefs," which is Neil Smelser's (1962) phrase for the tendency of social movements to offer the one and simple solution to the many problems of a complex world. Leninist regimes are "movement-regimes," to use Robert Tucker's (1961) fortunate formula. Against this backdrop, the impulse of social movements is to reclaim the institutional differentiations that are denied by Leninist regimes – between private and public, state and society, culture and politics, and to escape the clutches of utopia and prescribed unity.[8] This impulse to differentiate has been most clearly expressed in the post-revisionist Eastern European dissident movements, and "dissidence" thus understood may be looked at as the most consequent form of opposition in Leninist regimes. A *second* difference concerns the typical careers and impacts of social movements. In liberal democracies, the institution of citizenship leads social movements into the direction of reform and inclusion. In Leninist regimes, which are monocratic and exclusionist, social movements by definition contradict the constitutive regime principles, and defeat, temporary truce or regime breakdown are the more likely outcomes.

In light of these different logics of social movements in both regime types, one of the most perplexing features of the East German dissident movement is its blurring of Eastern and Western social movement discourses. Influenced by the "new social movements" in the western part of the divided nation, peace, ecology and Third-Worldism became major movement issues in East Germany, whereas the Eastern European discourse of human rights dissidence had notorious difficulties in establishing itself. But the very fact that human rights dissidence did appear, however incompletely, in the late 1980s indicates that also East German dissidents could not remain blind to the specific shortcomings of a Leninist regime.

Despite this deviation from the Eastern European pattern, East German dissidents faced the typical obstacles and dilemmas that all social movements in Leninist regimes had to face, and the following chapters will elaborate on some of them in great detail. The most fundamental obstacle is the very fact that opposition in Leninist regimes is illicit and illegitimate in principle, and subject to full-blown state repression. Only in a relatively late stage of Leninist regime development, which I define with Dallin and Breslauer (1970) as the "post-mobilization" stage, do organized and sustained opposition movements become possible at all. Two implications of this basic illegitimacy of opposition will be especially highlighted. First, the viability of social movements depends on the protection by actors or institutions that for historical reasons could maintain a limited degree of autonomy and independence from party controls. In East Germany, the support of the Protestant church was instrumental in the growth and consolidation of organized dissent. But, as I will show, the Church also helped to contain and neutralize the system-threatening implications of dissent. Secondly, much more than in liberal democracies, state repression becomes a key force that shapes the dynamics of social

movements. In East Germany, where the all-German politics of *détente* put certain limits on the use of overt state
repression, the surveillance and undercover manipulation
of opposition groups by the secret police has decisively influenced the internal dynamics and trajectory of these groups
– for instance, eight of the 16 founding members of East
Germany's leading human rights group, IFM, have now been
revealed as agents of the secret police. This inquiry will lead
us into a demonological world of deceit and manipulation,
in which the boundary lines between genuine and engineered
opposition, protest and collaboration, threaten to disappear
in the mist.

Chapter 1 introduces the theoretical framework of this
study. Following Philip Selznick (1952) and Ken Jowitt (1992),
I conceive of communist systems as "Leninist regimes." Fus-
ing assumptions of totalitarianism and modernization theory,
I point to the fundamental dilemma of Leninism as a political form of modern society: the maintenance of charismatic self-definition and monocratic control in an increasingly
differentiated and pluralistic society. In a second step, I
explicate the meaning of opposition in Leninist regimes,
and develop a typology of opposition movements (revisionism, dissidence, and nationalism).

Chapter 2 draws out the specific contours of regime and
opposition in East Germany, and elaborates why East Germany was not Eastern Europe. Among the factors that made
East Germany different are the National Socialist past and
the resulting problem of national identity in divided Germany; the "anti-fascist" foundation myth that entailed the
consent of the intellectuals; and the simultaneity, rather than
succession, of mobilization and post-mobilization regime practices. In the second part, three major episodes of protest
and opposition in 1953, 1956 and 1976 are compared and
related to the further development of regime and opposition.

Chapter 3 is on the peace movement, the first sustained
opposition movement in East Germany, which established
itself in the early 1980s under the roof of the Protestant
Church. Indicative of East German exceptionalism, peace,
not human rights, became the core motive of regime opposition, thus failing to tackle the Achilles' heel of a Leninist

regime and implicitly feeding the legitimacy of East Germany's "peace state" (*Friedensstaat*). This outcome was also conditioned by an all-German culture of *détente*, which made the "securing of peace" (*Friedenssicherung*) the pivotal moral and political preoccupation of the time.

Chapter 4 is about the attempt by a leading opposition group (Initiative for Peace and Human Rights, or IFM) to turn from peace to human rights opposition, and thus to make the step from "revisionism" to "dissidence" proper. This attempt succeeded only half-way. The crucial test became the rise of a phenomenon that would eventually cause the GDR to collapse: the rise of a massive movement of would-be emigrants. In refusing to adopt the plight of would-be emigrants and to build coalitions with those whose profane desire was freedom, IFM displayed not only its implicit regime loyalty, but also failed to tap the GDR's most explosive protest potential. Because the human rights group IFM became the main target of surveillance and undercover manipulation by the secret police, this chapter also discusses the impact of these covert forms of state repression on the targeted opposition groups.

Chapter 5 analyzes the forces that caused the sudden regime breakdown in 1989. Suggesting an exit- rather than voice-driven dynamic of regime collapse, I look at the futile attempts by opposition groups such as the New Forum to steer a process utterly outside of their control. I argue that Leipzig was not by accident the center of the revolutionary upheaval: only here voice- and exit-constituencies partially collaborated, thus preparing the "joint grave-digging act" (A. Hirschman) out of which the German revolution was made.

Chapter 6 comes back to the core question of this study: why there was no "dissidence" proper in East Germany. It explains this outcome through a combination of historical pull and cultural push factors. With regard to the first, German history, particularly the legacy of National Socialism, delegitimized nationalism as a counter-discourse to communist rule. With regard to the second, socialism had indigenous roots in German culture, which could be uniquely preserved in a regime that defined itself in these terms. This analysis suggests that a single-factor explanation of East

German exceptionalism would be incomplete, and that at different times and for different groups different factors were responsible for generating the same outcome: the unflagging commitment to the "revisionist" reform of communism.

I would like to thank Neil Smelser for his constant moral and intellectual support in the completion of this study. Various conversations with Veljko Vujacic were more stimulating than he probably realizes. A small grant by the University of Southern California facilitated the writing of Chapters 4 and 5. The final draft was prepared in the supportive atmosphere of the Center for German and European Studies at Georgetown University.

1 Social Movements in Leninist Regimes

Sidney Tarrow (1991) deplored the failure of Western social movement scholars to predict the revolutions that swept Eastern Europe in 1989.[1] On the one hand, this should not come as a surprise. Revolutions are by definition surprise events that take on the appearance of necessity only after the fact. Tocqueville's (1955:1) famous words on the French revolution, "so inevitable yet so completely unforeseen," well apply to the revolutions two centuries later. On the other hand, the neglect of social movement scholars to study movements in Leninist regimes is a serious one.[2] This may reflect that recent social movement theories are in serious ways incapable of understanding the changes in Eastern Europe. Now it becomes clear that recent theoretical paradigms such as resource mobilization or political process presuppose the existence of liberal-democratic rules and institutions, without explicitly saying so. The pragmatic give-and-take between rational actors, as depicted by resource mobilization theories (see McCarthy and Zald, 1977), models political conflict on the logic of economic exchanges – evidently reflecting the competitive and open style of conflict in the West for which there is no parallel in the East. Mobilization in Leninist regimes is the exclusive privilege of the political élite, impossibly an attribute of independent social groups. The same reservation applies to the notion of political opportunity, which is central to various political process approaches (see Tarrow, 1989). The notion of political opportunity presupposes a basic symmetry between, and legitimacy of, élites and conflict groups that align and realign themselves in shifting coalitions. This cannot be the case in Leninist regimes, where politics in the sense of legitimate interest conflict is abolished, or at least repressed.

Also the Western notion of new social movements is inappropriate to explicate the nature of social movements in Eastern Europe. Alain Touraine (1983), in particular, suggested

1

some parallels between Eastern and Western movements, both of which are seen as civil society movements that seek to contain encroachments by the bureaucratic state. This obscures the important difference that elementary citizenship rights are institutionalized in the West, while they are not in the East. The logic of conflict is essentially different in both cases: extending and deepening already existing citizenship rights, that is, reform; or introducing a new principle incompatible with the existing regime, that is, revolution. Not by accident, contemporary social movement scholarship has dropped the classic link between movement and revolution. This tacit reorientation reflects the high reform-elasticity of liberal democracies.[3]

Instead of mechanically reiterating the concepts developed for Western reform movements, we have to rethink our conceptual apparatus itself. Recent political process approaches come closest to recognizing the importance of state- and regime-structures for shaping the forms and careers of social movements (see Joppke, 1993). However, we must go one step beyond the usual comparisons within liberal democratic regimes and acknowledge the fundamental difference between types of regimes, in this case: liberal democratic and Leninist. An examination of the general features of social movements in Leninist regimes thus presupposes an explication of the nature of Leninist regimes.

The first part of this chapter discusses some character-defining elements of Leninist regimes, and draws out their implications for emergent social movements. The second and major part explicates the meaning of opposition in Leninist regimes, and outlines some typical forms and dilemmas of opposition movements. Though historically informed, the major purpose of this analysis is to clarify the logic of social movements in Leninist regimes. It will provide us with a set of concepts to draw the specific contours of regime opposition in East Germany.

LENINIST REGIMES

As Max Weber argued in his famous essay on the "objectivity" of social scientific knowledge, the theories and con-

cepts in the social sciences are eminently historical and constantly being transformed and remodeled in light of new
experiences and shifting "cultural problems" (Weber,
1973:214). The study of Soviet societies is a telling example
of the conditioning of theory change by changes of the underlying political reality. Dissatisfied with the rigidity and
political biases of the totalitarianism approach that dominated the American scene in the 1950s and 1960s, various
modernization, interest group, and complex organization approaches stressed the rationality and viability of communist
systems.[4] In this view, which became dominant at the height
of Soviet power in the 1960s and 1970s, the functional pre-
requisites of modernization could be adequately dealt with
by communist systems – communism was here to stay. In
the 1980s, fired by Gorbachev's reform attempts, a younger
generation of radical scholars proposed a new institutionalism
or state socialism approach that sought to understand communism from within its institutional structures and everyday life, thus abandoning the constant East-West comparisons
that had been inherent in previous theories.[5] The concept
of state socialism informing this approach refers to the coun-
ter-concept of capitalism and wants to convey that, despite
everything, socialism is still capitalism's future. "The struggle
for socialism is at its dawn, not its dusk," argue Burawoy
and Lukacs (1992:174) in their recent case for the potential "rationality" of socialist factory organization – a case that
seems all the more implausible after the Eastern European
revolutions.

Against this backdrop, the notion of Leninist regime comes
full circle and reinvigorates some tenets of the old totalitarianism approach, with its stress on parties, ideologies, and
monistic power structures.[6] In light of the breakdown of
communism, the Leninist regime approach has gained much
prominence, because it highlights the *precarious* nature of
communism and its *failure* to offer a viable organization of
modern society. Since the concept of Leninism refers to
the political form of communist systems, its counter-con-
cept is not "capitalism" but "liberal democracy." A comparison between Leninism and liberal democracy highlights the
distinct, and ultimately precarious, features of Leninism. In
Leninist regimes, legitimacy is based not on rational pro-

cedures but on charismatic action. Leninism is the rule of activists, crystallizing around the Communist Party, and it draws its organizational coherence and viability from the negative "combat" mission to eliminate opponents in its thrust for total power (Selznick, 1952). Whereas in liberal democracies political procedures are certain while political outcomes are uncertain, in Leninist regimes procedures are uncertain while outcomes are certain – it is clear *who* rules and *what for* he rules.[7] In this regard, the notion of legitimacy, which conveys rule by public consent, is misleading. Leninist rule is by definition illegitimate.[8] The communist cadre party, as the apex of the Leninist regime, is a "political warfare organization" (Tucker, 1961:284) and "organizational weapon" (Selznick, 1952) that seeks to seize and maintain total power by unconstitutional means of secrecy, subversion, and violence. The notion of Leninism adequately reflects the primary focus on the means rather than the ends of rule, which has haunted the Marxist tradition ever since (see Lukes, 1985).[9] Barrington Moore has put it well: "Lenin and his followers set out to achieve for humanity the goals of freedom and equality by means of an organization that denied these same principles" (Moore, 1951:81).

The notion of Leninism points to the fundamental dilemma of communist systems that undergo modernization: the maintenance of monistic power structures in an essentially pluralistic society with differentiated functions, multiple roles, and diversified group interests.[10] If the charismatically conceived party regime needs "combat environments" (Jowitt, 1983:277) to preserve its organizational integrity, these combat environments are increasingly difficult to obtain – sooner or later there will be no more hostile classes to annihilate. The greatest threat to a Leninist regime is the loss of combat task and "revolutionary momentum" (Tucker, 1961:286). In this moment, Leninist movement regimes face extinction: "Like a star that has ceased to give off light, an extinct movement-regime may go on existing for a long while without a revolutionary raison d'être..., [exercising] power in order to exercise power" (ibid.). Leninist regimes are by definition monocratic and endowed with a combat task – that is, totalitarian – or they cease to be Leninist. From this angle, Leninist regimes cannot be reformed, and their recent "mass extinction" (Jowitt, 1991) appears inevitable – the question becomes not *why* it happened but why it happened *so late.*

Leninist regimes incorporate a unique amalgam of traditional, modern, and charismatic elements. Lenin rightfully claimed to have "created a new type of State" (quoted in Friedrich and Brzezinski, 1965:116). As the opening article of the first Soviet constitution purports, the new state was a "socialist state of workers and peasants" that resulted from the "overthrow of the power of landlords and capitalists and the conquest of the dictatorship of the proletariat" (ibid.). The post-revolutionary Leninist state was not, like the post-revolutionary French republic, a political community of citizens with equal rights and obligations, but the instrument of functional groups that had seized power in order to transform society according to a utopian design. The most characteristic feature of Leninist regimes thus is the fusion of society and state. If the differentiation between autonomous spheres and subsystems, such as economy, polity and culture, is the hallmark of Western modernity, the Leninist counterproject is that of forced dedifferentiation. Its distinctively *traditional* feature is the arresting of spontaneous development and change in the name of an all-encompassing and unchanging view of the world that claims to penetrate society and individual in their totality – like the "truth language" of religious dogma (Anderson, 1983:14).

A distinctively *modern* feature of Leninist regimes is the incorporation of the masses into the polity, and the mobilization of society for an abstract and remote goal that is defined by the ruling élite's proclaimed "scientific" insight into the "laws" of historical development. Bertrand Russell once argued that the twin revolutions of modernity, the French and the industrial, gave birth to two conflicting principles, "freedom" and "organization" (Russell, 1934). If the message of 1789 was freedom, the message of 1917 was organization. The great counter-movement against Leninist regimes would thus occur in the name of freedom.[11] Leninist regimes are yet in another sense modern. Like liberal democratic regimes, they are based on the principle of popular rule (Prager, 1985) – as the Eastern European notion of "people's democracy" indicates. And in certain ways, one may consider Leninist regimes the direct inheritors of a Rousseauian concept of democracy, which proclaims an identity between rulers and ruled and is hostile to any autonomous intermediation between individual and state (Talmon, 1961). Whereas liberal regimes counterbalance the democratic fiction of unity and homogeneity with the principle of individual rights, Leninist regimes reject plurality and difference in the name of the people-as-one. If the people are one, so is the power that derives from them. It is thus a small step to the total appropriation of power by a party that claims to speak and act on behalf of the people as a unity. As Claude Lefort (1986:279) argued, in liberal democracies "the image of popular sovereignty is linked to the image of an empty place, impossible to occupy, such that those who exercise public authority can never claim to appropriate it." The Leninist project is precisely to occupy that "empty place" of power. And it does so on the basis of the Marxist claim that under socialism there is no longer any major cleavage and conflict line in need of independent representation – workers and peasants now *are* the unified people. The cognitive claim to have discovered the essential truth of history and societal development dispenses with the need to acknowledge and regulate political conflict.[12] No more hideous assimilitation between truth and power has been invented in the modern world.

However, the suppressed principle of difference would nevertheless reassert itself, and this is where the *charismatically* conceived party of élite activists moves into the picture. In fact, "difference" is part and parcel of the very constitution of the Leninist regime, which is, after all, a proclaimed state of "workers and peasants", not of dentists or airline pilots. As Juan Linz noted, the very existence of the Leninist vanguard *party* implied that it was only *part* of the political life, thus unwittingly acknowledging the modern principle of differentiation (Linz, 1975:199). From this paradoxical duality of proclaimed unity and unwitting difference follows a crucial characteristic of Leninist regimes. Unlike liberal democracy, Leninist regimes have a combat mission: to eradicate difference root and branch in their quest for the perfect society.[13] The proclaimed "people's" or "socialist democracy" presents itself in the martial language of struggle and combat against "class enemies" or "enemies of the people", thus perpetuating the principle of difference in the permanent attempt to extinguish it.[14]

In the precise sense of a unitary state whose mission is the permanent eradication of difference, Leninist regimes are totalitarian. However, as modernization theory has rightly objected, it is also important to differentiate between distinct phases and stages in the development of Leninist regimes. As one could reconcile totalitarianism and modernization theory on this point, the identification of distinct phases of development corresponds to the very nature of Leninist regimes. Unlike liberal democratic regimes, which are characterized by a plurality and indeterminacy of goals, Leninist regimes are imbued with a univocal teleology that drives them to actively create the future rather than to let it just happen. However, the changes resulting from forced development entail unintended consequences that affect the political regime itself and change its shape and operative tasks in decisive and unforeseen ways.

With Dallin and Breslauer (1970a), we can distinguish between three distinct phases of communist development: takeover, mobilization, and post-mobilization.[15] The *takeover* phase comes closest to Hannah Arendt's classic description of totalitarianism as a novel form of rule based on "ideology and terror" (Arendt, 1951: ch.13). Leninist regimes came to power either through indigenous revolutions, as in China, Russia and Yugoslavia, or through foreign military intervention, as in the countries of East-Central Europe. Since they came to power exclusively by force and violence, not by public consent, the first task of Leninist regimes was to wipe out and eliminate the old élites that could challenge the new rule. This was the heyday of terror, which became directed in arbitrary and unpredictable ways against whole sections of the population, without consideration of individual guilt (see Linz, 1975:217–28). Terror served not only the immediate consolidation of the new regime, but was inherently related to its ideological mission. Through the generalized fear and anxiety that it arouses in its potential victims, terror destroys all existing human bonds and old securities. It atomizes and individualizes the people, only to mobilize and reintegrate them for the purposes of the communist project. Terror is part and parcel of the great "canvas cleaning" that must precede the utopian project to build a new society (Popper, 1966:157–68). "You can't make an omelette without breaking eggs", said Lenin.

The *mobilization* phase is the heroic era of communist development. Lenin captured its essence in his famous phrase that communism was "soviet power plus electrification." Having consolidated itself by wiping out rivaling élites and removing the vestiges of the old society, the communist rulers set out to lay the fundaments of a new society. Since, contrary to Marx's expectations, the communist takeover had occurred in countries that were economically backward or destroyed by war, economic development and catching up with the developed countries of the West became the order of the day. As the term "mobilization" indicates, this was the phase when the whole society was geared toward a single goal – to build communism. This entailed the collectivization of agriculture, the massive build-up of modern industries and infrastructure, and systematic ideological indoctrination of the population in education and culture. Terror did not subside, but was now used more planfully for political control and change (Dallin and Breslauer, 1970:192). With regard to the mobilization phase, Leninism has been rightly characterized as a theory of politically driven development (Huntington, 1968:334–43) and maybe the only chance of underdeveloped societies to achieve a "breakthrough" to modernity (Jowitt, 1971).

In the *post-mobilization* phase the Leninist regime faces the complex and differentiated society that it has helped to create. As Richard Löwenthal (1970) outlined, communist regimes are plagued by a "dualism of goals" – to stick to its utopian project and to acknowledge the exigencies of modernization. In the post-mobilization phase, modernization wins out over utopia. The revolutionary élan of the rulers exhausts itself, and society pulls at its chains. Market principles such as prices and material incentives are reintroduced to counteract the rigidities of a totally planned economy. The inevitable differentiation of roles and proliferation of interests in a complex industrial society challenges the monolithic façade of a regime that looks increasingly "old". A new intelligentsia arises side-by-side of the old *apparatchiki*, defying dogma and the "correct line" in the name of rationality and efficiency (Konrad and Szelenyi, 1979). With the rise of a new "counter-élite" of professional experts, the institutions of economy and state are strengthened against the leading party (Ludz, 1972). Calculable forms of coercion and limited rule of law replace arbitrary terror. The total scope of political control decreases, and "zones of indifference" are increasingly tolerated (Dallin and Breslauer, 1970). In the post-mobilization phase, an implicit social contract between the rulers and the ruled replaces terror and ideology as chief mechanism of control and cohesion: state-guaranteed consumption and material well-being are exchanged for non-interference with the business of rule.

In its most significant shortcoming, modernization theory overlooked the fact that the post-mobilization phase poses a fundamental threat to Leninist rule. In light of a differentiated and pluralistic society, the monocratic pretension of Leninist élite rule is increasingly difficult to defend, and the Communist Party faces the threat of losing its combat task. As Richard Löwenthal (1976:104) put the dilemma, "Why should a party that no longer sees its task in transforming society by the annihilation of hostile classes continue to claim a monopoly of political decision?" Instead of spelling out the principal incompatibility of monocratic rule and differentiated society, modernization theory falsely assumed that both could very well coexist. Samuel Huntington (1970), for instance, draws a sharp distinction between "revolutionary" and "established" one-party systems, and considers the latter as a "new type of system with different characteristics" that was to be "judged by different criteria" (p.23). In this view, the scope of politics in the established one-party system simply diminishes, and the ruling party élite shrinks to a "Brahmanic caste" with merely ceremonial functions – without, however, abandoning its "monopoly of ultimate authority" (p.43).

In dropping the notion of totalitarianism, modernization theory became insensitive to the incompatibility between Leninism and modern social structures. Mirroring the practical reform attempts by a younger intelligentsia in the post-Stalinist thaw, modernization theory assumed that the pragmatic spirit of the "scientific-technical revolution" would inevitably draw the communist world into the global orbit of "industrial society" (Aron, 1967) – without conceiving the possibility of a concomitant regime collapse. Gyorgi Konrad and Ivan Szelenyi enshrined this reformist hope in their influential manifesto *Intellectuals on the Road to Class Power* (1974). In a reassessment twelve years later, Ivan Szelenyi explicates the hopes of the post-mobilization period: "As Soviet-type societies searched for a new identity in the post-Stalinist epoch and as the old-line bureaucrats loosened their grip on power, they considered sharing power with the intellectuals, who were excited by the idea of scientific planning, the scientific-technological revolution, and Marxism as a science" (Szelenyi, 1986/7:116). However, as Szelenyi now admitted, this hope proved premature: "We were wrong. The bureaucracy proved to be stubborn and less willing to share power and to compromise than anticipated" (ibid.). Striking a similar chord, Peter Ludz, in his landmark study of the changing East German party élite, admitted that the rise of an "institutionalized counter elite" of expert professionals did not "enlarge the sphere of democratic participation" (Ludz, 1972:409), and that the *nouvelle vague* of cybernetics and systems theory aimed at "the refunctionalization, not the annihilation, of ideological dogma" (ibid., 412). Reflecting on the reversal of reform hopes by Brezhnev-style neotraditionalism, Ken Jowitt saw the emergence of "amalgam regimes" that combined quasi-pluralist "inclusion" with restorative "mobilization" practices (Jowitt, 1975:89–96).

As these assessments indicate, the reform elasticity of Leninist regimes proved essentially limited. Therefore it would be misleading to abandon the concept of totalitarianism in favour of some version of authoritarianism, as some analysts have suggested.[16] Juan Linz (1975:264) defined authoritarian regimes by the lack of a comprehensive ideology, limited pluralism in the political sphere, and the non-attempt to mobilize society on behalf of a utopian goal. This is what Leninist regimes cannot be, at least not officially, without abrogating their constitutive principles.[17] Unlike liberal democracies, which are indeterminate with regard to goals and the direction of change, Leninist regimes cannot be reformed without being destroyed at the same time. In his scathing attack on a Western Sovietology that had precipitately abandoned the totalitarian model, Martin Malia (1991:288f) argued pointedly: "Totalitarianism does not mean that such regimes in fact exercise total control over the population; it means rather that such control is their aspiration." We will see that the Eastern European dissident movements of the 1970s and 1980s, which exposed the ritualism and hypocrisy in post-mobilization regimes as the Big Lie, could not be understood without the maintenance of the totalitarian *intention*.

The distinction between phases and stages of communist development is crucial for our purpose of delineating the space that is available for emergent social movements. In the take-over and mobilization phases, the prevalence of ideology and terror destroys the social space that is necessary for autonomous action. In fact, the ruthless persecution of difference and dissent is the very rationale of ideology and terror. But in the post-mobilization phase, some *de facto* toleration of unofficial thought and action becomes possible, even inevitable. Dallin and Breslauer (1970:198) observed that "the reduction of political terror has both strengthened the legitimacy of Communist regimes and significantly increased the amount of overt dissent". The taming of erratic and drastic coercion by limited rule of law has somewhat reduced the risks of dissent, and the toleration of niches exempt from political and ideological controls has opened up limited spaces for quasi-autonomous thought and action. The dilemma of *de jure* denial and *de facto* toleration of dissent and opposition is part of the difficult reality that Leninist regimes have to face in the post-mobilization phase. Ken Jowitt (1975) has located the social-structural origins of this dilemma in the emergence of "articulate social audiences." By this he means the educated urban strata with increasingly diverse and sophisticated demands, which the regime itself has helped to create through its project of forced development and modernization. Unlike "masses," these groups are "politically knowledgeable and oriented." But unlike "publics," articulate audiences are "restricted in their political behavior to those roles and actions prescribed by the regime itself" (p.71). Since these groups[18] could not be fully repressed without embarking on the precarious path of the permanent revolution, post-mobilization regimes had to reckon with limited but perennial patches of dissent and opposition.

The carriers of dissent in the post-mobilization phase have most often been intellectuals.[19] As is well known, intellectuals had played no small part in furnishing the communist ideology and putting it into practice. One could even argue that certain characteristics of the Leninist party, such as the strict separation between élite and masses and the nihilistic bracketing of tactical scruples in the fanatic pursuit of the ideal, reflect the distinct features of the Russian intelligentsia as an alienated and marginalized group with no ties to society.[20] However, in the wake of regime consolidation and the growth of an inert party and state apparatus, the intellectuals are increasingly pushed out of the citadels of power. Samuel Huntington (1970:36) noted that the "second generation of leadership comes out of the party apparatus and is largely composed of bureaucrats not intellectuals." This leaves the intellectuals with no other function but criticism, and in turn they "either keep strenuously away from political life or turn to open and systematic criticism of the regime" (Löwenthal, 1976:106). Because of the logocratic nature of communism, intellectuals are bound to be key actors in Leninist opposition politics. The transition from "revisionism" to "dissidence" as main mode of Leninist opposition politics, which I will discuss in the following, can also be read as the progressive disenchantment of intellectuals with the appeals of communism.

OPPOSITION IN LENINIST REGIMES

Considering the nature of Leninist regimes, the notion of opposition seems to involve a "contradiction in terms" (Skilling, 1968:294). Since conflict is officially abrogated as a principle of political life, and replaced by an essentialist concept of truth in whose possession the ruling party élite claims to be, any deviation from the "correct line" must assume the odour of "disloyalty" and "treason" (Schapiro, 1970:3). In addition, Leninist regimes never stripped off their origins in clandestine revolutionary sects acting in a hostile

environment, thus making them perceive the world in para-
noid terms of conspiracy and plotting. Adam Michnik correctly observed that "the communist system contains protest
in its ideological nature" (Michnik, 1985:46). Opposition,
even the most harmless and loyal one, becomes automatically couched as "counterrevolution" that must be held down
at any cost. Robert Dahl (1973:13) has captured the dilemma
of oppositionless states well: "If all oppositions are treated
as dangerous and subject to repression, opposition that would
be loyal if it were tolerated becomes disloyal because it is
not tolerated. Since all opposition is likely to be disloyal,
then all opposition must be repressed." Wherever it appears,
dissent and opposition is therefore bound to assume illegal
forms, and to be "movement" in the sense of lacking institutional grounding and recognition. And whatever substan-
tive issue they address, emergent movements are quickly made
aware of their illicit existence in a regime that does not
tolerate independent action. As Tony Judt (1988:205) observed in his reflections on dissident politics in East-Central
Europe, "there is almost no theme open to adoption by the
opposition which does not, sooner or later, bring the discussion back to rights and freedoms." Social movements in
Leninist regimes are not granted the modest preoccupation
with Western-style single-issue politics. Since their very existence contradicts the principles of the regime, social movements, as every form of independent action, have *by definition*
system-transcending implications.

What seems obvious in retrospect – that the crux of Leninist
regimes is their denial of individual rights and plurality –
became directly addressed by opposition movements only
after a long and arduous learning process. In general,
opposition movements in Leninist regimes faced two choices:
either to accept the normative principles of the regime and
try to make the latter live up to its ideals, *or* to invoke standards
of individual rights that are inherent in every form of free
expression and independent action, but that cannot be
accepted by the regime unless it abrogates its constitutive
principles. The first choice became known as "revisionism",
the second choice as "dissidence."

Revisionism

It is a common strategy of modern "proactive" social movements (Tilly, 1978) to invoke the normative standards inherent in polity and society, and to point to a bad reality
that does not live up to these standards. In the liberal
democracies of the West, social movements have invoked
the constitutional principle of citizenship to legitimize their
demands. This amounted to demands for equal rights and
participation by (or on behalf of) previously excluded groups,
or for extension of the spheres in which citizenship principles should be effective. Leninist regimes do not know the
concept of citizenship, and thus lack a mechanism to transform societal inequities and diverse group interests into legitimate political claims. It is the party that claims to represent
society as a whole, and inclusion and participation is something enforced from above rather than pushed for from below.
The functional equivalent to citizenship in Leninist regimes
is enfranchisement through the party. In normative regard,
freedom and equality are transposed from individually
invokable *rights* into the collective *promise* of communism. If
citizenship is about guaranteed equal rights in an imperfect
society where there is always inequity and conflict, communism is the promise of a perfect society in which claims for
equal rights have become obsolete because all sources of
inequity and conflict have been abolished. As Ernest Gellner
(1990:121) poignantly described the promise of communism,
"The Kingdom of God needs no constitutional law."[21]

However feasible this promise may be, "revisionist" movements from Trotsky to Bahro have invoked the communist
utopia to attack the bureaucratic and autocratic deforma-
tions of "real socialism."[22] Though, in formal regard, revisionist movements are equivalent to the citizenship movements
in the West, they are movements only in metaphorical sense.
Revisionism originates in the political apparatus and the
intellectual circles that revolve around it. Very much the
lament over the "revolution betrayed" (Trotsky, 1972), revisionism is limited to the intellectual élites and "vanguards"
that had a stake in it. The ensuing hybrid of reforming the
system through completing the "betrayed" revolution reflects
the inverted world of communism, where revolution has

become petrified as institutional dogma.

With the benefit of hindsight, it is certainly easy to ridicule the illusions of revisionism. But in a regime that even purged the notion of reform from its totalitarian vocabulary (Kusin, 1976:339), the revisionist challenge was a considerable one, and its protagonists were met with little courtesy by the party rulers.[23] In fact, since the early feud against "Social Democratism" (Lenin), the main target of Leninist combat was not the class enemy, but competing leadership groups. As Philip Selznick (1952:227) argued to the point, "the communists can compromise with the 'class enemy', they can even support him, but they dare *not* tolerate the political existence of those who may offer the target groups an alternative ideological leadership or who can effectively expose the totalitarian practices of bolshevism in power."[24]

Moreover, revisionism reveals a crucial characteristic of opposition movements in Leninist regimes: in a regime that lives by the book, opposition also proceeds by the book. In fact, revisionism is in the first instance an intellectual enterprise, and it consists of reading and rereading, interpreting and reinterpreting the sacred texts from which the regime derives its legitimacy. In a regime that is itself built upon an intellectual doctrine, the opposition also will naturally move on intellectual grounds. The secret exegesis of the humanistic young Marx becomes, like the reading of Goldstein's Book, a deadly threat to totalitarian rule, which is essentially "logocracy" (Milosz, 1953). In Leninist regimes, this is the one enduring insight of revisionism, intellectual opposition *is* political opposition.

In political terms, revisionism is within-system opposition that seeks to transform communism on its own grounds. Revisionism thus boils down to a "striving for democratic socialism" (Geremek, 1991:104), while not touching the principle of one-party rule. Historically, the Prague Spring of 1968 may be looked at as the epitome, and nemesis, of revisionism.[25] The quest for "socialism with a human face" was kicked off by a coalition of intra-party reformers and the intelligentsia in academia, media, and the arts. In fact, the Prague Spring was the historical hour of the "second generation socialist intelligentsia" (Bugajski and Pollack, 1989:43) that challenges the rule of *apparatchiki* in post-mobilization regimes. The Action Program of April 1968 advocated the democratization of the Communist Party, economic reforms, guarantees of civic rights and liberties, the strengthening of the institutions of the state against the party, and, most notably, complete independence of the media and freedom of culture (Kusin, 1976:356f). But more interesting than its entries are its omissions. The Action Program did not question the "leading role of the party," it did not advocate outright political pluralism, and it ruled out the possibility of opposition parties. This was not so much due to a Polish-style "self-limitation" to avert aggression from abroad. Rather, it betrayed the conscious attempt to stick to the parameters of "socialist democracy" – and this obviously included the pursuit of utopia by means of monistic power structures. The violent abortion of the Prague Spring prohibits us from knowing if "socialist democracy" would have been little more than a halfway house to Western-style liberal democracy with full-scale pluralism and multi-party system, *or* the beginning of a new round of ossified élite rule in a Leninist regime. Adam Michnik (1985:47) aptly characterized the dilemma of revisionism as being "transformed either into an accessory to power or a simple opposition group." The failure of revisionism in the Prague Spring would lead to a thorough transformation of the meaning of opposition in Leninist regimes.

Dissidence

"A spectre is haunting Eastern Europe: the spectre of what in the West is called 'dissent'." These are the opening lines of Vaclav Havel's famous essay *The Power of the Powerless*, which may be considered the Anti-Communist Manifesto of the Eastern European dissident movements. What is dissent? The *Oxford Dictionary* defines it as "refusal to assent."[26] Whereas revisionism "assented" to the normative principles underlying the Leninist regime, dissent (or dissidence) places itself outside these principles, claiming an elementary right of difference that is repressed by Leninist regimes. Though polite and moderate in tone, anti-utopian in its programmatic, and mostly limited to tiny circles of post-revisionist intellectuals, dissidence contains the seeds of revolutionary transformation – the regime cannot abide by the demand for plurality and difference unless it ceases to be Leninist.

The dissident perspective entails a novel interpretation of the structures of modern society, one that foreshadowed the end of Leninism. The socioeconomic distinction between capitalism and socialism gives way to the political distinction between open and closed societies.[27] In this view, the previous cartography of political positions in terms of left and right loses its meaning. In the stark words of Russian dissident Vladimir Bukovsky: "We are neither from the left camp nor from the right camp, we are from the concentration camp" (quoted in Michnik, 1985:91). Just as Western Sovietism abandoned the concept of totalitarianism, the Eastern European dissident movements of the 1970s and 1980s reintroduced it to denounce the closed and monocratic structures of communism (see Rupnik, 1988). As Adam Michnik (1985:47) wrote: "There is no such thing as a nontotalitarian ruling communism. It either becomes totalitarian or it ceases to be communism." Dissidence may be considered the highest form of opposition in Leninist regimes, because it recognizes the monocratic and irreformable nature of Leninism – indeed, the dissident perspective itself entails the theory of Leninist regimes that I introduced above.

The dissident phenomenon reflects the reality of post-mobilization regimes, where the utopian impulse has exhausted itself but lives on as mechanized ritual, and where "articulate audiences" strive to abandon their passive listener-status and become active "publics." While dissidence became a general phenomenon throughout post-1968 Eastern Europe, only in the case of Poland did it grow into a mass-based social movement. If we hesitated to call the revisionist opposition a movement because of its origins in, and basic allegiance to, the party state, the dissident opposition is certainly movement in that it orginates in society rather than the state apparatus. But its small size, fragmentation, and individualized quality violates our understanding of movements as a form of collective action. Rather than constituting a movement, dissidents are individuals that stand out in their personal courage and determination to resist prescribed unity. The dissident opposition is not a movement with leaders and members, program and organization, but the sum total of scattered and uncoordinated acts of individual resistance, thus both mirroring and counteracting the emasculation of society under communism.

Antipolitics

Dissidence entails a model of political activism that is directly contrary to the type of activism that feeds social movements in the West. Western social movement activism is *virtuoso* activism: it indicts the deficit of meaning and utopia in a differentiated and rule-based society. By contrast, Eastern dissidence is activism by default: it responds to the deficit of differentiation and legal rules in a society that is itself couched in the "movement" imagery of utopia and history-making. As in Havel's famous example of the greengrocer's refusal to put a party slogan into his shop window, dissidence begins by *not* doing certain things. As activism by default, dissidence lacks the activist pathos of "history making" that tends to accompany social movements in the West.[28] No one captured the meaning of dissidence as activism by default better than Adam Michnik (1985:11): "This war surprised you in the company of a pretty woman, not while you were plotting an assault on the Central Committee headquarters." This, of course, reflects the inverted world of communism, where *virtuoso* activism is a principle of the regime itself. Dissident politics is "antipolitics." The Hungarian dissident Gyorgy Konrad explains its meaning: "We have to liberate ourselves from politics like from an insect plague" (Konrad, 1984:211f). If the aspiration of Western social movements is to politicize spaces previously considered private or exempt from public scrutiny (e.g., Evans, 1980), the reverse logic of dissident politics is to contain the reach of politics that is by definition state-controlled.

Since the official space of politics is occupied by the communist rulers, dissident politics resorts to the prepolitical sphere. Not by accident, artists and literary intellectuals play such a prominent role in Eastern European dissident movements, from Solzhenitsyn to Kundera and Havel. While aesthetics offers a medium of expression untainted by political manipulation, the impulse and content of dissident politics is distinctively moral. The political division between left and right is replaced by the moral division between right and wrong. Havel has expressed this in his famous dictum that dissident politics is "living in truth." To be sure, the conjunction of politics and morality is an attribute of social movements as such, which always denounce existing power structures in the name of some "higher" moral standards of justice.[29] But in Leninist regimes, "living in truth" has some specific connotations that are without parallel in the West. First, "living in truth" reverses the traditional priorities of socialism, which subdues the individual and her choices in favour of the collective categories of class, society, or history. Dissident politics puts the individual up front (see Ash, 1989:191). Second, the resort to the prepolitical sphere of morality reflects the difficulty to find a language that is authentic and free from ideological manipulation. The very essence of totalitarianism is control that is "total" and includes the ritualization of language, the imposition of "correct" attitudes, and even the engineering of the past to fit the needs of the rulers. The great difficulty for opposition movements in Leninist regimes is to find a language and symbols of their own. If even collective memories and traditions succumb to the sway of the "New Faith" (Milosz, 1953), the center of resistance shifts to the individual sphere of morality. Dissidence rests on an elementary moral intuition to escape manipulation. "You simply straighten your backbone," Havel explains his greengrocer's small but momentous act of refusal, "and live in greater dignity as an individual" (Havel, 1990:65).

Most importantly, "living in truth" has political implications. It exposes the lie on which the regime is founded. Countering the totalitarian "lie" by the simple recovery of factual truth is a red thread of dissident thinking from Milosz to Solzhenitsyn and Kolakowski. Leszek Kolakowski (1983) has provided a chilling explanation of the lie's function in the totalitarian regime. By destroying historical memory and manipulating all information, the totalitarian regime destroys the very criterion of truth. If truth becomes the object of manipulation, a lie can become the truth, or rather, the notion of truth itself disappears: "This is the great cognitive triumph of totalitarianism. By managing to abrogate the very idea of truth, it can no longer be accused of lying" (p.127).

In post-mobilization regimes, where the utopian impulse has exhausted itself and lives on as a prescribed ritual out of touch with reality, the totalitarian lie becomes transparent and vulnerable. The dissident phenomenon arises in a situation where even the rulers have stopped believing in their mission to build a perfect society. "Then they were defending their program, today they are fighting for their privileges," says Adam Michnik (1985:37) in view of the Polish Jaruzelski regime, the first communist regime run by the military. If public life has degenerated into hypocrisy and mere ritual, the recovery of truth becomes the greatest possible threat. As Havel put it, "if the main pillar of the system is living a lie, then it is not surprising that the fundamental threat to it is living the truth. This is why it must be repressed more severely than anything else" (Havel, 1990:40).

Reflecting the post-revisionist mood in Eastern Europe, antipolitics rests on the paradoxical premise that communism cannot be reformed. In a strange combination of resignation and anticipation of things to come, antipolitics has given up any hope that change can be achieved through the party apparatus. Antipolitics is living as if the repressive conditions no longer existed. It does not so much address the power-holders as speak to itself. Tony Judt (1988:196) has put it well: "By simply living as though free, rather than demanding of the regime freedoms you know it will not or cannot grant, one creates the very social sphere whose existence one seeks." Tellingly, major dissident platforms such as the Czech Charter 77 or the Polish KOR, but also the East German Initiative for Peace and Human Rights (IFM), operated in complete openness and "legality." Charter 77 pioneered the practice of signing petitions and protest declarations with full names and addresses. This was at first an exemplary act of courage, which pulled down the veil of fear and anxiety that stifles public life in communist regimes.[30] But openness was also functional for the very maintenance of dissidence, because it created a protective cordon of publicity that even the regime had to respect.

Language of Rights and Recovery of Civil Society
The perennial issue of dissident politics is the reclamation of basic individual rights. Though against the grain of Leninist

regimes, focusing on individual rights became a viable strategy after the Warsaw Pact states had signed the Helsinki Final Act in 1975, which formally obliged the latter to respect basic civil liberties and human rights in the domestic realm.[31] In an ironical postlude to Marxist revisionism, Helsinki allowed the dissident opposition to confront the regime with its own futile claims. The decidedly nonprogrammatic and anti-utopian language of rights is aligned with the idea of citizenship, which refers to a political community of equal and free members.[32] Aware that Leninist regimes are at odds with the pluralism and individualism that citizenship entails, the dissident opposition sought to vindicate free spaces in which citizenship could be restored, if not *de jure*, then *de facto*.

The *de facto* restoration of citizenship in a nonofficial space exempt from state control is the true meaning of the much-celebrated recovery of civil society in Eastern Europe. In a regime one of whose main features is the systematic destruction of civil society, its recovery against the odds has at least two specific meanings. First, it refers to the resurrection of the private sphere. In her penetrating reflections on everyday life under communism, Slavenka Drakulic (1993:91–2) describes the beleaguered state of privacy: "To survive, we had to divide the territory, to set a border between private and public. The state wants it all public...What is public is of the enemy." Dissidents reclaimed what T.H.Marshall called "legal" citizenship rights, that is, a basic protection of the individual from encroachments by public authority, and the legitimate pursuit of action that is based on mere self-interest.[33] The second meaning of civil society is political, and refers to the creation of a genuine public sphere in which people are no longer subjects but "citizens" in the sense of fully enfranchised members of the political community.[34] The impact of the commandeered politicization of society in Leninist regimes is the exact negation of politics, understood with Hannah Arendt (1958) as the human activity that lives on speech, not force. In this sense, the true intention of "antipolitics" is the restitution of politics as a sphere of unimpeded public speech and expression (see Havel, 1988).

Establishing the private-public distinction and creating a

public sphere is the double thrust of the revival of civil society in Eastern Europe.[35] It is important to underline that this double task is essentially different from the parallel attempts by the new social movements in the West to strengthen civil society *vis-à-vis* the state.[36] With regard to the private-public distinction, constitutional guarantees of privacy and legal citizenship can, of course, be taken for granted in the West. Here the focus of social movements has been rather the reverse: to politicize the personal, and to turn private life-style issues into political ones (see Evans, 1980). With regard to the public sphere, the question in the West is not to create one, but rather to revitalize an already existing public sphere that is partially "colonized" by money and power (Habermas, 1981). In short, civil society exists *de jure* in the West, while at best *de facto* in the East. As Ralf Dahrendorf (1990:101) states laconically, citizenship in the East is "at heart rather than in the real world." It follows from this that the relation between civil society and the state in Leninist regimes is antagonistic and mutually exclusive, whereas this relation in liberal democracies is one of complementation and mutual penetration – witness the greening, feminization, or ethnicization of public policies in the West in response to new social movements. No such changes could be observed in Leninist regimes, where the only question was if, when, and how severely the state would strike back. The rise of civil society brought home that Leninist regimes could not be reformed.

Despite these general characteristics, the emergent contours of civil society looked different in each particular country.[37] In Poland, the strategy of social self-organization aimed at driving the party back into the state, giving rise to the most clearly developed, quasi-independent public sphere in Eastern Europe. In Czechoslovakia, an austere and unrelenting party state, and the reverse impotence of the dissident scene, entailed a spiritual and cultural resistance to the totalitarian presumption, crystallizing in an "underground" or "parallel culture." While in certain respects similar to Czechoslovakia, East Germany's emergent civil society took on distinctively counter-cultural contours – reflecting the general abstinence of the intellectual élite from opposition politics and the availability of an *ersatz* public sphere in West

Germany (see Chapter 4). In Hungary, the resurrection of civil society occurred in primarily economic terms, manifesting itself in the establishment of a "second market" of small private enterprises that was tolerated, and even supported, by the regime.

Nationalism

When Eastern European intellectuals turned from revisionism to dissidence, they fundamentally transformed the allegiances and orientations of opposition politics under communism. "For the first time," wrote Pavel Kohout shortly after the violent end of the Prague Spring, "I have the sensation of belonging to the nation."[38] In the wake of this traumatic event, the élitist and future-oriented "pursuit of the ideal" (Shils, 1970:35) gave way to the popular and past-oriented resuscitation of memory and history. Particularly the invocation of national identities provided a means to step out of the orbit of communism, and it made the dissident-intellectuals popular fixpoints and symbols of the aggrieved societies under communism. Nationalism has, in fact, been the most potent force in the break-up of communist regimes. Living in truth and antipolitics is a fine thing for intellectuals. But in the rare cases that opposition swelled into society-wide movements that shook communist rule at its foundations, it was couched in unmistakably nationalist colours – from the cry of Berlin workers in 1953 for national reunification, Hungary's "romantic nationalist rebellion" in 1956 (Armstrong, 1988:299), to Solidarity's resurrection of the "family that is...Poland" (Lech Walesa, quoted in Ash, 1983:28). When Vaclav Havel announced his election as President to an immense crowd of jubilant Czechs, Prague's Wenceslas Square was drowning in a sea of white, blue, and red – the colours of the Czechoslovak flag. Truly, the Eastern European revolutions of 1989 have been a rebirth of nations.

It was, at first, a gentle rebirth of nations, not least because the dissident intellectuals who had forged the concepts of human rights and civil society had also stressed their connection to the principle of national self-determination. Havel's dissident manifesto *The Power of the Powerless*, for instance, invoked the legacy of Tomas Masaryk's "working for the good of the nation." In fact, the restitution of the Czechoslovak First Republic of the interwar period provided a fixpoint for the dissident opposition, making the latter both the natural leaders of the "velvet revolution" and legitimate rulers of post-communist Czechoslovakia.[39] In Poland, the invocation of nationalist discourse by dissident intellectuals was even more pronounced, reflecting the tragic fate of Poland as a nation forever trampled and partitioned by foreign powers. Adam Michnik called Solidarity an "authentic movement of national rebirth," and he hailed the Gdansk Agreement of 1980 as the "Great Charter of the Rights of the Polish Nation" (Michnik, 1985:41,111). The readiness by dissident intellectuals to link their individualistic concepts of rights and antipolitics to the popular language of nationalism assured them a leading role in the mass movements that toppled the old regime, and it would contribute to the framing of nationalism in the distinctively civic terms of national self-determination.

This should not obscure that nationalism has a double face, a civic and an ethnic one.[40] Its *civic* face refers to the intra-group component of rights and plurality in the political community of citizens that since 1789 has been called "the nation." Until there is a world society, the national society remains the place in which citizenship rights are effective and guaranteed. As Ralf Dahrendorf (1990:135) put it, "the nation-state is to all intents and purposes still the repository of basic rights of citizenship." Whoever says "citizenship" must say "nation" and "nation-state" (as its institutional organ), because as yet no other collectivity and institution have been devised to house and enforce constitutional rights for individuals. This is the meaning of nation that was born with the French revolution and has remained a fixpoint of political modernization ever since. The Abbé Siéyès provided its classic formulation: "[A nation] is a body of associates living under common laws and represented by the same legislative assembly."[41]

The *ethnic* face of nationalism refers to the concept of nation as a collectivity of individuals with a common language, ethnic identity, and history. Empirically, civic and ethnic nationhood overlap: One is always citizen of a particular state that claims to represent a particular nation.[42] Whereas the civic component secures plurality and rights, the ethnic one provides identity and unity. The ethnic side of nationalism is usually invoked if we refer to nationalism as movement. In this vein, Ernest Gellner (1983:43) defined nationalism as "the striving to make culture and polity congruent." Nationalism entails movement if an ethnic nation wants to become a civic one by gaining independent statehood. In the case of East-Central Europe, ethnic nations sought to become civic ones, paradoxically, via recovering their civic legacies – Poland, Hungary and Czechoslovakia each had a brief, but collectively memorized, history of constitutional statehood that was crushed by Soviet occupation and Yalta.[43] The civic legacy, along with the relative ethnic homogeneity of these societies, conditioned a benign and largely civic nationalism that let 1989 appear as a "return" to the democratic revolutions of the modern epoch (Furet, 1990).

Nationalism is both inclusive and exclusive: "inclusive" with respect to the members of the in-group that are granted equal rights and status, but "exclusive" with respect to out-group members. The exclusive side becomes dominant in the nationalist movements that accompany, and fuel, the disintegration of multinational communist states, most notably Yugoslavia and the Soviet Union (see Vujacic and Zaslavsky, 1992). The accompanying ethno-national conflicts show the darker side of nationalism, which is entirely different from the predominantly civic nationalisms of East-Central Europe. In these multinational states, ethnic nationalism turns aggressive and violent because of the lack of civic legacies, long-engrained ethno-religious divisions, and the existence of ethnic minority groups in territories claimed by ethnic majority groups.[44]

While the empirical relationships between nationalism and communism are manifold, ranging from antagonism to alliance and substitution, both are in principle incompatible.[45] "The workers have no country," Marx wrote in the *Communist Manifesto*. Communism postulates the supranational category of class as the main allegiance and organizing principle in modern society, aiming at a world society in which all national boundaries are abolished. Not by accident, the Soviet Union was one of the few countries in the world without a nationality reference in its name. Communist alliances with nationalism were but tactical, from Marx's appreciation of national states and markets as centralizing and modernizing forces, Lenin's recognition that peripheral Third-World discontent was more likely to be articulated in national than class-based forms, to the attempts of post-mobilization regimes to use national symbolism as a remedy against ideological exhaustion. Despite such tactical alliances, which almost always worked to the detriment of communism,[46] Leninist regimes were generally hostile to national aspirations. "The struggle to overcome nationalism... is the most important task of Marxist-Leninists," stipulates the *Great Soviet Encyclopedia*.[47] This hostility stems not only from incompatible principles of allegiance, but also from incompatible temporal orientations. Communism is future-oriented, whereas nationalism seeks to mobilize the past.[48] In communist perspective, national identities and allegiances represented that gnawing principle of difference and remembrance of the past that had to be wiped out if utopian unity was to be achieved. A New Faith was to be instilled, and this required making, in the words of George Orwell, "all other modes of thought impossible".[49]

On the reverse, if communism was organized forgetting, the opposition to it was necessarily a "struggle of memory against forgetting" (Kundera, 1981:3), with national symbols and identities being the stuff out of which this memory was made. Along similar lines, one could argue with Clifford Geertz (1973) that communism violated the anthropological fact that humans complete themselves through culture, and not through culture in the abstract but through highly particular forms of it: "To be human is to be Javanese" (p. 53). In a world where cultural boundaries are drawn along national lines, nationalism was the inevitable response to the violation of cultural particularity by communism. This is particularly obvious in the case of East-Central Europe, where communism had few indigenous roots but resulted from Soviet military occupation. Opposition in East-Central Europe was necessarily couched in nationalist colours, because national collectivities were denied the right of autonomy and self-determination, and were relegated to quasi-colonial status (see Feher, 1988).

Dissidence and civic nationalism are closely related and interdependent. If one turned away from the "revisionist" quest for the true socialism toward the defense of elementary citizenship rights, one had to specify the collectivity in which these rights were to be effective. After all, one is a citizen not through membership in world-society, but through membership in a specific nation. The immediate responses to the end of the Prague Spring betray a shock-like recognition of this fact. After the "expulsion from paradise," says a former member of the Czech Charter 77, "the one-time critical loyalists finally found themselves in the same position as the rest of the nation".[50] This turn to the nation was not a difficult one for the intellectuals, because it could feed upon the "insurrectionary traditions" in Eastern Europe, in which aspirations for "national and individual freedom" were closely linked (Schoepflin, 1977:135). The dissidents thus resumed the traditional role of the Eastern European intelligentsias, who had always understood themselves as defenders of their small nations against Great Power rule (see Seton Watson, 1962).[51]

The link between dissidence and civic nationalism, or what Jacques Rupnik (1989:217) called the "belated reconciliation (of the intellectuals) with their nation", tends to be obscured today by the radically altered cleavage structures of postcommunist east-central Europe. Once communism had been overcome, the dissident and nationalist forces became split into opposite camps. Nationalism now took on exclusively ethnic contours, and became a repository for populist resentment against modernization and secularism, often in an odd alliance with unrepented or converted communists. In light of this changed constellation, Adam Michnik (1991:258f) now sharply distinguishes between "national self-defense," which refers to legitimate "aspirations to reclaim the national memory, to defend cultural identity, to have an independent state," and "nationalism" proper, which "amounts to intolerance." But as Michnik's distinction *also* conveys, the reassertion of the nation is an essentially positive component of the Eastern European transformation that cannot be reduced to its ethnic aberrations.

EAST GERMAN EXCEPTIONALISM

Following Ken Jowitt (1992:159–218), the Leninist regime world did not consist of sovereign nation-states but of Soviet "replica regimes," assorted around the sacred Moscow Centre like the segments in Durkheim's society of mechanical solidarity. East Germany was Moscow's quintessential replica regime because total military and moral defeat had wiped out the inertia of history and memory that elsewhere in Eastern Europe obstructed and withstood the communist imposition. East Germany exposes in crystalline form all the essentials of communist rule – its basic illegitimacy, which became enshrined in the Wall; its combat orientation, which found ample fuel, first in eliminating the remains of the Nazi past and, later, in outmatching the capitalist half-nation west of the Wall; its substitution of socialist for national identities, which expressed itself in a bizarre attempt to eradicate the German component from the regime's self-definition; and, ultimately, its inevitable extinction, which was nowhere as complete as in East Germany's disappearance from the map of existing states.

Devoid of a national foundation, East Germany was nothing but a Leninist regime, and socialism was elevated to a quasi-national, state- and society-defining ideology. This had important implications for the politics of regime opposition. As I will elaborate in the following chapters, the exceptionalism of East German regime opposition consists of the fact that the decisive step from revisionism to dissidence as highest form of communist opposition politics was not taken. Why? As I will elaborate in Chapter 6, there is no simple answer to a complex question. But the bottom line is that for historical and cultural reasons even a minimal form of civic nationalism was ruled out as a counterdiscourse to communism. In its most sympathetic reading, East German regime opposition became hostage to a regime that defined itself in exclusively socialist terms. If one opposed the socialist regime doctrine in dissident manner, one had to question East Germany's independent statehood. In a world divided into separate nation-states, each commanding their members' highest loyalties, the questioning of a society's independent statehood was akin to the disloyalty committed on behalf of a foreign power. In East Germany, the one who did not comply with the socialist creed had to appear as a "traitor" – that most universally despised figure in the modern world of nation-states (Anderson, 1983:82). East Germany's ultimate triumph as a Leninist regime was its imposition of socialism as a quasi-national imperative even on its opponents. In this regard, East Germany's was also totalitarianism's ultimate triumph: the lie had become the truth because all other modes of thought had indeed become impossible.

While the ultimate roots of East German exceptionalism are to be found in the peculiarities of German history and culture, the existing option to "exit" to the Western half of the divided nation functioned as an additional catalyst of regime loyalty. Albert Hirschman's (1970) theory of "exit" and "voice" as alternative responses by the clients and members of organizations and institutions to a decline in performance helps explain, not the mode, but some dynamic and organizational aspects of East German opposition politics. In East Germany, the equivalent to the dissident quest for the open society was to exit to West Germany, where everyone who managed to cross the Wall could pick up automatic citizenship. The exit option, which could be taken only individually, neutralized the appearance of antipolitical dissidence as a political claim. In this regard, the availability of exit did indeed "atrophy the development of the art of voice," as predicated by Hirschman (1970:43). In turn, the refusal of the exit option by committed voice oppositionists revealed, and solidified, their basic "loyalty" to the opposed regime, also as predicated by Hirschman (ibid., 78).

Albert Hirschman further mentions that voice is more likely to be taken in the case of "top-quality" goods that cannot be obtained elsewhere. This points to the basic limitation of the exit-voice model if applied to East Germany: it cannot explain why, in contrast to Eastern European dissidents, East German regime opponents continued to consider socialism a "top-quality" good. An explanation of the peculiar *mode* of East German regime opposition requires an appreciation of the historical and cultural context that made East Germany different, and that furnished the regime with a bonus of legitimacy that was exceptional in the communist world.

2 Regime and Opposition in East Germany

AN "ANTI-FASCIST" COMBAT REGIME

At first sight, the case of East Germany is not much different from the other countries of Eastern Europe, where Leninist regimes were imposed by Soviet military intervention shortly after World War II. To the degree that the concept of Eastern Europe reflects the bipolar geopolitics of the cold-war era rather than the historical or cultural traits of the region, East Germany also is Eastern Europe. But if we want to understand the specific contours of regime and opposition in East Germany, we must first recognize the fundamental ways in which East Germany is *not* Eastern Europe. As Joseph Rothschild (1989:IX) justified the exclusion of East Germany from his political history of Eastern Europe, "the (East) German Democratic Republic is indeed a state, but it is not a nation and is less than half a country." More importantly, East Germany was a successor-state to Nazi Germany, the hegemonic power to the West that invaded and occupied the small Slavic nations in the East.[1] Unlike Eastern Europe, where Leninist regimes were installed by sheer force, communism in Germany appeared as a positive "moral option" (Szczypiorski, 1991) that seemed to draw the adequate lesson from the defeat of Nazism.

Following Philip Selznick (1952), I argued that Leninist regimes internalize an ethos of combat. Germany after the war offered the ideal terrain for the establishment of a combat regime, which could concentrate its negative energies on the eradication of Nazism. "Anti-Fascism" provided the obvious foundation myth for a communist state in Germany.[2] As M. Rainer Lepsius (1989) has shown, all successor states to the German Reich faced the problem to demarcate themselves from the dismaying past, and to define themselves in non-nationalist terms. West Germany opted for a strategy of "internalization," which saw the Bonn republic as the legal

30

successor (*Rechtsnachfolger*) of the German Reich, thus shouldering the ensuing responsibilities and obligations. By contrast, East Germany opted for a strategy of "universalization": the Hitler regime was interpreted as a variant of fascism, which – according to Stalinist orthodoxy – was the inevitable result of decaying capitalism; by abrogating capitalism, all ties to the Nazi past could be cut, and the foundations were laid for the creation of a morally cleansed, "better" Germany.[3] This allowed the new state, in a rather ingenious twist, to rid itself of all burdens stemming from the Nazi past, while also utilizing this past in legitimating itself as the perennially "anti-fascist" combat regime.

Unlike liberal democracies, which provide a set of rules and institutions that are indeterminate with regard to who impersonates and follows them, Leninist [*sic*] regimes bear a strong charismatic imprint: they seek to perpetuate the "personal heroism" of their founders (Jowitt 1983:277). The formative experience of the communist leadership of East Germany was, indeed, the struggle against fascism and Nazism. As members of the prewar German Communist Party (KPD), many of them had participated in the Spanish civil war, had fought the rise of the Nazi movement in Weimar Germany, and then had faced imprisonment and death under Hitler, unless they managed to escape into exile. The Ulbricht Group, the nucleus of the new communist leadership, comprised veterans of the KPD who had survived Hitler (as well as the Stalinist purges) in Soviet exile.[4] As in the classic Bolshevist case, authority was claimed on the basis of action, not of constitutional procedures (Selznick, 1952:245). The heroic, and victorious, struggle against "Hitler-Fascism" (so went the official formula) justified communist rule, and this until its very end in 1989 (Knütter, 1991:22). By the same token, the charismatic basis of communist rule indicates its inherent limitations. Like all communist regimes, the East German regime did not dispose of institutional rules that allowed the orderly succession of new leadership generations. Not by accident, in East Germany's final hour those were still in charge who, like party chief Erich Honecker or the chief of the security police, Erich Mielke, had taken an active role in founding the regime under "anti-fascist" premises some forty years earlier. As one can conclude from Karl Mannheim's

(1952) seminal reflections on the problem of generations, without the "fresh contact" of new generations social change is either blocked or bound to become explosive. By 1989, the aged leadership was quite literally unable to understand the needs and motivations of the young generations who had grown up in relative security and prosperity, but now were fleeing the country in masses. "Socialism is so good that they want more and more," said the senile chief of the security police in a good example of generational myopia. "In my time we couldn't buy bananas, not because there were none, but because we had no money to buy them."[5]

As Philip Selznick (1952:318) demonstrated, communist strategy and tactics by definition "[elude] the need to win consent." In this regard too, defeated Nazi Germany offered an ideal terrain. The new leadership would approach its subjects from the suspicious distance of "reeducation," which legitimized its dictatorial practices. After all, the Hitler regime had not been overthrown by the German people themselves, but by the Allied forces. Since no resistance movement had challenged Hitler from within, the German people were accessories to his crimes (see Leonhard, 1955:288). Accordingly, before the people could become sovereign, they had to be educated for it (Dubiel 1991). Given the anti-fascist combat mission against the home population, any form of national communism, which could ease, if only for brief periods, the rigours of communist rule in Poland, Hungary or Czechoslovakia, was foreclosed in East Germany. Still in 1991, a leading communist of the first hour saw it as a lasting achievement of the withered regime that "our [*sic*] citizens have no resemblance with the fascist types that most of them had been in 1945".[6]

Its programmatic anti-fascism provided the East German regime with a moral bonus and quasi-legitimacy that was foreclosed to other communist regimes in Soviet-occupied Eastern Europe. In addition, until the building of the Berlin Wall in 1961, an element, however implicit, of choice kept the populace to the communist regime, even on the part of those who never felt much sympathy for the communist rulers. One of them, who only had to cross the Bernauer Strasse in Berlin to escape to the West, and who was then a theology student at the Free University in the

Western part of the city, explicates his motives for staying: "I always hated the communist system. But it was a conscious decision to stay in the East. This was partially because of family ties, but also because I felt an obligation to improve things there where I lived."[7] A Polish Jew, who had survived Auschwitz, defended her choice to move from Frankfurt am Main to East Berlin in more positive terms: "The GDR, so we thought, is an anti-fascist country, where one had the possibility to participate in something meaningful, where something was built that no longer resembled the old Germany".[8] Germany after the war, in however implicit and limited ways, offered the unique option to choose the kind of state in which one wanted to live, and in a country demoralized by defeat and guilt over the past, the messianic hope to build a "better Germany" on explicitly "anti-fascist" grounds made the East German state the obvious choice of many.

This element of choice, and ensuing loyalty, was most prominent among the intellectuals. Here was a state that purported to make a radical break with the criminal regime that had forced most of them into exile, and that put itself into the service of an *idea*. The Bonn republic, which confined itself to the stale and banal proceduralism of Western liberal democracy and, most appallingly, did not deny its legal continuity with the Germany of the past, could not still the romantic need for pathos and salvation – a core motif of the German intellectual tradition, and even more so after Hitler (see Stern 1961). For Johannes R. Becher, the expressionist poet and later minister of culture who had returned to East Germany from his Moscow exile, the new state was nothing less than the "Reich that is called Goethe," in which the old division between "spirit" (*Geist*) and "power" (*Macht*) was finally reconciled.[9] The score of exiled intellectuals who preferred East Berlin to Bonn is impressive indeed, including leading writers such as Berthold Brecht, Anna Seghers, Heinrich Mann and Arnold Zweig, noted literary critics such as Hans Mayer and Alfred Kantorowicz, and the philosopher Ernst Bloch.[10] In no other country of Soviet-occupied Eastern Europe did the intellectual élite so completely swallow the notorious pill of "Murti-Bing" (C.Milosz), which would make them obedient followers of communist rule. The Weimar-generation intellectuals, whose affiliation with the new regime was a matter of choice, not of imposition, would remain silent, or even side with the regime, when workers took to the streets in 1953, and they did not raise their voice when a younger generation of "revisionists" were put to show trials in 1956 (see Croan, 1962). Also later on, the leading intellectuals of the country remained conspicuously absent from opposition movements. Even in 1989, the intellectual élite, socialized in the post-war era but no less loyal to the communist state than the preceding Weimar generation, intervened only when the separate existence of the East German state was at risk. Quite tellingly, the proclamation "For Our Country," initiated by leading literary intellectuals such as Christa Wolf and Stefan Heym, conjured up the "anti-fascist and humanist values" upon which the communist state had been allegedly founded, and, likewise tellingly, the proclamation was also signed by leading communist functionaries (see Chapter 5).

The infatuation of intellectuals cannot deny the fact that in East Germany a communist system was erected that was as autocratic and totalitarian as any in the Soviet hemisphere. Alone, nowhere was it easier to conceal that fact. As Sigrid Meuschel (1992:40) put it aptly, "the anti-fascism formula accomplished the miracle to render the Stalinism in the GDR to oblivion. The terror was repressed, but the idea of an extraordinary mission survived." As throughout Eastern Europe, the Soviet-backed communist forces initially used the strategy of the National Front to hide their innate aspiration for total power. Walter Ulbricht, head of the Ulbricht Group, caught the Leninist logic in precise terms: "It must look democratic, but we must be in charge".[11] To fully understand this crucial point, it is useful to recollect the "operational code" (Selznick) of communist strategy and tactics. Historically, and depicted in social movement terms, communism stemmed from the split of the socialist movement into a social-democratic wing advocating legalist and electoral strategies and a Leninist-bolshevist wing shunning "rotten parliamentarism" (Lenin, 1932:41) in favour of the direct and unconstitutional seizure of power through cadre activism cum mass upheaval.[12] In contrast to social democracy, which puts program over office and is rather indifferent as to who holds power as long as its goals are served, the aspiration of Leninism is unabashedly élitist-activist: "To be a bolshevik is not simply to say that communism will win, but that *we* will seize the power, *our* nerve will not fail, to *us* will come the victory" (Selznick, 1952:113f). Since Leninism is by definition the business of élite activists, that is, of numerical minorities, it is always in fear of isolation and marginalization. Defying Blanquist élite combat for programmatic reasons,[13] Leninism's major strategic problem is to find access to the societal sources of power: isolation must be avoided and techniques devised for access and penetration of target groups and institutions (ibid., 77). This is the root of the United Front strategy, which is the seeking of tactical alliances with other "progressive" forces in the quest for total power. The purpose of these alliances is not the broadening of the communist power base, but the destruction of competing social forces.[14] "Unity," as Philip Selznick (ibid., 126) argues to the point, is the "most common, and most deceptive, of the communist slogans," because its exclusive purpose for the communists is the control and dismantling of its allies. As Lenin said, communists support other parties "as the rope supports a hanged man."

The struggle against fascism opened up the possibility to leap over the class lines of United Front strategy, and to establish "anti-fascist people's fronts" that also included "bourgeois" and other non-proletarian elements. In post-war Eastern Europe, the cross-class cutting "anti-fascism" formula was a rather ingenious device, since it allowed the Soviet-backed communist forces to tap social groups and structures that previously had been immune to their influence. This entailed, initially, some concessions to nationalist rhetorics and the pledge not to impose the Soviet model on societies with a bourgeois-democratic heritage – here lies the origin of the Eastern European notion of people's republic. The National Front strategy sometimes implied a complete denial of communist identity. For instance, the National Committee for a Free Germany, a Soviet-based organization of German exiled communists that tried to convert high-ranking prisoners-of-war to the communist cause, and in many ways the origin of the East German communist regime, rallied behind the black-white-red flag – the colours of Prusso-Wilhelminian militarism (Leonhard, 1955:244).

In East Germany, the National Front strategy fell on particularly fertile soil. Given the almost complete devastation of the country by war, and the eradication and delegitimation of the old political élites, the "joint work on reconstruction" (in Weber 1985:83) seemed more opportune than party conflict and competition for votes. Moreover, party conflict was negatively associated with the factionalism that had undermined and destroyed the Weimar Republic. Finally, the stress on unity and consensus dovetailed with the German political tradition, which Ralf Dahrendorf (1971:151) aptly characterized as a conflict-averse "desire for synthesis" (*Sehnsucht nach Synthese*). Wilhelm Pieck, first president of the GDR, evoked this tradition, when he favorably contrasted the "unanimity of parties and organizations (in the GDR)" with the "ugly struggle between egoistic parties [in West Germany]".[15] The communists did not even shy from nationalist language, stating that it was imperative to put "the fatherland above everything" or calling their effort at cultural renewal a "German movement" (see Pike, 1992:15f).

In the immediate post-war period, the major purpose of the National Front – to allow the communists to tap the sources of societal power – was not readily apparent. As in Czechoslovakia and Hungary, a *national* road to socialism seemed to be in the making, as indicated in the readmission of major pre-war parties, such as the Social-Democrats (SPD), or the founding of new ones, such as the Christian-conservative CDU and the national-liberal LDP. The refounded Communist Party (KPD) even propagated a "parliamentary, antifascist-democratic republic" instead of proletarian dictatorship (Weber, 1985:121), which was in part tactically motivated but also sprang from the orthodox view that the "bourgeois" had to precede the "socialist" revolution. The first Unity Front between the new parties, the so-called Antifa-Bloc, did not yet undermine the autonomy of the non-communist forces – even though the provision to reach decisions only by consensus apparently should prevent coalition-building against the KPD. But behind the pluralist façade, the Soviet Military Administration (SMAD) already secured the KPD most key positions in public administration, mass communication, and the security apparatus (ibid., 96–110).

The first step toward a Soviet-style one-party system occurred with the forced fusion between KPD and SPD and
the creation of the Socialist Unity Party (SED) in 1946. Here
the purpose of communist "blood-sucking," as Kurt
Schumacher, chief of the West-SPD, denounced the merger,
was already quite visible: the huge losses by communist parties in recent elections in Hungary and Austria had raised
the old specter of communist isolation, plunging the KPD
into a massive, Soviet-backed unity campaign. But a powerful historical motive easily obscured the more mundane reasons behind the campaign: the fateful historical split of the
German working-class movement, which had helped Hitler
into power, promised to be overcome.[16] Wolfgang Leonhard
(1955:387) noticed a "real, spontaneous enthusiasm among
the delegates" at the party foundation ceremony on 21 April.
Otto Grotewohl, leader of the SPD, hallowed his hand-shake
with KPD-chief Wilhelm Pieck: "When both of us went on
this stage, I became aware of the symbolic meaning of this
act. Wilhelm Pieck came from the left, I came from the
right. But we met in the middle" (ibid.). In fact, in the
beginning the SED was not yet a cadre but a mass party, it
rallied behind the doctrines of Marx, not Lenin, it stressed
the necessity of a German road to socialism, and all leadership positions were equally divided between former KPD and
SPD members.

Stalin's break with Tito in 1948 put an abrupt end to the
democratic-nationalist rhetoric and launched the overt Sovietization of East Germany. Whereas in Eastern Europe the
same transition was met with considerable resistance by
nationally minded communists (see Rothschild, 1989: ch. 3),
it occurred with relative ease in East Germany. Due to the
lack of a domestic resistance movement against Hitler, there
was no split among German communists between "local
undergrounders" and "Muscovites" that could have caused
infighting and opposition to Stalin's new line.[17] It also paid
off that the German KPD had always been the most doctrinary
and Soviet-dependent in Europe. Anton Ackermann, the early
champion of a German road to socialism, quickly delivered
the required auto-critique and professed his allegiance
to the "bolshevist party of the Soviet Union" (Leonhard,
1955:458). Robert Tucker (1961:283) once noted that in

Leninist struggle the combatted domestic order is treated "as though it were foreign." This was quite literally true in post-war Germany, where nationalism was discredited on principle, and where the exile experience had made the communist leadership obedient followers of Stalin – perfect conditions for erecting one of the most austere of all Leninist regimes.[18]

In 1948/9, the SED revamped itself as a Leninist cadre-party, purging the party leadership from former SPD members, introducing the principle of democratic centralism, abrogating the German road to socialism, and embracing the "great leader" Stalin instead. The National Front proper, which was founded shortly after the official proclamation of the GDR in October 1949, was little more than a stooge for communist one-party rule. It included two new parties, the National Democratic Party (NDPD) and the Peasant Party (DBP), both of which had been formed a year earlier as SED-steered satraps to neutralize a latent CDU/LDP opposition to sovietization. The National Front also included major mass organizations such as the Trade Union Council (FDGB) and the Young Pioneers, both of which had been SED-controlled from the beginning.

In this final phase, the United Front strategy shifted its function: once power had been seized, it became a means of effective control. All parties had to pledge their allegiance to the "leading role of the SED as the party of the working-class." The first "elections" in 1950, like all the following ones, were based on joint candidate lists of the National Front, which secured the SED an *ex ante* majority. Wilhelm Pieck defended the first unity list in both old and new terms: "The desire for peace unites the whole people, independently of ideology or class affiliation. In the struggle for peace all parties and organizations of the GDR have agreed upon a joint election list, because every splitting of the democratic camp would endanger peace. This we are taught by our past. Vote for the joint candidate list of the National Front, so that never again a mother will have to mourn for her son".[19] In the emergent cold-war era, the combat against fascism was gradually transformed into a "struggle for peace" (*Kampf um den Frieden*). In the Soviet hemisphere, the "anti-Hitler coalition" refashioned itself as a "world peace front," whose new enemy became "American imperialism." While flexible in the choice of its targets, without an enemy the combat regime could not be.

A STATE, NOT A NATION

Mirabeau once remarked about Prussia that it was not a country that had an army, but an army that had a country. About East Germany he might have said that it was not a country that had succumbed to communist rule, but communist rule that sought to create a country just for itself. Unlike the countries of Eastern Europe, the German Democratic Republic was a *creatio ex nihilo*, with no history and artificial borders to split rather than encompass a national collectivity. Pushing aside the inertia of nation and history, the new state was founded on nothing but sheer will-power, a triumph of Sovietism like the steel towns raised from nothingness. Next to the Soviet Union itself, the GDR was communism's most radical experiment of state- without nation-building. In the end, both were nothing but communist states – no wonder that both have since disappeared from the map of existing states.

The GDR (*DDR*), as the new state came to call itself, exposes in crystalline form the ambiguous relationship between communism and nationalism. Since German nationalism was discredited by Nazism, the canvas was perennially clean for communist rule. In this regard, optimal conditions existed: an explicitly nationalist opposition was unlikely to develop, or it would take the unpolitical form of individual exit to the western part of Germany. On the other hand, the case of East Germany also shows the fragility and precariousness of a Leninist regime that could not bolster its legitimacy by national symbolism and rhetoric. The GDR never lost the aura of being provisional and artificial, of a "state that must not be" (Richert 1964) and proverbial "satellite" of Moscow. Timothy Garton Ash once remarked that anniversaries were celebrated in the GDR "as if [each] were the last, like the birthday of a child born with a hole in the heart" (Ash, 1981:9). A state that could not arouse national loyalties was notoriously incomplete. An East German writer expressed the predicament of a nationless state well: "Take the word Austria, how well it sounds, or Scandinavia, England, France... And what does the word GDR tell us? An abstract concept? Can one love a country with such a name?"[20]

East Germany's problem of national identity is instructive, because it demonstrates that communist regimes cannot exist within, but also not without a national framework. Their ideology defies national allegiances, while their institutional stabilization requires them. Ernest Renan once said that "the existence of a nation is an everyday plebiscite" (Renan, 1964:10). While all communist regimes are precisely not nations in their obvious refusal to stand the test of the "everyday plebiscite," East Germany's special predicament was the existence of a concrete measure for its incapability to command national loyalties: West Germany. Before the building of the Berlin Wall in August 1961, which may be considered the GDR's "secret foundation day" (Staritz 1985:138), one-sixth of the population had insisted on their "everyday plebiscite" by fleeing to the West. Exit became the mutilated form in which East Germans expressed their desire for national self-determination. The building of the Berlin Wall epitomized the decisive "natural defect" of the GDR (Glässner, 1988:123): its negative but constitutive fixation on the Federal Republic.

In his interesting study of kinship and "nationness" in both post-war Germanies, John Borneman (1992) argues that each state tried to build its own identity in an "intimate process of mirror-imaging and misrecognition" (p. 4). The anthropologist's penchant for dual classifications obscures the asymmetrical quality of state-building in East and West. Already the official foundation of the GDR in October 1949 was a reaction to the proclamation of the Bonn republic a few months earlier, and it would remain so from remilitarization to *détente,* all of which were Western initiatives that forced a fundamental redefinition of Eastern identity. Based on an anthropological definition of "nationness" as "a subjectivity, not contingent on an opinion or attitude, but derived from lived experience within a state" (ibid., 338 fn. 11), Borneman concludes that "by 1989 there were two German nations" (p. 311). This bold statement leaves one wondering what by 1990 had happened to one of them. If one defines nations *à la* Foucault as state-controlled kin-ship and lifecourse patterns, one must overlook the histori-cal inertia that may prevent states from forming nations in their image.

In this context, it is important to note that initially there was a contest between both post-war states over the legit-imate representation of the German nation. But once it re-alized that it could not win this contest, the East German regime went over to erase the German component from its self-definition. It is often forgotten today that until the coming of *détente* in the early 1970s the communist regime pursued a German unity course with sometimes starkly nationalist connotations. Already the "anti-fascist" Unity Front of 1945 was founded with the explicit purpose "to save the nation" (in Hacker 1987:44). Since "capitalism" was held respon-sible for the rise of fascism, the "leadership of the nation" had passed on from the bourgeoisie to the working class. As Otto Grotewohl, who had led the SPD into the merger with the KPD, said, "only the German working class can be the leader and representative of the German nation arising from the ruins of the past" (ibid., 45). From this perspec-tive, the Bonn republic was denounced as a "vassal govern-ment" of the Western powers, which had "split" the nation. On its Second Party Conference in 1952, the SED succumbed to a distressingly nationalist and anti-Western tone that was not unfamiliar to German ears: "The national liberation struggle against the American, English and French occupiers in Westgermany (*Westdeutschland*) and for the overthrow of the vassal government in Bonn is the task of all peace-minded and patriotic forces in Germany" (ibid., 46). The "anti-fascist" combat orientation was invoked to justify the regime's all-German claims. As Walter Ulbricht stated in 1960, "the le-gitimate German state can only be the one that fights in the tradition of the Anti-Hitler tradition against the rebirth of German militarism and fascism" (in Ludz, 1977:231).

In light of this, James McAdams (1993:25) rightly says that, initially at least, "the national ideal was probably as dear to the East German elite as it was to that of the FRG." But one must not forget that in a Leninist regime questions of value are forever subordinated to those of strategy and tactics. As a first-hand expert on communism clarified, "the Commu-

nists are not *nationalists*; for them, the insistence on nationalism is only a *form*, just like any other form, through which
they strengthen their powers" (Djilas, 1957:100). The regime
resorted to nationalist discourse only as long as it served
the early United Front strategy and the later Soviet-initiated
campaign against the "secessionist" Adenauer regime. Once
it threatened the socialist identity of the regime, nationalist
discourse was dropped.

How could it be invoked in the first? First and foremost,
the theme of unity, overdetermined by German history and
political culture, was equally central to communist and
nationalist discourse. This elective affinity made it almost
unavoidable for communists to exploit popular attitudes that
had been well-nurtured by Nazism. Accordingly, the recently
founded Socialist Unity (*sic*) Party presented itself as the
"genuinely national party of the German people" (quoted
in Pike, 1992:177). But secondly, the KPD-Comintern theory
of fascism itself left open the possibility of a positive identification with the German nation. If Hitler was merely a puppet
of the monopoly capitalists who had "enslaved" the German
people, there were two Germanies, "One hated, one loved!/
One sworn to the Hitlers/ The other true to itself."[21] Officially abandoned after the war because of its apparent
implausibility in the face of unflagging popular support for
Hitler, the notion of two Germanies reappeared in the attempt by the communist regime to claim the allegedly
untainted German cultural heritage, "the Germany of great
thinkers, scientists and poets, whose labors have enriched
the world's culture."[22] Along these lines, the regime celebrated
a Goethe Year in 1949, a Bach Year in 1950, a Beethoven
Year in 1952, and a Schiller Year in 1955. Thomas Mann
(1960:1146) had persuasively argued against such attempts
that there was "only one [Germany], whose best, through
devil's ruse, had turned into its worst." In a striking confir-
mation of this famous diction, also the "good Germany"
claimed by the communists contained a distressing amount
of evil. Particularly when utilized as a weapon against the
West-oriented Bonn republic, this cultural nationalism was
infused with motives previously exploited by Nazism, distinguishing the "folkish" national culture of Germany from
the "rootless cosmopolitanism" and "cultural barbarism" of

the West, not even shrinking back from overt anti-Semitism.[23]

On the political terrain, the building of the Berlin Wall was the first concession of defeat in the struggle over representing the German nation. If the nation was there where peoples' feet would carry them, it was in the West. The Wall brought home that communist regimes are the exact negation of the "everyday plebiscite" that constitutes a nation, replacing the citizen by the subject, the "equally impotent" (Dahrendorf, 1971:435). Party chief Ulbricht defended the "cordon sanitaire" in revealing terms: "It is common knowledge that drug addicts are isolated from addicting drugs for their own interests and for their recovery. Likewise, we have separated from West Berlin many of those citizens who had become confused by the swamp [of West Berlin]. I am convinced that in the majority of cases this sickness will prove curable".[24] The Wall, sometimes belittled as a necessary condition of stability or even legitimacy,[25] epitomized that the GDR was by definition an "illegitimate state" (Naimark 1979: 549). It also reinforced the regime's perennial fixation on the western part of the country. After all, it could constitute itself only by an act of *delimitation* from the West. No such dramatic demarcation from the East was obviously necessary to found and stabilize the Bonn republic. The Wall was certainly consistent with a regime based on combat; consequently, though no less absurd, the Wall became officially referred to as "anti-fascist protection wall" (*anti-faschistischer Schutzwall*). But it stood as an all-visible symbol that the state could only exist by preventing its populace from leaving. After the Wall, the SED-regime still claimed to defend national unity, but now conceded the existence of two separate states. This became enshrined in the Constitution of 1968, which defined the GDR as a "socialist state of German nation" (*sozialistischer Staat deutscher Nation*).

Geopolitical *détente* brought a decisive turn in the regime's position on the national question. Once again, a Western overture forced a fundamental reorientation of Eastern identity. As part of its new *Ostpolitik*, the SPD/FDP government under Chancellor Willy Brandt was ready to trade a *de facto* recognition of the GDR's sovereignty for a partial opening of the "iron curtain." The rationale of this new chapter of Bonn's *Deutschlandpolitik* was that the goal of national unity,

firmly enshrined in the Basic Law, was better served by
relaxing the relationship between both German states, instead of insisting on the ever more unrealistic goal of state
unity. The rapprochement of the split nation at the level of
everyday exchanges was rightly perceived by the communist
regime as a serious threat. In an implicit acknowledgement
that the legitimate representation of the German nation was
with the West, the all-German claim was suddenly dropped,
and all references to German national identity were systematically eradicated and purged. From now on, the communist regime no longer claimed to be German, and the plain
acronym "DDR" came to be used as if it were the name of
a separate nation. While the *détente* philosophy of "peaceful
coexistence" finally brought the GDR the long-desired recognition on the international scene, domestically it undermined the strategy of state consolidation through seclusion
from the West.[26] Aware that it could not win the test of
national loyalty, the regime sought to bolster its socialist
identity. How could the second German state justify its existence if not in socialist terms? Socialism became a kind of
ersatz nationality. The new Constitution of 1974 dropped
all reference to Germanness, and the state now defined itself, like the Soviet Union, in non-national terms as a "socialist
state of workers and peasants." In the same document, the
perennial Soviet satellite moved back to square one by pro-
fessing its "eternal friendship with the Soviet Union" (see
Staritz, 1985:211). A deliberate strategy of delimitation
(*Abgrenzung*) hammered down that capitalism and socialism
could not mix. The anthem could no longer be sung, since
its text referred to "Germany, united fatherland" (*Deutschland,
einig Vaterland*); the German Academy of Sciences was renamed "Academy of Sciences of the *DDR* ", the German Union
of Journalists became the "Union of Journalists of the *DDR* ",
Radio Germany (Deutschlandsender) was now called Radio
DDR, and so forth (see McAdams, 1985:103).

The paradoxical attempt of nation-building through eradi-
cating the national component culminated in the new doctrine that a "socialist nation" was in the making, which had
nothing in common with the "capitalist nation" in the West.
This position, elaborated by party ideologue Alfred Kosing
(1976), entailed that two German nations existed separately

from one another, thus blunting by conceptual *fiat* the threat of a national rapprochement. Obviously aware of the implausibility of the two-nation thesis, Kosing made a further distinction between "nation", which was defined by class, and "nationality", which was defined by ethnicity – thus reintroducing the German component through the back door. When SED-chief Erich Honecker was asked how to fill out a passport application, he responded along these muddled lines: "Citizenship-GDR, nationality-German".[27]

This inconclusive tinkering at the problem of national identity did not convince the East German population. In 1975, more than two-thirds of the population did *not* consider West Germany a foreign country, as suggested by the communist leadership (Ludz, 1977:224). Wavering in the nationality question only underlined the regime's notorious artificiality and lack of legitimacy. No plausible concept of nation could be established if the "everyday plebiscite" was denied. Moreover, the attempt to engineer a national identity was caught in a contradiction. As the Latin word *natio* conveys, nationhood implies continuity and tradition. "Thinking about one's nationality is thinking under the spell of the origins" (Sloterdijk, 1990:80). The (German) origins, however, the regime had *grosso modo* swept away, with the broom of "anti-fascism". If socialism was a future-oriented thing, then it was especially so in the GDR. The GDR always remained what it had been from the outset: a state, not a nation.

The GDR was the only communist regime in Eastern Europe where overt regime nationalism had to be absent, while many of its covert aspirations could not, appearing instead in curiously subverted forms. When national communism sought to soften the yoke of Soviet hegemony in Kadar's Hungary and Gomulka's Poland, East Germany did not go untouched. Walter Ulbricht's exposition of the GDR in the 1960s as a socialist show-case of technological prowess and economic strength had unmistakably regime-nationalist undertones – suggesting that the leadership role in the socialist camp was about to be passed on from the Soviet Union to East Germany. But tellingly, the East German way of articulating nationalist aspirations was hyper-socialism, as in Ulbricht's bold claim that the "socialist human community" (*sozialistische Menschengemeinschaft*) had already been realized,

but only in the GDR. Also Ulbricht's astonishing feud with
Moscow over his refusal to accept the first Western *détente*
overture, which ultimately caused his downfall, smacked of
nationalism in disguise. "Coming from any other leader,
[Ulbricht's] policy would have been seen as one of nationalism," J.F.Brown (1988:248) stated in obvious amazement, "but
the GDR and nationalism seemed incompatible notions."

Whereas regime nationalism would ease the rigors of communist rule in Eastern Europe, the East German display of
independence from Moscow under the late Ulbricht had to
be directed against the home population, whose obvious
interest in the humanitarian benefits of *détente* made it implicit allies of Moscow against the own rulers. When *détente*
had finally become accepted under Honecker, but threatened to be buried by the mounting superpower rivalry of
the early 1980s, a similar quasi-nationalism appeared again
– with reversed roles. In astonishing defiance of the Soviet
line, the GDR refused to cut its ties with the West, citing a
"German responsibility for peace" (Honecker). This complete turnaround is only *prima facie* surprising, because by
then the East German regime had learned to exploit *détente*
for purposes of regime stabilization (see Chapter 3).

FROM MOBILIZATION TO POST-MOBILIZATION

Leninist regimes are intrinsically geared toward mobilization and combat. As mobilization regimes, their aspiration
is the all-out penetration and activation of society in the
name of a single, overarching goal.[28] As combat regimes,
they are poised for permanent struggle – an enemy always
has to be defeated.[29] In this light, terror is not a deplorable
deviation, but the adequate *modus operandi* of a regime that
struggles rather than governs, confronts rather than represents society.[30] The problem is that mobilization and combat,
though constitutive for Leninist regimes, are also self-termi-
nating. Effective resistance becomes eliminated or neutralized over time, and the mobilization drive yields, at least
partially, the modernized and equalitarian social structures
it aimed at. At this point, Leninist regimes are forced to
"make peace with society" (Löwenthal, 1976:101). They must

meet the functional exigencies of an industrial economy, recognize and arbitrate between the multiplicity of interests in a differentiated society, and find a form of quasi-legitimacy that moderates the activist-terrorist pretensions.

At this post-mobilization stage, Leninist regimes face a fundamental dilemma: regime consolidation requires the relaxation of total control and engineered change; giving in to this need, however, militates against the regime's constitutive principles. As Ken Jowitt (1983:277) characterized the combat need, "as charismatically conceived and organized units, Leninist parties require combat environments to preserve their organizational integrity." In a regime that replaces the rule of law through arbitrary élite discretion, no stable formula to reconcile the conflicting requirements of regime consolidation and charismatic self-definition could be found. Spasmodic fits of reform and repression, increasing regime ossification and corruption, and sustained dissidence and opposition came to characterize the post-mobilization stage of Leninist regimes.[31]

In Soviet-occupied Eastern Europe, the transition from mobilization to post-mobilization has often been interpreted as a "return to diversity" (Rothschild, 1989) or "organic rejection" (Brzezinski, 1989) of Soviet rule. After the forced annexation and assimilation to the Soviet Union, with streamlined one-party systems and Stalinist terror, followed the cautious reassertion of national independence, forging a kind of community of destiny between the national communist rulers and their subjects. In nationless East Germany, the demarcation line between mobilization and post-mobilization had to be less clear-cut. Until 1961, the moderating impact of the open Western border prevented the terroristic excesses that had accompanied the Sovietization of Hungary or Czechoslovakia, particularly after Stalin's rift with Tito. However, the lack of a national platform to unite rulers and ruled also made the subsequent de-Stalinization efforts less thorough in East Germany than in the other Eastern European countries. Ulbricht would rule his communist state with iron claw and consistency from the late 1940s to the early 70s, unmoved by the periodic turmoil and dramatic leadership successions in neighbouring Poland, Czechoslovakia, or Hungary. Though never in the full grip of unmitigated terror, East Germany never fully escaped the doctrinary and monolithic spell of mature Stalinism either.

Like almost everything in East Germany, the particular contours of mobilization and post-mobilization must be seen in the context of the other German state. Since socialism was the only justification for the separate existence of the GDR, it could not be compromised or relativized in any way. Situated at the frontline between socialism and capitalism, East Germany offered almost ideal conditions for permanent mobilization and combat. There was no scarcity of imagined enemies and subversive plotting to feed the conspiratorial fantasy of the communist rulers, and to keep the apparatus in constant vigilance and combat readiness. As, for instance, the gargantuan size of its secret police apparatus attests, the GDR was the ultimate combat regime of the Soviet hemisphere.

On the other hand, the GDR also could not escape the exigencies of post-mobilization. In the most highly developed and industrialized country in the Soviet bloc, the regime had to be particularly adaptive to the requirements of a differentiated modern society. High living standards and consumption levels were necessary to counteract the insidious comparisons with the western part of the nation and its "economic miracle." But bolstering consumption and the quality of life was bound to be permanently frustrated by the higher-developed and more prosperous West. Moreover, the lessening of ideological rigor and combat readiness threatened the very existence of the socialist GDR, and thus had to be always counteracted by ultra-repressive measures that are more typical of the mobilization stage.

As a result, mobilization and post-mobilization were simultaneous aspects rather than clear-cut temporal sequences in East German communist development. In this vein, Thomas Baylis (1974:XII) correctly observed the "simultaneous adherence to inconsistent if not contradictory visions of society" in East Germany, arguing that "the aspiration toward total mobilization and control coexists rather *illogically* with a growing awareness of the demands of diverse social forces" (emphasis added). Only, "illogical" this coexistence was not. It precisely reflected the German situation, a nation divided into capitalist and socialist halves, which created the perennial need for the GDR to define itself in exclusively socialist terms. But the peculiarities of the German case also helped to bring out more clearly than elsewhere a dilemma that all Leninist regimes had to face: their simultaneous need to confront and to accommodate to their societies.

The New Economic System

The simultaneity of confrontation and accommodation is already visible in the first major episode of post-mobilization in East Germany – which occurred directly after the building of the Berlin Wall. The Wall, that ultimate symbol of communist mobilization and domestic warfare, had ironic consequences. Now that exit was no longer feasible, it became both necessary and possible to "integrate" the population more positively, and to forge at least a "partial identity between party and people" (Ludz, 1970:11). Only now some belated and rather cautious attempts at de-Stalinization were made. The Soviet dictator's monument in East Berlin disappeared, and streets, factories and cities were renamed. Limited rule of law was introduced, with a more independent judiciary and a "state protected" sphere of privacy and family life (Weber, 1985:355f). Because of the exit-induced shortage of skilled labor, ideological indoctrination was scaled down in education and academia. A brief cultural thaw brought critical artists to prominence, such as novelist Reiner Kunze or song-writer Wolf Biermann, and Western authors could be published in *Sinn und Form*, East Germany's major intellectual platform.

A sweeping reorganization of the economy became the core of this post-Wall reform period. The New Economic System (NES) of 1963 was the first major attempt to mitigate the rigidities of the planning economy in the Eastern Bloc. Marketlike devices for allocating resources and stimulating performance were introduced (so-called "economic levers"), including price, cost, profit, and sales (see Baylis 1974:233–60). The role of material incentives in economic performance, once branded as capitalist vestige, was upgraded. Not ideology, but technical competence (*Sachlichkeit*) should henceforth guide political and economic decision-making. The party apparatus was restructured according to a new "production principle." This principle divided the party along functional rather than territorial lines, granted more autonomy to local units, and aimed at replacing the old *apparatchiki* by a new brand of young professional experts (Ludz, 1970:35). When the "end of ideology" was proclaimed in the West, the East also came under the spell of the "scientific-technological revolution."

The New Economic System was East Germany's hour of the technical intelligentsia. This was also the group most highly represented among those who had fled the country before (and after) the Wall.[32] The self-styled "socialist achievement and consumption society" (Ulbricht) should evidently win them back. How well did this succeed? On the one hand, the privileges and career chances now available to the technical intelligentsia did bind them closer to the regime, and this group would largely abstain, now and in the future, from protest and opposition politics. As J.F.Brown (1988:236) put it aptly, "the technocrats became for the GDR what the officer corps had been for Imperial Germany." On the other hand, the political gains of the technocrats were rather limited. The apex of communist power, the politburo, remained firmly in the hands of *apparat* men and ideologues.[33] Only in the Central Committee of the SED and the Council of Ministers did experts and professionals make some inroads. Refuting Peter Ludz's (1972) influential thesis of the "institutionalized counter-elite," Thomas Baylis (1974:264) cooly observed that "no titanic struggles between technocrats and apparatchiki have taken place." Also in the GDR, the intelligentsia was certainly not on the road to class power.[34]

The fate of the New Economic System is instructive, because it indicates the inherent limits to post-mobilization practices in the GDR. Most reforms were soon reversed and abandoned. The "production principle," which had opened up the SED to the expert élite, was abolished in 1966 (Ludz, 1972:409). Fearing a spillover from economic reform to political liberalization, as happened in the Prague Spring, the conservative party leadership reemphasized the old virtues of "democratic centralism", with top – down party and state authority in economy and society (Baylis, 1972:50).[35] Most importantly, the techno-pragmatic language of system analysis and cybernetics, which had become *de rigueur* in the late

1960s, threatened to undermine the primacy of politics and ideology. Where was the enemy in all this? Party meetings came to resemble "economic conferences," the *apparatchiki* complained, and there was a precarious lack of ideological leadership (Staritz 1985:162). If science had been elevated to the primary productive force, how could the leading role of the party as vanguard of the working class still be justified? Mellowing the ideological front in technocratic terms would make the GDR just a copy of the Federal Republic, and a notoriously deficient and imperfect one at that.

From Ulbricht to Honecker

The leadership change from Ulbricht to Honecker in 1971 put politics and ideology back to the front seat. With Honecker, the ultimate *apparat* man came to power, one who had supervised the building of the Wall and whose "expertise" was in matters of party organization and security affairs. Doctrine replaced pragmatism, and – in an apparent hiss at the previously pampered intelligentsia – the working class was reasserted as the "chief" force of production in socialism (Baylis, 1974:258). Ulbricht's late fancy of the emergent "socialist human community" was rejected for its harmonistic and apolitical implications. As Honecker rightly figured, there was no bigger threat to the leading party than the loss of its enemy. As if to reconfirm that communist rule was first and foremost "conspiracy in power" (Brzezinski 1989), the new leader admonished his comrades that "the cultivation of socialist consciousness must always be bound up with the struggle against bourgeois ideology," and that "imperialism will use all means available to impair the socialist development of our republic".[36]

The new stress on ideology and combat must be seen in the context of *Ostpolitik* and *détente*. Under Ulbricht, the seclusion and isolation of the GDR from Western influence allowed a relative lessening of ideological rigor. The partial opening of the Wall due to *détente* reasserted the imperative of socialist self-definition. The Western overture of national *Annäherung* had to be countered by socialist *Abgrenzung*. After the Basic Treaty of December 1972, the country was swamped with Western visitors, and the everyday communications between the two Germanies intensified to an alarming degree. In 1977 alone, a total of 7.7 million West Germans visited the GDR. Telephone calls from West to East were up from 500 000 in 1969 to 9.7 million in 1975. By 1976, sixteen Western newspapers, journals, and radio and TV networks had offices in East Berlin, exposing the country to public scrutiny like no other in the Soviet bloc (Zimmermann, 1978:35–8). The GDR became transparent and receptive to Western influence, and the intensified human contacts threatened to reawake an all-German consciousness. What choice did the besieged rulers have but to hammer out socialist distinctiveness? "Peaceful coexistence," so the populace was told in a major exercise of Leninist Newspeak, was a form of "class struggle."[37]

Delimitation (*Abgrenzung*) became the regime's response to the lure of *détente*. The leading role of the party and of Marxist-Leninist doctrine, never in question, was rhetorically reinstated. At the workplace, party agitation regained primacy over technical expertise. The regime preached internal vigilance, and security-related matters took top priority – the secret police (*Stasi*) is really the child of *détente*. Military education was introduced in the schools, and state chief Honecker admonished his youngsters to "hate [the] enemy with the same passion and conviction with which [you] love and trust a friend" (quoted in McAdams, 1985:132). The new category of *Geheimnisträger* (carrier of secrets) prohibited employees of party, state, and other "sensitive" areas to have any contacts with Westerners. Admission to universities, relatively liberal under Ulbricht, was tightened along lines of ideological proficiency and "correct" class origins (Ludz, 1977:55f).[38]

I argued above that mobilization and post-mobilization elements appeared simultaneously in East German communist development. In fact, the reaffirmation of doctrinary zeal under Honecker was accompanied by a large-scale attempt to increase the general quality of life. If the populace was to give up the dream of reunification and forfeit political liberalization, it was to be rewarded with the highest consumption level in the communist world. The formula to accomplish this was the "unity of economic and social policy." It became codified in the Constitution of 1974: "The further raising of the material and cultural living standard of the people... is the decisive task of the developed socialist society" (quoted in Naimark, 1979:559). Behind the facade of ideological *Abgrenzung*, Honecker's East Germany adopted the most typical feature of post-mobilization regimes: the trading of political non-interference for economic well-being. If socialism under Ulbricht was still the future-oriented thing that stressed investment and deferred gratification for the vague promise of bliss, Honecker's "real existing socialism" had lost the power of transcendence. It stressed instead the virtues of normalcy and of the life here and now. Consumption, not production, was the new focus. An ambitious housing program provided 600 000 new or renovated units between 1971 and 1975, and aimed at some 770 000 additional units by 1980 – not a small thing in a country of only 16 million people (Zimmermann, 1978:26). Minimum wages, old-age pensions, maternity leave, and health-care benefits all increased significantly. Basic living-costs, such as rents and food prices, were kept at state-subsidized minimum levels, and the more refined tastes were courted by so-called Intershops, in which imported luxury goods could be purchased with Western currency. In another curious counterpoint to the mantra of *Abgrenzung*, even the watching of West German television was no longer outlawed, and the state and party chief himself promised to diversify the domestic entertainment options.

In everyday experience, the result was the "double life" that is so typical for post-mobilization regimes. And nowhere was the contrast between doctrinary pretension and private life-styles more extreme than in the GDR, a country based on nothing but a doctrine, but also the richest in the Soviet bloc. "Nowhere in Eastern Europe," writes the most astute of the area's observers, "is the life with two languages and two opinions, the art of the double tongue, so widespread and perfected... Here is a society of split people in a split nation" (Ash, 1981:205f). Günter Gaus (1986), romanticizing somewhat, has described the state-tolerated life in the shadow as "niche society." In the private niches of the *Schrebergarten* or the *Landhaus*, which were not the privilege of a few but amenities of the many, most East Germans made peace with their regime. Close observers even discovered the contours of an emergent "state identity" (*Staatsbewusstsein*) among East Germans (Gaus, 1986:124f). While it did not add up to a separate national identity, it fed upon a natural pride about hard-won material achievements.[39] In similar terms, Peter Ludz, the *éminence grise* of Western GDR scholars, found the rise of a specific "GDR-consciousness", which he defined as "self-awareness, a pride in achievement, and scepticism toward the West and especially toward West Germany" (Ludz 1970:30).

In fact, the 1970s were the heyday of the GDR's obvious emancipation as a sovereign, stabilized state that seemed to have shed the previous curse of artificiality and temporariness. Demography helped. By 1971, 60 per cent of the population were politically socialized in the GDR, and only 25 per cent still carried a personal memory of Weimar and Nazi Germany (Staritz, 1985:207f). The GDR seemed to have produced a socialist young generation that was fully integrated and loyal to the regime. Surveys by the Leipzig Youth Institute show that in the 1970s "socialist convictions and value orientations" were shared by a wide majority of the GDR youth (Friedrich, 1990:26). For instance, in 1975, 86 per cent of the interviewed apprentices (*Lehrlinge*) and 95 per cent of students professed their allegiance to Marxism-Leninism; in the same year, 95 per cent of the former, and 98 per cent of the latter, were to some degree "proud to be a citizen of the socialist GDR" (ibid.,27,30).[40] From findings like these, Western GDR scholars concluded that the GDR was here to stay – even without Soviet bayonets. "The long-term prospects for the development of a durable and viable political culture," so John Starrels and Anita Mallinckrodt (1975:57), "are good."

Less obvious at the time, but no less effective, was the seamier side of the niche society, the syndrome of apathy, fear and cynicism entailed by a "double life" of forced acclamation and compensatory withdrawal. A citizen movement activist, who before 1989 had never crossed the line of outright opposition, explains: "This whole system was built on *Angst*. However repressed and latent, this *Angst* was always there. You could not name it. But this dull feeling (*dumpfe Gefühl*) in the stomach was with you all the time. Of course, we lived in 'niches'. But in the end, the long arm of the party reached you also there. Life in the niches was life in deceit. At the latest, reality would catch up with you at the workplace, where your colleagues were spying on you."[41]

Moreover, the alleged regime loyalty had to be brittle indeed, because – as both Gaus (1986:125) and Ludz (1970:30) admitted – it rested on a defiant demarcation from a more prosperous and patronizing West. The popular "GDR-consciousness" (Ludz) was a product of resignation rather than genuine allegiance, and it replicated the GDR's basic design flaw: its compulsive fixation on the West. Also life in the niches fed parasitically upon Western inputs, from the regular "fake escape" (*Scheinflucht*) via Western television to the hard currency that was necessary to provide the spare things and services that made life in communism tolerable. As in all post-mobilization regimes, political compliance was traded for economic well-being (Baylis 1972). A decline in economic performance, even a relative one (an ever-present threat where the measure was Europe's most powerful economy), was bound to spell serious trouble. Richard Löwenthal (1976:107) argues that, due to the absence of "institutional procedures," the "legitimacy" of post-mobilization regimes rests on "uniformly good performance." Economic crisis, so one may extrapolate from this, would amount to an implicit breach of contract, and threaten to conjure up a legitimation crisis which Neo-Marxist critics of late capitalism could only dream about (see Chapter 4).

Finally, post-mobilization entailed a more assertive society. As Dallin and Breslauer (1970:81–144) outlined, the flipside to partial regime loyalty in post-mobilization regimes is the rise of dissidence and opposition. In his description of the East German niche society, Günter Gaus (1986:160–5) noted a new assertiveness and propensity to "stick one's head out of the niche" – from the increased number of written appeals (*Eingaben*) and complaints to the party and state authorities, the post-Helsinki flood of exit petitions that were brought forward with an unprecedented air of self-assurance and determination, to the first peace initiatives urging for domestic reform and political liberalization.

OPPOSITION

As we saw above, Leninist regimes do not know the concept of opposition. An East German source tells us why: "In socialist states, there is no objective social or political basis for an opposition. This is because the working-class, in alliance with all other working people (*Werktätigen*), is the dominant class, whose basic interests are in harmony with the interests of the other classes and strata" (in Staritz, 1987:95). In reverse, one could argue that an effective challenge to Leninist rule requires the reverse alliance between the major groups and classes in society.[42] In the dramatic upheavals of Eastern Europe, this reverse alliance did come about, if only for a moment: Hungary 1956, which was a coalition of party reformers, the "revisionist" intellectuals of the Petöfi Club, and students and workers who took to the streets of Budapest; Prague 1968, where workers proved their allegiance to Dubcek and his intellectual allies in culture and academia by standing up against Russian tanks; and Poland 1980/1, of course, the apotheosis of intellectuals joining ranks with striking workers (see Rothschild 1989:ch.5).

Only in East Germany, the reverse alliance of society against the regime did not happen. In 1953, intellectuals remained indifferent, or even sided with the regime, when workers revolted against higher work norms. In the post-Stalinist thaw of 1956, workers stood aside when intellectuals and students mobilized for reforms. After the expatriation of song-writer Wolf Biermann in 1976, not even students bothered to join the few literary intellectuals who had pulled themselves together for a, rather polite, protest note. If compared with its Eastern European neighbours, East Germany stands out in the flatness of its oppositional landscape.[43] Why? First, and most importantly, there was no language of nationalism that could have united latent and manifest protest groups. As a result of the delegitimation of nationalism, and lured by the regime's "anti-fascism" façade, East German intellectuals remained "captive minds" (Milosz), accomplices of the regime rather than catalysts of opposition. In addition, the available "exit" option weakened the "voice" potential, prohibiting the growth and consolidation of regime opposition. Finally, a monolithic party apparatus did not generate sufficient impulses of reform and remained relatively untouched by the waves of national communism that periodically rocked the party states of Eastern Europe. A closer examination of three major protest episodes will illustrate these factors.

The Workers' Uprising of 1953

Of all protest episodes in the GDR, the June revolt of 1953 came closest to being a national upheaval against a regime that was seen as a "collaborationist" and "colonialist" tool of a foreign power (Brandt 1970:205). It was also the only time that workers, and mostly they, would mobilize against the regime in a major way. But, as recent investigations have revealed, what began as a workers' strike came very close to a genuine revolution. Drawing on the recently opened records of the state security police, Armin Mitter and Stefan Wolle (1993) call the June revolt a "revolutionary upheaval" that, without Soviet military intervention, "would have inevitably resulted in national reunification" (p.160). Indicative of the magnitude of the upheaval, some 500 000 people participated in a country-wide strike and demonstration wave that seized almost 600 factories and 373 cities and villages, particularly in Saxony and Thuringia – the industrial heartland of central Germany with a strong social-democratic and communist tradition (Diedrich, 1991). In some cities, such as Görlitz, local town-halls, police headquarters, and prisons were stormed, leading to a complete collapse of the local state and party structures. A bizarre secret police record catches the anarchic mood of that time: "The whole village (of Wendemark) sits drunk in the local pub and toasts to Adenauer" (in Mitter and Wolle, 1993:72). In response to the upheaval, martial law was declared in 167 of 217 districts and counties, more than 6000 demonstrators were arrested, and almost 100 people were killed – among them 40 Soviet soldiers who were executed after they refused to follow orders (ibid.,105). So deeply engrained became the June experience in the memory of the communist leadership that almost forty years later, on the eve of the GDR's collapse, the "Comrade Minister" of state security worried in a secret meeting if "June 17 (would) break out tomorrow" (ibid.,125).

The story of the 17 June revolt has often been told, but a few points are worth recalling. In contrast to later de-Stalinization waves in Poland and Hungary, no intellectual debate had preceded or galvanized what must be seen as a spontaneous and genuine workers' uprising (Baring, 1972:77). The initial economic demand to revoke a ten per cent increase of the work norms, raised by the construction workers on East Berlin's Stalinallee, quickly spilled over into the political demands for free and secret elections and reunification with West Germany.[44] But the flip-side to the virtue of spontaneity and authenticity was the vice of having no program or leaders. Arnulf Baring (1972:76) even argued that the movement "faded away" more than being put down by Soviet tanks. While the June revolt became commemorated in the West as a "people's uprising," its social basis was much narrower, being confined to a core of young industrial workers, particularly in the construction industry. Farmers, middle strata, and the technical intelligentsia mostly stayed away (ibid.,52f). This is not surprising, because these groups had been made some explicit concessions in the previous revocation of the disastrous "Construction of Socialism" program of 1952, while only the ten per cent increase of work norms had remained untouched – no small provocation in a state where workers were allegedly the ruling class.

The intellectual élite also stayed away from protest. For one, pampered as they were by individual contracts, high incomes and other state-guaranteed privileges, the intellectuals were rightly perceived by workers as being "bought off" by the regime. In fact, in this first workers' rebellion against a workers' state in Eastern Europe, many intellectuals sided with the regime. For the Weimar generation of intellectuals who had made the GDR their home of choice, the "anti-fascism" myth made the regime sacrosanct. As Sigrid Meuschel (1991:33) argues pointedly, "the intellectuals participated in the pedagogical mandate of the party *vis à vis* a society deemed unready for democracy." Even Stefan Heym, the noted writer, denounced the June revolt as a conspiracy of "fascist eight-penny boys" (in Noack, 1991:57), thus adopting the official labeling of the revolt as a "fascist putsch attempt." Opposing the regime would have amounted to a

betrayal of the fabled Buchenwald Oath, "Never Again!",
that is, the "anti-fascist" founding myth of the GDR (see
Brandt 1970:147–8). Its nationalist undertones, in any other
Eastern European country the point of greatest proximity
between intellectuals and the people, made the June revolt
the point of greatest distance between both. Heinz Brandt,
a party intellectual sympathetic with the uprising, aptly described the lack of a collective identity and of basic
symbolisms, such as songs and slogans, among the workers.
But when the German anthem was raised at one point, the
party intellectual (a Jewish-communist prisoner at Buchenwald
in May 1945) admitted to feeling "most disturbed." "I felt
this was the last thing that belonged here" (ibid.,216). Almost forty years later, in the streets of Leipzig, the response
by intellectuals to the appearance of the German flag would
be strikingly similar.

The response of the intellectuals to the June upheaval
displays the peculiar pattern of partial criticism and principal loyalty that characterized their general attitude toward
the regime then and in the future. Surveying the individual
responses by some prominent literary intellectuals, such as
Berthold Brecht, Stefan Heym, or Hans Mayer, one can detect
at least four recurrent motifs: a fundamental distrust of the
home society, which not long ago had cheered to the Nazis
and still was seen as volatile and unready to speak for itself;
an identification with the communist rulers and their interest
in containing the dangerous situation; the framing of the
upheaval in the binary terms of fascism versus antifascism,
which left no other possibility but to condemn it; and, finally,
the hope for a "great discussion" with the ruling party about
past "mistakes."

First, it is astounding to see how much the Nazi past determined the perception of the present. When Berthold
Brecht interrupted his stage work on 17 June to assess the
escalating situation on Unter den Linden, he saw only the
"sharp, brutal figures of the Nazi era, which had not been
seen in such numbers for years, while they had always been
around" (in Mohr, 1982:87). He also detected the many
"Western bicycles," and "agents" who had been allegedly
brought in by the West to stir up the masses. On the same
day, Brecht felt the need to send "solidarity" letters to

Ulbricht, Grotewohl and Semjonov, the Soviet commander in East Germany. Later he defended this unusual show of support: "I felt united with the party when... it was attacked by the fascist and war-mongering mob. In the struggle against war and fascism I have always stood on your [the party's] side" (ibid., 88). Also for Hans Mayer the "true stake" on 17 June was "fascism or antifascism," and he compared the uprising to thè *Kristallnacht* when Jewish synagogues and stores were destroyed and set on fire by plundering Nazi hordes: "No doubt, on 17 June 1953 the Soviet Union had once again averted the threat of fascism (in Germany)."[45]

These statements are a stunning demonstration of the regime's success in binding the intellectuals via its proclaimed "anti-fascism". For the Weimar generation of intellectuals, "anti-fascist" East Germany was the last and permanent refuge after so many years of persecution and restless wandering. How would life have been without the GDR, asks Stefan Heym in his autobiographical reflections: "It would have been like so many times before, without home and protection, with no place, no country left where one could still find refuge" (Heym, 1988:569). And Heym expresses the fundamental dilemma of the one who had made the GDR his country of choice: "Since he has chosen its side, he is bound up with this fragile republic, its prosperity is his, but also its ruin" (ibid.,570).

The choice of this "fragile republic" entailed a loyalty to the state, not to the society it claimed to represent. Like Brecht, Stefan Heym took 17 June as an occasion to express his solidarity with the communist rulers. "The Western agents have found fertile soil for their subversive intents," he writes to the Soviet Marshal Sokolovskij, "because we are dealing with Germans here" (Heym, 1982:150). Heym continues: "The basic fact in Germany is that the German workers have *not* made a revolution in 1945. Of course, they were tired of the war. But they also did not want a new social order" (ibid., 151). This distancing of intellectuals from the home society has been typical in post-Nazi Germany, not only in the East. Still in 1988, Heym confessed that he "never much liked the Germans" (Heym, 1988:574) – an amazing statement by a fellow-national that would be inconceivable in any nation but the German after Nazism.

Consistent with this negative view of the home society, the June upheaval appeared as a betrayal of the well-meaning leadership by an ungrateful populace. "How ashamed I feel!" is the characteristic title of a propagandistic poem by Kurt Barthel ("Kuba"), the president of the Writers' Union. Of course, authentic intellectuals such as Brecht or Heym always resisted such unconditional kowtowing to the powers-that-be, and they combined their solidarity declarations with cautious regime critique.[46] In his address to Marshal Sokolovskij, for instance, Stefan Heym carefully points out that the deeper "cause" of the June upheaval had to be found in the dismal living conditions "within the GDR" (Heym, 1982:152). Berthold Brecht, in his solidarity address to party chief Ulbricht, also called for the "great discussion, so necessary now, about the mistakes committed on all sides" (in Mohr, 1982:88). Alas, the "great discussion" never came.

The June upheaval did, however, galvanize an internal party opposition. At one time, a party faction around Rudolf Herrnstadt, a member of the Ulbricht Group and editor of the party newspaper *Neues Deutschland*, and Wilhelm Zaisser, chief of the security police, even seemed to have Moscow's backing to depose the badly damaged and unloved Ulbricht (Baring 1972:106–10). But this remained an élite intrigue behind closed doors, unconnected to any group or force outside the party apparatus. Heinz Brandt's (1970:218) remark remains true that "no Gomulka, no Nagy" appeared to capitalize on the sudden opening. Ulbricht's temporary weakness even became his strongest asset. Removing Ulbricht spelled the prospect of uncontrollable turbulence and regime breakdown, so that Moscow finally rallied in his support. Moscow's satrap emerged from the June upheaval greatly strengthened.

The Post-Stalinist Thaw of 1956

The second protest episode, in the wake of Khrushchev's secret speech before the 20th Party Congress in the Soviet Union, began, like elsewhere in Eastern Europe, as a revolt of party intellectuals against the Stalinist *apparatchiki* (Griffith, 1962:227). But in contrast to Poland and Hungary, the East German revisionist opposition did not galvanize a national upheaval against communist rule. In 1956, East German workers remained passive – demoralized by their defeat in 1953, but also acquiesced by regime concessions such as lower prices for consumer goods, better housing conditions, and a shortened work-week (Weber, 1985:283). In its attempt to contain the revisionist virus, the regime skillfully fed popular resentment against an intelligentsia that was perceived as élitist and privileged. Carola Stern (1963:198) aptly paraphrased Ulbricht's strategy: "Don't provoke workers, but bring them up against students and other intellectuals; all existing resentments between both groups must be utilized." Along these lines, "workers' fists" – in the form of factory combat units (*Betriebskampfgruppen*) – were mobilized to hold down a wave of unrest at the country's universities (Jänicke, 1964:171).

University students, quiet in 1953, were at the forefront of opposition in 1956. Quite interestingly, the student opposition was concentrated in medicine and veterinary faculties, most notably in Leipzig and Berlin (Richert, 1967:ch.7). Traditionally minded and financially secure, these students of mostly "bourgeois" family backgrounds first spoke out against the Marxist-Leninist *studium generale* and soon went over to mobilize mass action outside the university. Ernst Richert (ibid.,188) reports "most serious clashes" between rebellious students and regime forces at the Baltic Coast in Greifswald, where several hundred medical students were arrested, and in Berlin, where 25 per cent of the enrolled veterinary students were relegated from the university. The harsh clamp-down and successive doctrinary tightening of university life led to a mass exodus of non-communist students and faculty to the West, turning East German universities into the "spiritual cemeteries" (Richert) that they have remained ever since.[47]

In general, however, the East German thaw was far less dramatic than the ones in Poland or Hungary (Klessmann, 1991:56). Its protagonists remained fragmented and basically loyal to the Ulbricht regime – as if aware that even moderate revisionism threatened the very existence of the GDR. Robert Havemann, the charismatic philosopher-physicist who would emerge as East Germany's major dissident of the 1960s and 1970s, professed that no one but Ulbricht "could successfully cope with [the] complicated task [of liberalizing the GDR] without jeopardizing the existence of the GDR" (Brandt, 1970:262).[48] Ernst Bloch, philosophy ordinarius at Leipzig, and in 1957 removed from the university for his heretical views, still refused to criticize the regime openly because this would only revalorize "Atlantic unfreedom" (Meuschel, 1991:33).[49] In a similar way, Stefan Heym (1988:600) felt inhibited to brand Stalinist terror because this would relativize the Nazi crimes.

Melvin Croan (1962:244) observed that the revisionist opposition was carried not by the intellectuals of the Weimar generation, but by a younger intelligentsia that only responded to the SED's own invitation to "creativity" during a period of doctrinary relaxation. One pillar of revisionism was the Institute of Economic Sciences at Humboldt University, where the economists Fritz Behrens and Arne Benary propagated the introduction of market principles into the planning economy (Jänicke, 1964:104–10). Both loyal regime supporters, Behrens and Benary quickly repented, and they were relegated to the Academy of Sciences in order to keep them away from students. Seven years later, many of their ideas became official policy in the New Economic System. The second, and best remembered, pillar of revisionism was a group of young philosophers and literary intellectuals around Wolfgang Harich, then a philosophy professor at Humboldt University and editor-in-chief of the *Deutsche Zeitschrift für Philosophie*, and Walter Janka, chief of the Aufbau Verlag, a liberal publishing house among whose more prominent authors were Georg Lukacs and Thomas Mann. In fall 1956, Harich published a "platform" that called for a sweeping reform of party and society, most notably all-German elections and reunification – without questioning, however, the leadership role of a "reformed SED" (Weber, 1985:290).[50] Harich was soon arrested and put on trial. Ernst Richert (1967:151), otherwise well-tempered he, ridiculed the "absolute dilettantism" of this "conspiracy." Harich had openly used Western media for propagating his conception of a "special German road to socialism," and he even thought that his ideas could be discussed within the SED "in complete legality" (in Fricke, 1984:121). At his trial, Harich delivered one of the more memorable auto-critiques, "thanking" the state security forces for his imprisonment, and calling himself a "run-away horse... ripe not just for the ten years demanded by the *Herr* state prosecutor, but ripe for the gallows".[51]

The shallowness of this "opposition" stemmed also from the fact that the still-open border to the West made the revisionist struggle an infight among loyal communists, incapable of striking a popular chord. Gustav Just, editor of the intellectual weekly *Sonntag* and co-defendant in the trials against the Harich-Janka group, dryly commented thirty years later that he could have spared himself much trouble by simply exiting at the "next subway stop" – which would have left him in West Berlin.[52] This exit the revisionists did not take. As Robert Havemann wrote to his imprisoned friend Heinz Brandt, a communist renegade who had been spectacularly kidnapped in the West to face trial in East Berlin: "In your place I would have preferred prison in the DDR to living in a clerico-fascist restorationist state" (Brandt, 1970:252).

While never openly articulated, nationalist aspirations were nonetheless present in the revisionist opposition. In fact, 1956 may be looked at as the "last historical chance" (Gustav Just) for a German road to socialism. Not by accident, the leading reform advocate at the party top, politburo member Karl Schirdewan, had spent the Nazi years in a German concentration camp, thus reviving a latent schism between Muscovites and local undergrounders in the SED (Stern 1963:209). But indicative of the lack of a national base in the GDR, Schirdewan and his small band of followers in the politburo did not seek rank and file support in their drive to oust Ulbricht, and even less did they try to build bridges to the pockets of revisionism outside the party (Croan 1980:145). Instead, like Herrnstadt and Zaisser before them, the Schirdewan group turned to Moscow for support. But the barely aborted revolution in Hungary left Khrushchev with little taste for further experiments, and so he dropped his previous favorites. As in the workers' revolt, Ulbricht emerged from a serious challenge greatly strengthened, capitalizing once more on the ever-precarious condition of his artificial state. His later heir, Erich Honecker himself, delivered the indictment against the party rebels. Never since has an internal party opposition raised its head in the SED.

The Intellectual Exodus of 1976

One may read the history of the GDR opposition as the successive elimination of protest groups, each of which had its separate moment in history, but all of which failed to bring about the reverse alliance of society against the regime. After their failed revolt in 1953, workers, the officially ruling class, fell into a protracted silence. Students and the university intelligentsia, at the forefront of the thaw of 1956, disappeared thereafter as agents of change. Literary intellectuals had their turn in 1976, in response to the expatriation of song-writer Wolf Biermann. The Biermann expatriation and the intellectual exodus that followed are significant in at least two regards. First, never before had intellectuals so openly defied the regime. Second, the regime discovered that manipulating the "exit" valve was an effective means to combat its "voice" opposition – a strategy that would become ever more pronounced and perfected in the remaining years of the GDR.

Literary intellectuals play a crucial role in communist opposition politics. The written word often compensates for the lack of an institutionalized political opposition. Leninist regimes are perverse *républiques des lettres*, in which poetry and prose attain the function of talking truth to power, in however indirect and disguised ways. As Jurek Becker, a prominent casualty of the Biermann episode, puts it, writers in socialist countries are expected to be a "guide for living"[53]. In East Germany, however, a "siege mentality" (Volkmer, 1979) and socialist commitment also tied the literary intellectuals close to the regime. But by the mid-1970s, a post-Weimar, second or even third generation of intellectuals had entered the literary field, who were socialized in the late Nazi or early post-war years and for whom the "anti-fascism" formula became less effective to secure automatic compliance.[54] For them, the socialist order was no matter of pure choice, but something one had grown up within and that one had to adjust to. These post-Weimar generations, which stretched from Christa Wolf (b.1929) to Volker Braun (b.1939) and Christoph Hein (b.1944), remained emphatically pro-socialist. But in their work and politics they would defend the claims of the individual for self-fulfillment and participation in society, if necessary, against society. Volker Braun expressed the hopeful creed of these younger intellectuals: "Here rules the experiment and not stiff routine" (in Emmerich, 1989:218). This had to bring them on a soft collision course with the regime.

The two decades that separated the revisionist opposition of the 1950s and the intellectual exodus of the mid-1970s had passed by without notable opposition. The building of the Berlin Wall in 1961 was met with "demonstrative silence" (Jänicke, 1964:211) by those who had mobilized for reforms a few years earlier. The writer Stefan Hermlin even defended the Wall as a step towards blocking the "aggressive path" of the "most dangerous state in the world": West Germany.[55] Most intellectuals took the Wall as a "chance" to finally achieve the long-desired "great discussion" with the ruling party.[56] The Prague Spring of 1968 was the next significant date that failed to leave an overt imprint. Christa Wolf even publicly defended the Warsaw Pact invasion. Covertly, however, the end of the Prague Spring caused a deep depression particularly among the younger East German intellectuals, and it became the formative experience for a tiny dissident scene.[57] Considering the upheavals in Prague and Warsaw and the student revolts in the Western world, the GDR's domestic landscape in the late 1960s was still one of "ideologico-political sterility" (Croan, 1980:147). Dissent was limited to a small circle around the young Wolf Biermann, whose biting prose and satire had led the regime to prohibit his public performances since 1965, and communist veteran Robert Havemann, who had been relegated from Humboldt University in 1964 after a series of highly popular lectures that criticized doctrinary Marxism-Leninism. Proximity to, if not involvement in, the Biermann-Havemann circle became an indispensable initiation mark for authentic regime opposition.[58]

Intellectual acquiescence was helped by the fact that the early Honecker years brought a remarkable liberalization in cultural life, initiated by Honecker's famous remark that there should be "no taboos" with regard to the styles and contents of art and literature (Jäger, 1982:135–58). Modestly critical literary work by Christa Wolf, Volker Braun or Heiner Müller could be published. Ulrich Plenzdorf's play *The New Sufferings of Young W.*, which assailed the plight of bored youth in real socialism, was performed in sold-out theatres throughout the GDR. As in the early 1960s, *Sinn und Form* reemerged as a platform for aesthetic debate of astonishing openness. And in countless quasi-independent youth clubs satire, poetry, and jazz and rock music were offered to engaged and enthusiastic audiences, articulating and integrating impulses of the Western beat and youth movement that the Wall wasn't high and tight enough to keep out of the GDR.[59] Honecker seemed to have realized his promise to make life in socialism more colourful and entertaining.

But the *détente*-induced strategy of *Abgrenzung* and ideological tightening eventually prevailed. In a major example of the rhapsodic oscillation between mobilization and post-mobilization strategies, the clamp-down came in the year of 1976 – soon after the signing of the Helsinki Accords and an international Communist Party conference in East Berlin that had carried the virus of Western reform communism ("Euro-Communism") into the GDR.[60] In an apparently concerted action, the protagonists and carriers of cultural liberalization were quieted. By the end of the year, most youth clubs had been forced to shut down. Reiner Kunze, the only writer of rank who had openly protested against the violent abortion of the Prague Spring, was forced to leave the Writers' Union, because he had published a critical collection of prose, *Die wunderbaren Jahre*, in the West.[61] With the expatriation of Wolf Biermann in November, the cultural clamp-down reached its dramatic peak, but also its unexpected turning-point. The GDR's literary élite, including Christa Wolf, Stefan Heym, Heiner Müller, Volker Braun and Jurek Becker, most of them in leading positions in the official Writers' Union, came out with a protest resolution, which underlined the *chansonnier*'s socialist loyalty and "asked to reconsider the chosen measures" (in Jäger, 1976:1235).

While polite and rather subdued in tone, this concerted protest of the literary intelligentsia was unprecedented. It is all the more impressive because it united representatives of all intellectual generations, including former exiles like Stefan Hermlin or Erich Arendt. More than a hundred writers and artists came out in support of the original protest note. The regime responded with a new strategy. Whereas the revisionist opposition of the 1950s faced (mostly moderate) prison sentences, the literary opposition was put before a new alternative: to endure prosecution and professional discrimination – or to leave for West Germany. In one of his *Letters from Prison*, Adam Michnik mused about an offer from his jailers to exchange iron bars for "Christmas on the Côte d'Azur" (Michnik, 1985:68). If the "victory of truth over lies" made Michnik choose prison, in the German case the exit-alternative was more easily taken. What "truth" might have been served by toiling in a country that was nothing but a communist state? Within a short time, a heavy portion of the GDR's literary and artistic élite had left, most notably the younger ones, who felt less committed to the "anti-fascist" foundation myth. In this context, Stefan Hermlin, who had spent the Nazi period in Swiss exile, drew a sharp distinction between two sorts of refugees: "These people [leaving the GDR in the wake of the Biermann protest] are mere *Ausreiser* (departees), leaving with nice papers... and often with a friendly hand-shake... Refugees are only we. Only we, no one else. Only we Antifascists" (quoted in Emmerich, 1989:254). Needless to add, the "anti-fascist" refugee never left the GDR.

The post-Biermann exodus caused an intellectual drought from which the GDR never really recovered. Any future opposition would be peculiarly nameless and devoid of support from intellectual leaders. Those who did not leave made themselves unavailable through anxious withdrawal into an "inner immigration" or cynicism – such as Christa Wolf and the celebrated playwright Heiner Müller, respectively. A Vaclav Havel could not exist in East Germany. In general, Timothy Garton Ash's observation remains true that the most puzzling question raised by this protest episode is not why it was possible at all, but why it remained such a short-lived and muted affair, unable to penetrate more deeply into society (Ash, 1981:115–16). Ash compares the public riot that followed in Warsaw when, during a period of intellectual ferment, a play by the national hero Adam Mickiewiczs was prohibited to be performed, to the absolute lack of critical reaction in East Berlin, when Heinrich Heine's *Wintermärchen* suffered the same fate at the very time of the Biermann affair: "No public protest followed. No students demonstrated. The Humboldt University kept sleeping" (ibid.,119).

This lack of protest reflects that the intellectual opposition in the GDR remained caught in the narrow orbit of revisionism, that is, a basic loyalty to the regime. Whereas the Prague Spring had led to a fundamental reorientation of intellectual opposition politics in Eastern Europe, a similar turn from revisionism to dissidence proper failed to come in the GDR. Several protagonists of the Biermann protest quickly withdrew their signature in fear of "false friends" – the label for conservative anti-communists in the Federal Republic. In the West, Biermann himself left no doubt about his communist loyalty, and he deplored his fall from "rain into manure" (*vom Regen in die Jauche*).[62] Robert Havemann, who was put under permanent house arrest after Biermann's forced departure, never tired of referring to party chief Honecker as his "comrade of the anti-fascist resistance movement" (in Faust 1980:168), and from his frugal home in Grünheide he continued to preach an austere communist utopia" without cars and television sets (Havemann, 1978).

East German intellectual revisionism reached its apotheosis in Rudolf Bahro's *Die Alternative*, published in 1977. Quite interestingly, Bahro, a previously little noticed party technocrat whose subsequent imprisonment made him an international *cause célèbre*, had conceived the plan for his Trotskyist assault on bureaucratic party rule right after the Soviet invasion in 1968.[63] The Hungarians Andrew Arato and Mihaly Vayda dryly commented on Bahro's plea for a rejunivated Leninist avantgarde movement that it "belongs to the Eastern European past" (Arato and Vajda, 1980:167). In fact, when Eastern European intellectuals had long turned to antipolitics and the recovery of civil society, East Germans still believed in the possibility of reforms from within the party-state. The road from Harich to Bahro has been an extremely short one (see Weber, 1978). Arato and Vajda point right to the root cause of this anachronism: "To demand... the restoration or creation of civil society is to demand what the FRG already (or still) has, a condition under which the division of Germany loses its legitimacy. But to demand unity even by implication, *seems* to place the dissident in the camp of the German right" (Arato and Vajda, 1980:175). Due to the lack of a legitimate discourse of nationhood, there was no alternative to socialist revisionism.

At the same time, a different movement emerged whose single goal was to achieve what most intellectuals were anxious to avoid: to get out of the GDR. That both movements could not, and would not, merge became the principal crux of East German opposition politics. The view of critical writers who were granted unlimited visas to the West, and who combined socialist rhetoric with soft regime critique, must have been infuriating for the growing number of common people who implicitly knew that antipolitics in East Germany meant leaving for the West. Upon signing the Helsinki Accords, the Honecker regime saw itself confronted with a massive wave of exit petitions. As Karl Wilhelm Fricke (1976:1135) commented on the estimated 120 000 individual exit petitions by 1976, "civic courage and risk-taking have increased in [East Germany]." In fact, this desire for mobility and self-determination reflected the rise of "articulate audiences" (Jowitt, 1975) in a post-mobilization regime. But due to the individualized nature of exit, its constituency was almost impossible to organize – especially in a Leninist regime.[64] The intellectual opposition, on the other hand, kept deliberate distance from those whose simple desire was liberty.[65] While a welcome device to get rid of the intellectual opposition, the exit valve broadly applied threatened to destabilize economy and social structure – the Wall, after all, had been built to prevent just that. In a seemingly ingenious *divide et impera* strategy, but probably more born out of necessity, the regime prevented from leaving those who wanted to leave, while forcing to leave those who pleaded for reforms and showed no intention of leaving. As will be elaborated in Chapter 4, the ensuing schism between exit and voice greatly diminished the capacity of regime opposition in East Germany.

3 Détente and the Peace Movement

In the early 1980s, the end of geopolitical *détente* and the fear of nuclear Armageddon gave rise to broad peace and disarmament movements throughout the Western world. Among Eastern European dissidents, the peace issue was less warmly received.[1] Czech dissident Vaclav Havel (1985:28) found the view of Western peace fighters who risked so little and feared so much "mildly pathetic", and he denounced the "ideological opportunism" of those who placed the securing of peace above all other moral and political goals. From a Czech perspective, "peace at any price" smacked of the "spirit of appeasement" that had made this country the first victim of Nazi Germany (Hauner, 1990:103). More importantly, human rights was the major focus of the post-revisionist Eastern European dissident movements, and taking on the peace issue only threatened to blur the agenda. As Havel (1985:31) clarified the priorities of Eastern European dissidence, "respect for human rights is the fundamental condition and the sole genuine guarantee of true peace."

Only in East Germany, peace, not human rights, became the focus of the domestic opposition scene. Whereas previous regime opposition in East Germany had remained sporadic and episodic, the peace movement became the first organized and sustained opposition movement.[2] Situated at the borderline between East and West, East German dissidents had to be especially receptive to Western influence. In a curious reflection of Western social movement discourse, a noted East German dissident sociologist even called the peace movement in his country a "new social movement" that addressed "global" instead of "class-specific" issues.[3] Embracing the peace issue prevented East German dissidents from tackling the Achilles' heel of Leninist regimes head-on: the denial of elementary citizenship rights. The peace issue even forged a partial alliance between movement and party-state, which found a new combat task in the advocacy

71

of peace and disarmament and extolled itself as a "peace state."[4] The rise of the peace movement underscores the maintenance of revisionism in the East German opposition scene.

The previous history of East German regime opposition shaped the contours of the peace movement. The intellectual exodus after the Biermann affair had eroded the opposition scene. Whereas Eastern European dissident movements had strong intellectual leadership, the East German peace movement was almost devoid of it (Kroh, 1988:7). The death of Robert Havemann in 1982 marked the divide between the old intellectual opposition and the new leaderless and nameless peace movement. The literary intellectuals who refused the exit-option made themselves unavailable. A key opposition figure of the post-Havemann era complains: "We had no leaders. In order to get more public recognition, we constantly tried to recruit prominent intellectuals, such as Stefan Heym or Christa Wolf. But they always declined."[5] Not intellectuals, but disaffected youths who resisted the "double life" and hypocrisy in a post-mobilization regime carried the peace movement (Wensierski and Büscher, 1983:134; see also Mleczkowski, 1983). In this regard, the label of "new social movement" is not all that inaccurate. The early 1980s saw the rise of an alternative youth culture, particularly in big cities such as East Berlin, Dresden and Leipzig, that showed striking parallels to the youth culture in the West. Often the privileged sons and daughters of party members and functionaries, the youthful followers of the peace movement opted out of mainstream society, whose control mechanisms no longer seemed to be effective. A young woman expresses this sentiment at the 1982 Dresden Peace Forum, the first country-wide gathering of the East German peace movement: "I am nineteen years old, yet I've got nothing left to lose" (quoted in Wolschner, 1982a:40f). A movement of disaffected youths, the peace movement, like all previous regime opposition, failed to enlist broader segments of the population and to penetrate more deeply into society.[6]

Despite its countercultural outlook, the peace movement still sought the "dialogue" with the regime. For Robert Havemann, until his death the *éminence grise* in the peace movement, the GDR was still the "better" Germany, and he hoped for a "dialogue with a small group of people in the politburo" (in Kroh, 1988:32). When Eastern European dissident movements had long given up the hope, East German dissidents still wanted to reform communism from within. In fact, the very notions of dissent and opposition were initially rejected by those who *de facto* practiced them. On the one hand, this hesitation had tactical reasons, because any form of organized opposition had to provoke massive state retaliation. But more important was the underlying loyalty to the regime. A dissident despite himself explains: "We had trouble with the notions of dissidence and opposition. We did not want to abolish the socialist system; we wanted to reform it."[7] Despite the generational and social divide that separated the intellectual opposition of the Biermann-Havemann era from the new peace movement, they were revisionists all.

THE CULTURE OF DÉTENTE

The fact that peace, not human rights, became the focus of East German opposition politics was conditioned also by the all-German context of *détente*. The attempts by both Germanies, in the early 1980s, to defend the fruits of *détente* against the mounting superpower rivalry created an atmosphere in which the securing of peace attained top priority. "Peace," "community of responsibility," and "security partnership" became the watchwords at that time, equally used in Bonn and East Berlin. As foreign observers noted with some concern, under the mantle of *détente* a cautious German–German rapprochement seemed to be in the making – one that undermined the West-integration of the Federal Republic and brought new legitimacy to Honecker's regime (Ash, 1990c). Ferenc Feher and Agnes Heller (1986:57) commented on this deceptive prelude to German unification that "once again in German history, nation and freedom part ways." A closer look at the culture of *détente* will help to put the East German peace movement into context.

In reunified Germany, the impact of *Ostpolitik* and *détente* has become the subject of heated debate. Did *détente* "secure peace in Europe at the cost of liberty in the East," as one of its critics put it,[8] or did *détente* create the necessary space without which the dissident movements of Eastern Europe would not have been possible in the first, as one of its proponents claims?[9] The question is difficult to decide, but in different phases and contexts *détente* probably did both. Brandt's *Ostpolitik* started as the simple desire to acknowledge post-war Germany's eastern borders, thus providing the necessary complement to Adenauer's *Westpolitik* (Griffith, 1978). But its hidden agenda was national reunification, and thus counter to the premises of West integration.[10] Egon Bahr's concept of "change through rapprochement" (*Wandel durch Annäherung*) unwittingly fed the peculiar erosion of the boundaries between democracy and communism, which came to characterize the culture of *détente*.[11]

The debate over the stationing of American medium-range nuclear missiles in Western Europe brought this "boundary erosion" to the open (see Herf, 1991). For Egon Bahr, one of the most perceptive and visionary German post-war politicians, geopolitical security in the nuclear age was possible only as common security, which could not be reached against but only with the communist regimes. Moreover, Bahr replaced the division between the Western and Eastern blocs, democracy and communism, with the division between nuclear and non-nuclear powers. This suddenly put the two Germanies into the same camp of non-nuclear powers (Bahr, 1981). The feeling of shared victimization by the superpowers led to a cautious rediscovery of a common national identity. Not by accident, Günter Gaus (1981:45) stated on the eve of the missile debate that "the Elbe is a German river, not Germany's border." In no other country in East and West was the fear of nuclear war more urgently, even hysterically, expressed than in the two Germanies. The often repeated saying that "a war must never again start from German soil" acquired an almost "shamanistic significance," as Timothy Garton Ash (1990c:80) said in obvious irritation. German guilt fueled a zealous attempt to make the world safe for peace, which was received by Germany's Western neighbours with considerable unease.[12] In the German–German rapprochement, the "national" interest in peace blurred the boundaries between the two political systems. Equilateralism – an equal distance to the two superpowers

– became the dominant mindset, which Richard Löwenthal defined as a "loss of the understanding that the conflict with the Soviet Union is *not only* a conflict between two great powers and their associates, but also a conflict between freedom and tyranny" (in Ash, 1990c:90).

The West German peace movement is the genuine child of *Ostpolitik* and *détente,* and it expressed overtly what the political élites had to formulate more covertly. For the peace movement, the danger came from Washington, not Moscow, whereby equilateralism was even turned into a reverse unilateralism that favoured Moscow. The denunciation of the nuclear *pax Americana* unleashed the anti-Americanism that had been latent in the German left since the anti-Vietnam demonstrations of the late 1960s.[13] Anti-Americanism was only the reverse side of the notorious anti-communism that defined the political culture of early post-war West Germany. As Peter Brückner (1978) argued to the point, opposition in the FRG existed in the form of a state, the GDR. In reaction to being denounced as agents of communism, opposition movements from the student movement onwards developed an equally notorious anti anti-communist disposition. Jeffrey Herf scrutinized this disposition in a disturbing look at the "people's front" (*Volksfront*) student coalitions at West Germany's universities in the 1970s – "now as before, the common enemy stands on the right," as a typical pamphlet of that time said (in Herf, 1991:77). From here it was no big step to draw an insidious line between "hawkish" Washington and "dovish" Moscow.

Next to equilateralism, if not reverse unilateralism, nationalism is the second feature of the culture of *détente* that became more directly articulated by the Western peace movement. The emergence of left-wing nationalism, though limited to a small intellectual élite in the peace movement, still had to be surprising, because nationalism had previously been the turf of the German right. Its left-wing proponents were quick to underline that this nationalism inherited the "libertarian tradition of the anti-Napoleonic Wars," while shedding the "narrow-mindedness of Wilhelminian nationalism" and the "excesses of Nazism" (Brandt and Ammon, 1981:24f). The rise of the peace movement and its institutional complement, the Greens, was accompanied by a search for identity and the rediscovery of regional folkways, dialects, and *Heimat.* In the Euromissile debate, this new sensibility easily turned nationalist. This was a nationalism that carried the boundary erosion of *détente* to the extreme, aiming at a neutralized, reunified, and socialist Germany decoupled from the existing geopolitical alliances – the newest version of the old idea of a German *sonderweg* between East and West. In other words, this was a nationalism that put a wedge between Germany and the West, and placed the "national interest," disguised in the Euromissile debate as the "peace" or "survival interest," above a commitment to Western-style liberal democracy. A leader of the Green Party bluntly articulates the motive of neutralist nationalism: "If there is only the alternative between... becoming dependent on the USSR, living like in the GDR, and fighting like its peace movement, or programming the... extermination [*Ausrottung*] of the Germans..., then our choice is clear: *in dubio pro* life..." (Stolz, 1981:28). Ferenc Feher and Agnes Heller (1986:41) aptly characterized this rather bizarre scenario as the "worst possible conclusion of WW II."

Irrespective of its nationalist implications, the culture of *détente* placed the securing of peace above all other political goals, and thus inadvertently worked against the Eastern European dissident movements. This became clear in West Germany's response to General Jaruzelski's clamp-down on Solidarity in December 1981. The peace movement responded with silence, eager not to disturb its shaky alliance of Protestant Church, Greens, Social Democrats, and the Moscow-oriented German Communist Party (DKP). In the political élite, the proponents of *détente* even defended the declaration of martial law, arguing that this step was in the interest of "stability" in Europe. Klaus Bölling, Bonn's political representative in East Berlin, said: "According to a general consensus in East and West, peace just is a higher good than paragraphs devoted to the idea of freedom" (in Ash, 1990c:100). Egon Bahr, the architect of *Ostpolitik*, even invoked Weber's ethic of responsibility to denounce the combined demand for peace and human rights as a dangerous "ideologization" of politics – admonishing the beaten Poles that "a nation's right to self-determination has to rank below the preservation of peace" (in Meuschel, 1983:12). In a telling, and probably not accidental, symbolism martial law was declared on the day when Chancellor Helmut Schmidt convened with SED Chief Honecker at Lake Werbellin, north of East Berlin. Arguing from an Eastern European dissident perspective, Ferenc Feher and Agnes Heller (1986:42) found that "German Social Democracy has never had... darker days than the ones in which Schmidt and Honecker together 'felt regret' about what 'had to happen' in Poland," and they deemed Europe under the shadow of a "new Rapallo."

What impact did the culture of *détente* have on East Germany's regime opposition? On the one hand, the "peace first" rhetoric in East and West was almost impossible to evade. It established an uncontested hierarchy of moral and political concerns. Accordingly, regime opposition in the 1980s would understand itself as peace movement, not as human rights movement. Tellingly, Poland's Solidarity movement played almost no role for the development of East German regime opposition.[14] On the other hand, Western proponents of *détente* considered the Honecker regime, not its opposition, as their interlocutor. In this respect, the Eastern peace movement, which *qua* movement had to provoke periodical state repression, appeared no less a risk to stability than Poland's Solidarity. So it cannot surprise that East German dissidents have always deplored the lack of moral and political support from the West. Contacts with Social Democrats or Greens were rare, and it was mostly journalists who provided the shield of publicity that would protect peace activists from overly harsh state repression.[15] Once in the West, exiled dissidents often carried the stigma of anti-communism and they received little sympathy from Western fellow-intellectuals. Jürgen Fuchs (1984:164), expatriated in 1977, explains why: "Western intellectuals are reminded by us (dissidents) of an error and a betrayal: the error that communist one-party rule is the road to a better future. And the betrayal to have struck an alliance with these new rulers." Even the leadership of the West German peace movement tended to ignore its Eastern counterpart (Wolschner, 1982b). The minimal consensus in the Western movement was the prevention of NATO rearmament, and any deviation from this goal threatened its broad alliance structure that included Moscow-oriented communists. In striking parallel to the political élite, the German Peace Society (DFG/VK) – a core organization of the Western peace movement – considered the SED-official Peace Council (*Friedensrat*) its main address in East Germany, not the unofficial opposition movement. Tellingly, in 1982 the Peace Society's journal *Zivilcourage* refused to print an article on the repression of the Eastern peace movement, arguing that this was an "insignificant problem" (*Kleckerproblem*) (ibid., 30).

HONECKER'S "PEACE STATE"

Visiting the GDR in the 1980s, a striking contradiction would be among one's first impressions. Upon passing the inquisitorial border controls at East Berlin's Friedrichstrasse or elsewhere, the most likely type of person to see in the streets would be men in military uniform. In 1983, 1.2 million GDR men and women were under arms (including 400 000 Soviet troops stationed in the GDR, the National People's Army, border guards, and armed militia). This amounts to 11 soldiers or militiamen per square kilometer – the GDR was the most militarized society on earth (Asmus, 1983b:305). Walking on to Alexanderplatz, the visitor would make a second, and somewhat dissonant, observation: the huge emblem of a white dove carrying a twig of myrtle, accompanied by the words BERLIN – CITY OF PEACE.

How can these two observations be reconciled? In the course of the Euromissile debate, the "securing of peace" (*Friedenssicherung*) became the GDR's premier "state doctrine" (Weber, 1985:498). In response to the 1979 NATO "double-track" decision to install Pershing II and cruise missile rockets in Western Europe if no agreement about the reduction of Soviet SS-20 could be reached, the SED regime, in alliance with Moscow, launched a massive disarmament campaign and openly supported the goals and practices of the West German and Western European peace movements. The securing of peace offered the regime a new and welcome combat task in the face of new challenges. On the economic front, severe shortages of basic consumer goods in 1982 and 1983 entailed a first crack in the implicit social contract with the populace. The energy cost explosion after the second oil crisis had put a heavy strain on the GDR economy, making it ever more difficult to maintain the costly state-subsidization of basic consumer goods, such as food and housing.[16] On the ideological front, the Polish Solidarity movement spelled a communist identity crisis that threatened to spill over Poland's borders. The quest for peace injected new life and meaning to the communist cause; it allowed the regime to divert attention from the looming economic crisis and to realign regime and society around a common cause. This effort was not without success. Günter Gaus (1989:127) states that "no other issue has more united the East German populace with the regime than the disarmament issue." Surveys indicate that the regime's peace campaign temporarily reversed a secular decline in regime identification, particularly among the country's youth (Förster and Roski, 1990:40). In short, *détente* helped the regime to new stability.

This success in presenting the GDR as a "peace state" is striking, if one compares claim and domestic reality. As in all communist societies, military education and organization were central mechanisms of social control. In fact, militarism is inherent in the combat ethos of Leninist regimes. As Milovan Djilas (1957:95) put it, "Founded by force and violence, in constant conflict with its people, the communist state, even if there are no external reasons, must be militaristic." If politics is internal class struggle, military action is external class struggle; and because the internal enemy had already been defeated, the real enemy now was external – in form of the "capitalist states." From Kindergarten on, paramilitary training (*Wehrerziehung*) was an integral part of socialist education. Sixth and seventh-graders had to participate in paramilitary maneuvers, which were organized jointly by the youth pioneer organization "Ernst Thälmann" and the National People's Army, and which included joyrides in miniature tanks and improvised war battles; eighth-graders were summoned up to the "Hans-Beimler Contests," which included sportive disciplines such as rifle shooting, the throwing of hand grenades (*Handgranatenzielwurf*), and climbing ropes. An instruction booklet for physical educators reads like applied body disciplining *à la* Foucault (or shows that the GDR was indeed Germany): "Great emphasis is to be given to exact commands and their obedient execution. Discipline and order... are equally relevant in sport and military service. Strict physical education... instills in students a disposition for disciplined behavior" (in Ehring and Dallwitz, 1982:20).

In a shrill counterpoint to its peace campaign, the regime even tightened the screw of domestic militarization. In 1978, military instruction (*Wehrkunde*) was introduced as a mandatory subject in the ninth and tenth grades of the GDR's college-track high schools. In 1982, a new Military Service Law stipulated that in the case of war women were to be included in the draft. Parallel to this, a massive ideological campaign was launched to increase military vigilance and "hatred of the enemy," which included the swamping of the country with cheap, and previously outlawed, war toys. These measures were in obvious contradiction to the official peace rhetoric – a contradiction that, in fact, triggered the rise of the East German peace movement. What are the causes of this increased emphasis on domestic militarism? First and foremost, this was part of the general strategy of delimitation (*Abgrenzung*), which should counteract the *détentist* mellowing of socialist distinctiveness. Second, the militarization of education and schooling was obviously an attempt to tackle the rising problem of youth integration – a move that probably aggravated the problem it was designed to solve. Finally, the number of male births between 1963 and 1974 had declined by 40 per cent – more had to be achieved with less, calling for intensified military training and alertness (Kuhrt, 1984:33).

How can the apparent contradiction between peace rhetoric and actual militarization be reconciled? For the regime, there was no contradiction. The regime only followed Lenin's doctrine of international relations, according to which "peaceful coexistence" was a "form of class struggle." In this view, capitalist states were inherently aggressive and "imperialist," whereas socialist states were peaceful by definition. An SED-pamphlet explains: "Socialism and peace are identical. No one in socialism profits from military armament, no one is interested in occupying foreign lands and resources and in violating the sovereignty of other peoples" (in Ehring and Dallwitz, 1982:14). But "durable peace," so the pamphlet continues, requires the "strengthening of our defense capability" (ibid.). Because of the inherent aggressiveness of capitalism, peace had to be imposed on capitalism, and this was contingent upon the military superiority of socialism. In fact, before the Euromissile debate, the Warsaw Pact leaders frankly admitted that with the installation of SS-20 missiles the communist bloc had finally reached its long-desired military superiority in Europe (Kuhrt, 1984:23). And, in general, a war was justified, so long as it served the socialist cause. Two Soviet authors celebrate the aesthetics of a socialist war: "A war for the defense of the socialist fatherland is beautiful ... Such a struggle ... incites strong and pure passions in the soldier, and unfolds in him true beauty and humanity" (Milowidow and Safranow, 1978:71).

Given this militarism potential of Leninist regimes, Honecker's presentation of his state to the world as a "peace state" was no small feat. But besides doctrinary commitments, Honecker also had a very material interest in *détente*, because the stability of his regime had become dependent on its benefits in many ways. This became clear in the GDR's moderate response to the final stationing of NATO missiles in fall 1983 (see Asmus, 1985; McAdams, 1988). Whereas Moscow launched an aggressive campaign against the "revanchist" Bonn government, East Berlin opted for a reconciliatory response of "damage limitation." When Moscow realized its threat to respond to the NATO measures through stationing a new set of short-range nuclear missiles, Honecker did not conceal his dislike of this "devil's stuff" (*Teufelszeug*) on GDR territory. Honecker's attempt to exempt the German–German relations from the rough winds of geopolitics resulted in the most serious clash ever between Moscow and East Berlin. While Honecker had to cancel a long-planned visit to Bonn because of Andropov's veto, he simultaneously received a delegation of the Green Party and the West German peace movement, appealing "in the name of the German people" not to slip into a new "ice age" (in McAdams, 1985:188). These were unexpected words from a previous champion of proletarian internationalism and one of Moscow's most faithful friends. So much had Honecker become affected by the culture of *détente* that he was increasingly perceived in the West as a "German" communist leader (see Gaus, 1986).

While in the West *détente* had raised the hope of a national rapprochement, in the East it was seen as an opportunity to stabilize a forever fragile regime. In foreign policy, one of *détente's* fruits was the long-desired international recognition of the GDR. In 1984, the year of the clash with Moscow, Honecker excelled as a European spokesman for peace, being courted by Western leaders like Pierre Trudeau, Bettino Craxi, and Olaf Palme. In economic regard, the fruits of *détente* were more ambiguous. By the 1980s the GDR's economy was critically dependent on West German credit and hard currency transfers. Already in the 1970s, West Germany had become the GDR's second largest trading partner, after the Soviet Union. In the 1980s, the annual West German cash transfers for transit, mail delivery and prisoner exchanges amounted to DM 4 billion – which represents 10 per cent of East Germany's produced national income or two-thirds of its annual industrial investment, exceeding the yearly allocation for defense (Michel, 1987). As several observers pointed out, East Germany's mini-*détente* of 1984 was also motivated by its quest for two huge West German bank credits, which reestablished the GDR's creditworthiness on financial markets after three years of post-Poland '81 isolation (see Baylis, 1986:383). While *détente* thus helped the East German regime to new stability, it also made it more dependent on the West. This, in turn, obliged the communist rulers to moderate their approach to the domestic regime opposition. Herein lies the truth of Egon Bahr's (1992) observation that the politics of *détente* created a "free space" (*Freiraum*) for dissent and opposition.

THE ROLE OF THE CHURCH

The rise of the East German peace movement was conditioned by several factors. First, the West German peace movement provided a model that could be emulated in the East. Tellingly, the first independent peace mobilization in the East occurred just after the Western movement had taken off in a series of nationwide campaigns and mass rallies in 1981. Second, the SED's own campaign against the NATO double-track decision of 1979 created widespread fear of nuclear war, making peace and disarmament the pivotal concerns of the time. Third, the apparent contradiction between peace advocacy in foreign policy and domestic militarism provided an obvious target of opposition. Fourth, in classic revisionist manner, regime claims could be held against a flawed reality. For reasons of consistency and credibility, the regime, which supported the peace movement in the West, could not totally repress a peace movement within its own borders. But fifth, and maybe most importantly, an independent institution existed that had adopted the peace issue from early on and later provided a shelter for autonomous peace groups: the Protestant Church.

In their classic study of totalitarian rule, Friedrich and Brzezinski (1965) argued that "there are islands, islands of separateness, in the totalitarian sea" (p. 279). Due to the lack of a civil society in Leninist regimes, opposition movements could not thrive without these "islands of separateness," such as – most famously – the Catholic Church in Poland. In East Germany, the Protestant Church was the only institution free of state control. But unlike in Poland, where the Catholic Church became a refuge for the suppressed nation, the role of the East German Protestant Church was more ambiguous. In a post-mobilization regime, the communist rulers were no longer out to raid the "islands of separateness" but were ready to use them for purposes of "inclusion" (Jowitt, 1975) and peace-making with society. In the East German case, the regime learned to use the Protestant Church as a device to neutralize domestic discontent and opposition. Opposition was tolerated as long as it remained within the church, but it faced stiff persecution as soon as it stepped outside the church. A true creature of the culture of *détente*, the church thus walked a thin line between cooptation and opposition. The further trajectory of regime opposition can then be reconstructed in terms of its gradual (and eventually incomplete) emancipation from church tutelage.

East Germany was the only country in Eastern Europe with a Lutheran majority population.[17] Considering the traditional Lutheran Doctrine of the Two Kingdoms, which preaches unconditional submission to worldly authority, the church was an extremely unlikely advocate of regime opposition.

But parallel to the Lutheran strand, there was also a strong Calvinist strand which was less hesitant to take a political stance (see Goeckel, 1990:ch.2). As the Confessing Church (*Bekennende Kirche*), this Calvinist strand – represented by eminent theologians such as Karl Barth and Dietrich Bonhöffer – had already spearheaded the resistance to Hitler. In particular, Bonhöffer's concept of the "Church for Others" suggested a special obligation of the church to defend the weak, marginalized, and persecuted in society. Not a monolithic organization, the East German Protestant Church was organizationally and territorially divided into three Lutheran "Bund" churches in the South, and five Calvinist "Union" churches in the North. Whereas the Lutheran churches, such as Saxony/Dresden and Thuringia, remained bastions of submissiveness, the Calvinist churches, most notably Saxony/Magdeburg and Berlin-Brandenburg, became receptive to, however cautious, regime critique.

In most other Eastern European countries, such as Czechoslovakia, Hungary and Bulgaria, the churches were systematically disassembled and subjected to strict party control. Besides Poland, only in East Germany could the church retain its institutional integrity and relative autonomy. When the GDR was internationally shunned and isolated in the 1950s and 1960s, an independent Protestant Church provided the regime with dearly needed ersatz recognition, most notably through the church's inter-German ties and its membership in international organizations such as the World Council of Churches and the Lutheran World Federation. Moreover, the confessional homogeneity of East Germany made it difficult to play off the churches against each other, as it happened in confessionally divided Hungary and Czechoslovakia. Finally, and most importantly, the democratic and decentralized internal decision-making structures of the Protestant Church prohibited any straightforward cooptation (Goeckel, 1990:ch.9).

In the 1970s, the church–state relations underwent a sea change, which prepared the church's active role in the later peace debate. Through cutting off its organizational ties to the Evangelical Churches in the West, the Eastern Church removed a stake of long-standing contention with the regime. The previous church strategy of hibernation and seclusion gave way to a more active strategy of participating in society. In 1971, church leader Albrecht Schönherr, Bishop of Berlin-Brandenburg, coined the famous concept of the "church within socialism." According to this concept, the church should find its place "in this given society, not separated from it, nor in opposition to it" (in Goeckel, 1990:173). This formula was tailor-made for the "inclusion" needs of a post-mobilization regime. In March 1978, a "summit" (*Gipfeltreffen*) between the church leadership and Honecker sealed a thorough rapprochement between church and state. For the first time, the state officially acknowledged the relative autonomy of the church, pledged that it would no longer discriminate against Christian youths in education and professional training, and granted the church certain privileges such as regular television access and integration of the clergy into the pension system (ibid., 242f). In turn, the church obliged itself to play a "critical-stabilizing role" in socialist society, as church secretary Manfred Stolpe put it (ibid., 269). Klaus Gysi, State Secretary for Church Affairs, summarized the new relationship in revealing terms: "Our real intention is to make the church feel at home in our republic and to gradually win over its potential both for the stable internal development of our republic and for our peace policy" (in Asmus, 1983b:322).

On both sides, the motivations for this church–state rapprochement differed. The church sought to counteract a dramatic loss of membership, which was partially due to the general march of secularization, but also resulted from the multiple discriminations that church members had to endure in education and employment. Whereas in 1950 the protestant church membership was 14.8 million, by 1978 membership was down to seven million (ibid., 322). In the early 1980s, the ratio of practicing protestants in the GDR was estimated at 20 per cent of adults, and only ten per cent of youths (Zander, 1989:220). If the churches opened their doors for dissenters and peace groups, they did so also because they were empty. For the regime, the quasi-corporatist integration of the churches should help extinguish the lingering flame of societal unrest, particularly after the Biermann expatriation and a series of youth riots in several cities of the GDR (Wensierski, 1981:24). Moreover, courting the church was part of a general attempt to bolster the regime's legitimacy through recovering, rather than repressing, historical and cultural traditions. Tellingly, party chief Honecker made himself the chair of the Luther Committee that was to prepare the 500th birthday of the church reformer in 1983.[18]

Critical church involvement in peace issues had been longstanding. After the introduction of the general draft in 1962, the churches had pressed hard for a substitute military service without weapons, which was introduced in 1964. The so-called *Bausoldaten* (construction soldiers), who were organized and counseled by the church, may be considered a nucleus of the peace movement (Eisenfeld, 1978). In 1973, construction soldiers founded the Peace Seminar in Königswalde near East Berlin, which met twice a year and was the first of its kind in East Germany (Meusel, 1988). In the late 1970s, the churches opposed the introduction of military education in schools, propagating instead an Education for Peace. In 1981, a Dresden-based church initiative proposed a Social Peace Service to replace the previous construction soldier service. Most importantly, the churches provided the organizational and thematic clues for the emergent peace movement, such as the Peace Decades (*Friedensdekaden*), which were held annually since 1980 at the local level, or, since 1982, the annual Peace Workshops (*Friedenswerkstätten*) in East Berlin, which attracted peace and other opposition groups from all over the GDR.

Push and pull factors in the churches' critical peace engagement are hard to disentangle. Wolf Biermann once said that there were three ways to escape the GDR: across the Wall, through suicide, or into the church.[19] To study at one of the two Protestant Church seminars at Naumburg or East Berlin was one of the few ways of getting a decent education without compromising oneself ideologically. The increasingly critical engagement of the churches mostly originated from a young generation of theologians and priests "by default."[20] When the churches took on the peace issue, they became attractive also for secular dissident constituencies. Over time, the initiative would shift from the church itself to these outside groups, which looked for church connection for the purely instrumental reason of gaining protection from state repression. The result was to carry the conflict between regime and opposition into the church, where an unrestive and critical "basis" of peace circles and friendly young priests became pitted against a more conservative and accommodating church leadership.

A good example is the career of the Peace Circle (*Friedenskreis*) of the Evangelical Student Parish (ESG) in East Berlin. Founded in 1977 by former construction soldiers, the ESG Peace Circle underwent a major transformation around 1980, when portions of the non-church opposition scene of East Berlin sought entry. A member describes the transformed Peace Circle as a mixture of "Christians, Marxists and Anarchists."[21] The ensuing politicization of the Peace Circle, which became one of the most radical opposition groups in East Berlin, moved the nervous ESG to cancel its affiliation in 1982. But being kicked out of the church would have spelled the certain end of the opposition group. So a new parish had to be found, which was dependent on approval by a friendly priest. After two years of unsuccessful inquiry, the church parish of Friedrichsfelde near East Berlin finally agreed to host the homeless Peace Circle. The young local priest, Gottfried Gartenschläger, had himself been part of East Berlin's "alternative" culture scene for many years, and he still was fond of playing the guitar in a rock band when not on sacral duty. Over the years, the regional church leadership of Berlin-Brandenburg followed with increasing unease the unorthodox mores of priest and Peace Circle, which became a magnet for dissent and opposition in the capital. In early 1989, the church leadership yielded to the incessant pressures by the local party state. The Reverend Gartenschläger was "banned" to the countryside, far away from East Berlin. Without the priest's sponsorship, the Peace Circle lost its hold in the church, and it soon disbanded.[22] To be sure, not all of the church-dependent peace circles that flourished from the early 1980s on were so explicitly political in orientation like the one in Friedrichsfelde. But the tendency was the same everywhere: outside groups seeking the protective "roof" of the church, and forcing the latter to play a moderating role in the conflict between regime and opposition. The East German sociologist Detlev Pollack (1990) aptly describes this constellation: "The church became the place in which the denied and suppressed problems and tensions of society were articulated and carried out" (p. 12).

The ambivalent role of the church in both expressing and containing conflict was evident from the start. In early 1982, a Dresden-based peace group distributed flyers throughout the GDR, which called for a peace rally at the site of the destroyed Liebfrauenkirche, to commemorate the anniversary of the Allied bombing of Dresden in 1944. Five thousand individuals, whom a sympathetic source described as "young drop-outs, many with long hair" (Ehring and Dallwitz, 1982:70), attended what became the first unofficial and independent peace mobilization in the GDR. However, at the last moment the Saxon Bishop Johannes Hempel could persuade the organizers to cancel their original plan of holding an unofficial public march, and to participate instead in a church-sponsored Peace Forum. Hempel had the backing of the local party authorities, who were apparently interested in avoiding a confrontation (Asmus, 1983b:312). After the official ending of the Peace Forum, a faction of the participants nevertheless held a non-church sanctioned procession to the Liebfrauenkirche, with lit candles – thus anticipating the symbol of the mass demonstrations in fall 1989. This was the first unofficial peace demonstration in the history of the GDR.[23] As in the Peace Forum that was henceforth held every February in Dresden, the church provided a platform for independent peace groups, but it also neutralized and staled their impact by subjecting them to church discipline and keeping them out of the public. "You can all come, even as already existing groups," church secretary Manfred Stolpe stated, "but you must respect two conditions: the creedal obligation (*Glaubensbindung*) of the church, and the final responsibility (*Letztverantwortung*) of the respective church parish, particularly with regard to public activities" (in Zander, 1989:322). A young church worker expressed this containment function of the church more bluntly: "If the party only knew how much we sometimes have to discipline these young people, they would be thankful to us" (Wensierski and Büscher, 1983:131). In fact, the party knew. In the jargon of the secret police, the disciplining and containment of opposition groups by the church was referred to as the "theologization" (*Theologisierung*) of "hostile-negative activities" (see Mitter and Wolle, 1990).

STATE RESPONSE

The peace debate provided a temporary remedy for the greatest threat to a Leninist regime: the loss of combat task. Party-engineered peace mobilization rejuvenated the original features of a "mass-movement regime" (Tucker, 1961), in which the whole populace becomes enlisted in a single, overarching cause. When confronted with the existence of an unofficial peace movement, the communist rulers pointed out that the whole country was an official peace movement. "There cannot be a pacifist movement because the government's policy is pacifist," said a high party functionary (in Asmus, 1983b:302). The "official" peace movement was organized in the party-controlled Christian Peace Conference (*Christliche Friedenskonferenz*) and the Peace Council (*Friedensrat*) of the GDR. But even the "unofficial" or "independent" movement was enlisted in the state's peace campaign. Party chief Honecker declared to a delegation of the Green Party: "This independent peace movement in the GDR has the great advantage that it exists in a state that pursues the same goals" (in Kuhrt, 1984:8).

In practical terms, the regime responded to the independent peace movement with the double strategy of accommodation and repression. Accommodation aimed at either recruiting unofficial peace groups into the official peace campaign, or neutralizing them within the Protestant Church. Repressive measures such as imprisonment and expatriation were directed at all those groups and initiatives that mobilized outside the churches or touched upon certain taboo themes, such as national unity or the status of Soviet military occupation.

Accommodation

The peace-state image and parallel support of the Western peace movement suggested an accommodating response to the independent peace movement in the home country, even though the very existence of the latter ran against the grain of a Leninist regime. Church-related movement activities were generally tolerated. After all, the church took great pains in stressing that it understood itself as part of the *official* peace movement.[24] In addition, the regime stressed the "unity of all peace forces" and sought to recruit also independent pacifists and Christians into the statist "peace front" (in Wensierski and Büscher, 1983:110). An important role in this accommodation policy fell to the Free German Youth (FDJ), the official youth organization. The FDJ held numerous discussion rounds with church groups and independent pacifists, and even invited the latter to participate in its annual May rallies. The FDJ eagerly replicated, and altered, the slogans and symbols of independent peace groups. For instance, the opposition call to "Make Peace Without Weapons" was transformed into the official slogan "Make Peace Against NATO-Weapons." The FDJ also played to the taste of the youthful peace audience, for instance, in a series of "Rock for Peace" concerts.

There was a deliberate attempt to preempt and vindicate all symbolisms that could have provided strength and unity to the emergent peace movement. For instance, after the surprise rally by independent peace groups at the ruins of Dresden's Liebfrauenkirche in 1982, the SED was anxious to avoid a repetition of this embarassing event in the next year. In 1983, the SED itself staged a mass rally of 100 000 at the site. In an obvious attempt to claim the ruin's symbolism and reassert the party monopoly on the peace issue, the FDJ stationed a "guard of honor," complete with flags and eternal flame, in front of the ruins until late in the night, thus trying to discourage unofficial peace activities (Asmus, 1983c:2). Nevertheless, 1000 participants of the church-backed Peace Forum '83 staged a candle rally as they had done the year before. In the following years the strange contest over this peace shrine repeated itself, with an obvious imbalance of forces. But when in 1985 a metal fence shielded the battered church building from illicit access, indefatigable peace demonstrators simply placed their candles on top of its iron bars (Zander, 1989:292).

Repression

Whenever independent peace groups dared to move outside the church, they faced stiff state repression. The best known example was the conflict about the "Swords to Plowshares" emblem in early 1982. The emblem, which was first used during the second church-based Peace Decade in November 1981, shows a smith forging a plowshare from a sword, framed by the Old Testament verse. A more inconspicuous symbol could hardly be found, because it was based on a socialist-realist sculpture donated by the Soviet Union to the United Nations in 1946.[25] When the emblem rapidly spread as a public symbol of the emergent peace movement, the regime showed no tolerance. Teachers were advised to confiscate all "Swords to Plowshares" book-marks, and the police would stop anyone on the streets who carried the sticker on their clothes. Radio GDR called the carriers of the incriminated symbol "blind, deaf, and hypocritical," and the FDJ journal *Junge Welt* dismissed the goal to "make peace without weapons" as a "suicidal illusion, if one considers the aggressive intentions of imperialism" (in Ehring and Dallwitz, 1982:63). In a typical move, the church was finally allowed to use the symbol, but only in its internal affairs. Throughout the 1980s, the incriminated socialist blacksmith remained the central symbol of East German regime opposition.[26]

The dire consequences of lacking church support became felt by the independent peace movement of Jena, a university and industrial town in the southeast of the GDR. In Jena, dubbed by a reliable source as the "original home of the East German peace movement" (Rüddenklau, 1992:32), an extremely state-obedient and conservative church coincided with one of the most state-defiant youth and dissident scenes of the GDR (Asmus, 1983d). Jena had a lengthy history of clashes with authority, dating back to the workers' revolt of 1953. The city was the home of a number of critical writers, such as Jürgen Fuchs, and the basis of a notorious anarchist youth scene. Jena was also said to have the highest rate per capita of applications for emigration to the West. At the same time, the Protestant Church of Thuringia, which had championed the rapprochement with the state in the 1970s, was one of the most conservative in the GDR, and certainly unwilling to provide a shelter for independent peace groups. This created a situation ripe with potential conflict. In November 1982, 80 members of the Jena Peace Community (*Friedensgemeinschaft*) staged a two-minute protest on the city's main square, during which they formed a silent circle and unrolled a banner with the word "peace" on it. After a second silent protest in December, all participants were rounded up by the police. The event became widely publicized by the Western media, making the phrase "Jena Peace Scene" (*Jenaer Friedensszene*) almost a household word in the Federal Republic. The church distanced itself from the protests, stating that "there were no activities outside the church for which it could be held responsible" (Bishop Leich, quoted in Zander, 1989:324). Bowing to the negative publicity in the West, the local authorities had to release their young prisoners after a short while. While prevented by the watchful eyes of the Western media from inflicting harsh prison sentences, the regime resorted to a no less effective measure known since the Biermann affair: expatriation. In June 1983, Roland Jahn, who later became known as one of the most outspoken exile-dissidents, was deported to the West, handcuffed and locked into a train toilet. By late 1983, most other members of the Jena Peace Community had landed in West Berlin, some voluntarily, some against their will (Asmus, 1983e). Exit wiped off Jena from the map of regime opposition. Eager to control this restless turf, after this the watchful local authorities even banned the traditional town carnival (Zander, 1989:325).

Where church affiliation was lacking, Western media publicity increasingly helped stabilize independent peace groups. This became evident in the case of the Berlin-based Women for Peace. As an opposition group, the Women for Peace are significant in several regards. This was one of the first peace groups in the GDR that tried to escape church tutelage. Most of its members were recruited from the dense dissident scene of the Prenzlauer Berg district of East Berlin, a run-down working-class quarter just north of the city center, which may be considered the topographical center of East German regime opposition in the 1980s (see Chapter 4). Some of the pivotal figures during the regime breakdown in 1989, such as Bärbel Bohley and Ulrike Poppe, made their step from tacit disapproval to explicit opposition as members of Women for Peace. The group was formed in October 1982 in response to the introduction of the female draft. After their start as a conventional signature-gathering campaign, the Women for Peace increasingly experimented with symbolic forms of public protest. A member describes the insecurity of the state in dealing with female protesters: "They always looked for the man in the background, the 'wire-puller' (*Drahtzieher*). They were not used to dealing with women. This was new to them."[27] The Women were also the first opposition group to use the Western media for their purposes, and to seek the contact with the Greens and the Western peace movement. In December 1983, these Western contacts became the pretext for arresting the core members of the group, and charging them with "high treason" (*landesverräterische Nachrichtenübermittlung*).[28] This was no small thing, but a "crime" that carried a maximum of 12 years in prison. The sudden arrests were part of a massive raid on the independent peace movement in late 1983, when the defeat of the Western peace movement had released the regime from all tactical restraints (Asmus, 1984:2f). But the assault on a group already widely known in the West had to backfire. What had first incriminated the group turned out to be its greatest asset: its public presence. After an unprecedented Western media blitz and the intervention of political leaders such as Willy Brandt and Olaf Palme, the arrested Women were released, and all charges had to be dropped. Gerd Poppe, the husband of Ulrike Poppe and himself a major figure in East Germany's regime opposition of the 1980s, outlines the significance of this event: "We used all our international contacts to release the prisoners, and we were much surprised how effective this was. We noticed that state repression could no longer remain secret. Western publicity became our best protection."[29]

Not only action in public, but also the touching of certain taboo themes provoked a harsh state response. An example is the so-called Berlin Appeal of February 1982, which asked for the denuclearization of Europe and the "withdrawal of all occupation troops from Germany."[30] This touched upon two taboo themes in East Germany: national unity and the status of the Soviet military stationed in the GDR. This was too much even for the churches, which recommended not to sign the appeal that was circulating widely in both Germanies. In fact, the crypto-nationalism of the West German peace movement found few parallels in the Eastern movement, perhaps in an implicit understanding that nationalism would question the existence of the GDR. The young author of the Berlin Appeal, Rainer Eppelmann, was one of the more iconoclastic figures in the East German peace movement. A Protestant priest in East Berlin's Samariter parish, Eppelmann had become known for his so-called Blues Masses, which were full-scale rock concerts within church walls that attracted thousands of young people from all over the GDR. Eppelmann was strongly disliked and shunned within the East Berlin opposition scene, partly for purely personal reasons, but maybe also for his uncompromising stance toward the state. His taboo-breaking Berlin Appeal brought Eppelmann a police arrest, if only a short one. This was a rare measure to be taken against a priest, because priests were almost untouchable in the GDR, and thus could risk more than others.[31] But few were as daring as the Reverend Eppelmann.

PEACE AND HUMAN RIGHTS

Eberhard Kuhrt (1984:81) rightly states that the "system-threatening potential" of the East German peace movement consisted in its implicit human rights dimension. As I outlined in Chapter 1, it is a general characteristic of social movements in Leninist regimes that independent action, whatever concrete issue it addresses, must sooner or later deal with its incrimination by the party-state, and tackle the denial of elementary citizenship rights. East Germany is no exception to this. But the special German context made the turn to human rights dissidence a particularly difficult one. Nevertheless, because domestic militarism, rather than nuclear geopolitics, provided the starting-point of independent peace mobilization in East Germany, the human rights dimension was present from the beginning, if only implicitly. The impulse to make human rights an explicit focus originated from an incriminated movement basis that had to endure severe state repression. After their deportation to the West, members of the Jena Peace Community declared: "Human rights and peace are indivisible for us. Where individuals are persecuted by the state because of their political, religious, or pacifist convictions, as in the countries of Eastern Europe, there can be no peace" (in Kuhrt, 1984:80). The experience of a party-state that did not respond to the unrelenting "dialogue" offers from below, but that, on the contrary, incriminated and persecuted independent peace activists, had to be disillusioning. In fact, the repressive state helped create what had not been there before: a self-conscious opposition. A member of Women for Peace describes this process: "In the beginning, I did not see my peace engagement as being in opposition to the state; it was more like setting a different accent while pursuing a common goal. But the hoped-for dialogue never happened. By being incriminated and persecuted, we were pushed into a frontal opposition to the regime. This is how we discovered the issue of human rights."[32]

But the obstacles to sharpening the human rights dimension within the peace movement were formidable. The concrete experience of injustice at the movement basis did not yet entail a program and a cause. There was no language to make human rights violations a more prominent concern. The programmatic élites in the peace movement – the intellectuals and the churches – practiced the "peace first" rhetoric so typical for the culture of *détente*. As indicated above, the direct involvement of prominent intellectuals in the independent peace movement was negligible. But intellectuals played an important role in framing the stakes and issues of the peace debate. In the early 1980s, a series of highly publicized meetings between writers from both Germanies became especially important in this regard. The first "Berlin Meeting for the Strengthening of Peace" convened in East Berlin on 13 December 1981 – the day when martial law was declared in Poland. The previously issued "Appeal of the Writers of Europe" had set the terms of the meeting: "Nothing is more important than the preservation of peace."[33] The Berlin Meeting, officially sponsored by the East German Academy of Arts and the Academy of Science, and attended by the cream of East and West Germany's literary intellectuals, exposed in minutiae the culture of *détente*. Dissidents like Robert Havemann had not been invited. The dramatic Polish events were almost ignored. Günter Grass was among the few who confessed "concern about what is happening in Poland," but he quickly added that "capitalism, too, is inherently sick and producing nothing but its own crises" (Krüger, 1982:134).

The second Berlin Meeting, which took place in April 1983 in West Berlin, stood under the direct impact of the arrests in Jena. The relationship between peace and human rights inevitably became the dominant theme. But Stefan Hermlin, head of the East German Writers' Union, declared from the beginning: "The discussion about human rights is noble and important. But I am not prepared to confound this question with the concerns of the peace movement" (Krüger, 1983:30). No East German writer at this meeting dared to criticize the communist government. Not even Stefan Heym, who took a temporary lessening of the state repression in Jena as "a victory... of the reformers in the GDR leadership, [which] has to be acknowledged as such" (ibid., 132). But also Bernt Engelmann, head of the West German Writers' Union, refused to "decapitate the Soviet chicken," and to muddle the peace agenda with human rights questions (ibid., 134). As the form and substance of both Berlin Meetings indicate, the East German intellectual élite sided once more with the party-state, not with its grass-roots opposition. But in doing so, East German intellectuals only acted out the culture of *détente*.

So did the churches. Despite multiple tensions between the churches and autonomous peace groups, the churches provided the cognitive framework for the peace movement.[34] This begins with the notion of peace itself. No concept in East German opposition politics has been as central, and enigmatic, as the notion of peace. Even when the peace movement had long passed its zenith, "peace" was still the unifying symbol for the new ecology or human rights groups that emerged in the second half of the 1980s. The churches introduced a broad notion of peace that was not limited to geopolitics, but referred to the individual sphere of everyday life (see Kuhrt, 1984:ch.4). According to this broad notion of peace, there was a direct connection between "peace-creating" (*friedenschaffend*) action in the private sphere and the peace between states. "Peacelessness" (*Unfrieden*) had to be rooted out from the bottom up, and everybody could get into the act. The churches also introduced a distinction that henceforth became a *chiffre* for human rights demands: "external" vs. "internal peace." The 1983 Synod of the Evangelical Churches in Potsdam stated that "internal and external peace are indivisible" – meaning: no peace without democracy. While this may be interpreted as a barely disguised plea to respect human rights, the position of the churches on this issue is still more complicated.[35] The 1981 Human Rights Report of the Evangelical Churches espouses a "holistic" (*ganzheitlich*) understanding of human rights, according to which the "individual" could not be separated from the "social" aspect (Kuhrt, 1984:81). According to this understanding, individual human rights have no unconditional validity. The plus in social rights in socialism thus partially compensates for its neglect of individual rights. Moreover, this neglect is seen as only temporary, resulting from the anxiety of the communist leadership in a hostile environment. Therefore, the emphasis had to be on strengthening the neglected component of individual rights.[36]

This holistic understanding of human rights, according to which there is no *a priori* incompatibility between liberal democracy and communist rule, is logically connected to the *détente* concept of security partnership, which the churches wholeheartedly embraced. At the 1982 Synod in Halle, the churches passed the resolution "Against the Spirit and Logic of Deterrence," which defined the church position in the nuclear debate and became influential also in the peace movement. In this programmatic statement, the current militarization of domestic life and lack of democracy is seen as a result of the geopolitics of deterrence (*Abschreckungspolitik*). As the theologian Hans Tschiche (1981) argued, the communist rulers' "trauma of being threatened" (*Trauma der Bedrohung*) was the main cause of their undemocratic ways. So take away this threat through "security partnership", and domestic liberalization will naturally follow. This was the church version of *Ostpolitik*'s "change through rapprochement."

This position set the terms for the emergent peace movement, both positively and negatively. On the positive side, the peace movement also never questioned the intrinsically "peaceful" and defensive character of Soviet foreign policy. The East–West conflict resulted from erroneous perceptions and mutual anxieties, not from the different principles and structures of both political systems. Most importantly, the assumption of a democratic potential inherent in "real social-ism" fed the reformist and regime-loyal disposition of the peace movement. On the negative side, the concept of se-curity partnership implied the decoupling of the peace and human rights issues, and thus worked against the peace movement *qua* movement. At the 1984 Synod in Greifswald, the churches declared that "all open questions must be sub-ordinated to the main task of preserving peace" (in Zander, 1989:272).[37] Because the concept of security partnership was defined at the level of inter-state relations, domestic oppo-sition movements entered the scene as potentially "desta-bilizing" factors. "This smacks of Metternichian politics," remarked the dissident theologian Edelbert Richter (1988:89). For the peace movement, the phalanx of security partner-ship was almost impossible to penetrate, because it had equal support in the West. A former Dresden peace activist ex-plains: "I was against the concept of security partnership, because it allowed to cover up the real problems in the GDR, which were in the area of human rights violations. But security partnership was the heart of national policy (*Deutschlandpolitik*), also in the West. Eppler, Bahr, and all the other Western politicians invited by the church reiter-ated the same position: 'Peace is the first human right', 'peace first, everything else second'. The SPD said it, the church said it, and, of course, the SED said it too. But even most peace groups said it. If you did *not* say it, you were denounced as an 'enemy of detente' (*Entspannungsfeind*)."[38]

The East German peace movement could partially escape the grip of German *détente*, when its Eastern European neigh-bours launched the concept of a "bloc-transcending" peace movement (see Poppe, 1988). Because Eastern European peace movements developed out of human rights dissidence, the linkage of peace and human rights was never in ques-tion there (see Tismaneanu, 1990a). The look toward the East allowed East German peace activists to loosen the debilitating fixation on the West, and to shed the *détente*-dogma of security partnership. Only now a truly "independent" peace movement emerged, even though it was confined to largely conceptual developments among a tiny number of dissidents.[39] But whereas in Eastern Europe "bloc transcendence" meant the reassertion of national self-determination, this could not be in East Germany, the nationless state. For East German dissidents, "bloc transcendence" meant the transformation of the peace movement into a "movement for emancipation in the broadest sense," which addressed "Third World, environmental, women's, [and] human rights" concerns – in that order.[40] The shadow of East German exceptionalism was long, all too long, and the peace movement remained its prisoner even in the attempt to escape it. In a clear case of *détentist* boundary erosion, the "industrial system", rather than a dictatorial regime, was built up as the main target of opposition.[41] This was not so different from the parallel attempts of the church to expand its peace advocacy toward Third-Worldism and ecology.[42] From this angle, the regime breakdown of 1989 must appear as the most unlikely, if not undesirable, of all events, and it would certainly take forces other than the peace movement to make it happen.

4 The Incomplete Turn to Human Rights Dissidence

Situated at the boundary between East and West, East German opposition politics was always exposed to conflicting, if not contradictory, influences. The peace movement of the early 1980s obviously followed the Western model of new social movements and its system-indifferent emphasis on "global" and "survival" problems. In the mid-1980s, however, East German opposition politics became more receptive to the Eastern model of human rights dissidence. After their failure to prevent a new round of nuclear rearmament in 1983/4 and in light of the obvious unwillingness of the party state to enter into a "dialogue" with its opposition, East German peace activists looked for new modes and fields of activity. The turn to the East became especially attractive with Gorbachev's glasnost and perestroika. This allowed the opposition to confront the regime with a new and unexpected round of claims that the previous "peace first" rhetoric was ineffective to contain.

The turn to the East was further conditioned by a rapprochement, however cautious, between the Western peace movements and the Eastern human rights movements. Since its Berlin meeting in 1983, the European Conference for Nuclear Disarmament (END) – the clearinghouse of the Western peace movements – actively promoted a dialogue with Eastern European dissident groups such as Charter 77.[1] The call for a "*détente* from below" and for an "open European dialogue across the bloc frontiers"[2] helped reconcile what previously had seemed irreconcilable: the Western quest for peace and the Eastern quest for civil rights and national self-determination.[3] In the wake of this East–West rapprochement, East German peace activists became exposed to the Eastern European human rights discourse. This provided a language to articulate the own negative experience of a grass-

100

roots movement in a Leninist regime.

The formation, in 1986, of the Initiative for Peace and Human Rights (IFM) became the catalyst for the turn to human rights dissidence. While emerging out of the church-backed peace movement, the IFM was the first opposition group in the GDR that deliberately positioned itself outside the churches.[4] In form and content, the IFM was modeled on the Czech Charter 77. Three speakers signed as responsible for the group, to which everyone could belong who "openly propagated its goals and signed its documents" (Templin and Weisshuhn, 1991:153). Like the Charter 77, the IFM sought to create a public sphere through acting as if it already existed – all of its appeals and statements were accompanied by a list of supporters, with full names and addresses. This made the signatories vulnerable to state repression but at the same time created a cordon of publicity that increasingly functioned as a substitute for lacking church protection. In another similarity with the Charter 77, the IFM claimed to abrogate utopia in favor of an "open society" with guaranteed civil liberties (Templin, 1989:60). Its "politics from below" no longer "leered at the favor of the rulers," but instead sought to promote the self-organization of society (Templin, 1988:75). As one of IFM's declarations states, "democratization" and the creation of "legal statehood" (*Rechtsstaatlichkeit*) were the group's two major goals (IFM, 1987).

The comparison with Charter 77, evoked by IFM activists themselves,[5] is instructive. In fact, Czechoslovakia was not unlike East Germany in certain regards – both were rigid communist regimes complemented by apathetic and impassive societies, opposition being confined to tiny circles of dissident intellectuals. But equally instructive are the differences. First, consider the different stature of the leadership of Charter 77 and IFM. The three first signatories of Charter 77 included Jiri Hajek, foreign minister under Dubcek, Jan Patocka, a famous philosopher, and Vaclav Havel, the country's leading playwright. This is as if Christa Wolf, Ernst Bloch, and a major party reformer had conjoined to openly challenge the SED leadership – but Christa Wolf, the celebrated writer, was still a faithful party member (until the summer of 1989); Ernst Bloch, the famous Christian-Marxist philosopher of hope, had long exiled to the West (without ever renouncing his allegiance to the communist cause), and there was never a major party reformer in East Germany. Instead, the leadership of IFM reflected the peripheral status of East German regime opposition in the 1980s. The first three signatories, Ralph Hirsch, Peter Grimm and Wolfgang Templin, were completely unknown outside East Berlin's small dissident scene, and in moral stature and influence could not measure up to the Czech Chartists. This was not the country's political and cultural counter-élite (such a thing the GDR did not have), but its youthful counter-culture.[6]

In a second regard, too, the comparison with the Czech case is instructive. The human rights platform of Charter 77 was the uncontested center of dissident politics in post-1968 Czechoslovakia. In East Germany, the turn to the human rights issue occurred belatedly, and it remained heavily contested within the opposition scene. Rather than concentrating on human rights dissidence, opposition politics diversified in the mid-1980s – ecology and Third-Worldism being two equally favored ersatz issues after the peace movement had passed its zenith.[7] Moreover, the notion of peace remained the umbrella that united the diverse opposition groups, reflecting also the fact that most of these groups remained closely tied to the Protestant Church.[8] Tellingly, East Germany's major ecology group, founded in 1986, called itself "*Peace* and Ecology Group of the Zion Parish" (better known as Ecology Library), while the acronym IFM stood for "Initiative for *Peace* and Human Rights" (emphasis added). Even among those who embraced the "neuralgic" human rights issue (Templin and Weisshuhn, 1991:149), there was disagreement about the meaning and implications of this turn. A group of self-styled "social revolutionaries", which called itself "Gegenstimmen" (Counter-Voices), criticized the "sectarian decoupling of the human rights from the peace issue" (quoted in Rüddenklau, 1992:59). The Gegenstimmen favoured a "socialist" interpretation of the human rights problematic, and particularly objected to the extensive use of the Western media as pioneered by IFM.[9]

But even IFM, contrary to its verbal claims, remained caught in the old ways. In the GDR, where socialism was the state-defining doctrine, the shadow of revisionism was hard to escape. To renounce the socialist creed meant questioning the existence of the GDR, and IFM, like all other East German opposition groups, tried hard not to be denounced as "state enemy" (*Staatsfeind*). An IFM leader admits: "We stood firmly on the ground of socialism (*auf dem Boden des Sozialismus*). We wanted a democratized socialism, not the restoration of capitalism in the GDR."[10] Antipolitics could not exist in the GDR, and the revisionist hope of entering into a "dialogue" with the communist rulers remained constitutive also for IFM. Tellingly, IFM's first major activity was an "Open Letter to the Party," which tried to assist the SED's policy finding process at the 11th Party Congress. Which was a detailed overview of major problems in family and education, culture, welfare, the environment, and security policy, accompanied by concrete suggestions for improvement. The Open Letter concludes with the plea to establish an "independent peace council" to "harmonize the interests of state and society" and to stimulate the "open discussion" between both.[11] Needless to say, the Party did not bother to respond.

There is a third regard in which the comparison with the Czech case helps sharpen the contours of emergent human rights dissidence in East Germany. As Vaclav Havel indicated, the notion of dissident was a creation by Western journalists. In fact, human rights dissidence in Czechoslovakia was critically dependent on Western media publicity, which forced the Husak regime to temper its ways with the opposition. But by the mid-1980s, when the novelty of dissidence had worn off and all Western eyes were fixed on the more dramatic reform experiments in Hungary, Poland and the Soviet Union, the conditions for human rights dissidence had actually worsened in Czechoslovakia. A Czech dissident even wondered whether Charter 77 could have been launched at this time, because "sufficient international attention and pressure does not now exist."[12] Until the Velvet Revolution in 1989, Chartists were subject to full-scale state repression, which included harsh prison sentences and physical police brutality. Not so in East Germany. No other communist regime was more tightly in the grip of *détente* and more dependent on Western cash-flows than the East German one.

East German oppositionists could count on the steady presence of the West German media, preserving them from the non-domestic "issue-attention cycles" (A. Downs) that plagued the cause of the Czech dissidents.[13] By the mid-1980s, East German oppositionists no longer had to fear harsh prison sentences. Eager to maintain its "peaceful" façade in foreign policy and "coalition of reason" slant in inter-German relations, the party state resorted to "political" means to hold down its opposition – which meant tight observation by the secret police and the active manipulation of opposition groups by undercover agents and spies. This was complemented by the steady threat of deportation to the West as well as tight travel restrictions (so-called *Republikhaft*) – the entire IFM leadership was barred from leaving the GDR, in order to undercut their contacts with Eastern European dissidents. In sum, from the vantage point of overt state repression, the conditions for regime opposition were more favorable in the GDR than in Czechoslovakia.

THE "PARALLEL CULTURE"

As outlined in Chapter 1, the recovery of civil society was a major goal of Eastern European dissident movements. In Germany, the difficult history of civil society, both as a concept and as a reality, is notorious. Hegel's pejorative definition of civil society as realm of only "partial" interests (*Not- und Verstandesstaat*) that had to be kept in check by an "impartial" state remained effective (see Dahrendorf, 1971:214–31). From this angle, the GDR, more than the Westernized Bonn republic, inherited the "statist" fixation of German political culture – the catchy notion of Red Prussia contains more than a grain of truth (see Ash, 1981).

    Under these conditions, the attempts by an increasingly "Eastern-Europeanized" opposition to recover civil society against an imperious party state would necessarily be difficult. The comparison with the Czech case is again instructive. Not by accident, the dissident circle around IFM adopted the Czech notion of parallel culture to denote its attempt to rebuild civil society (see Rosenthal, 1988a). In both countries, an impotent dissident scene faced a rigid party state, so that a Polish-style confrontation between society and state was out of the question. But if a close observer of Czechoslovakia could say that "the whole cultural life of the nation exist[ed] ... *only* underground" (Wyatt, 1984:6), this was emphatically not the case in East Germany. The intellectual élite remained in an ambiguous position of skeptical yet loyal distance to the communist rulers. In Ralf Dahrendorf's term (1971:299), the leading East German intellectuals inherited the German tradition of the "classical intellectual" who combined apolitical inwardness with a basic affirmation of the powers-that-be.[14]

Clever state policies helped reinforce the loyalty of the intellectual élite. Since the Biermann affair in 1976, artists were granted generous travel visas (so-called *Künstlervisa*), which allowed them to move freely between East and West. After a temporary clamp-down in 1979,[15] the regime showed remarkable restraint *vis-à-vis* its leading artists and intellectuals. In the late 1980s, when the regime otherwise excelled in its rejection of Gorbachev-style glasnost, the Writers' Union openly debated the abolishment of censorship. This, however, did not bring the literary intellectuals in any closer contact with the grass-roots opposition. When, in the late November days of 1987, the 10th Writers' Congress convened in unprecedented openness to demand an end to censorship, the security police raided the Ecology Library, a bastion of East Berlin's emerging "parallel culture"[16] – and the writers did not feel compelled to issue a protest note. This epitomizes the half engineered, half self-imposed dissociation between East Germany's intellectual élite and the "parallel culture."

In order to understand the emergent "parallel culture" it is important to know more about its prime location: East Berlin's Prenzlauer Berg district. Since the early 1970s, the shabby former working-class district just north of East Berlin's Alexanderplatz, once the home of Heinrich Zille and Käthe Kollwitz, had become the premier address of young artists, dissidents, and drop-outs.[17] When the previous "mainstream" inhabitants, frustrated by the adventurous housing conditions in East Berlin's most run-down corner, moved out to the new satellite city of Marzahn or elsewhere, the country's counterculture moved in – or it would develop as such in the greenless quarters between Schönhauser and Prenzlauer Allee. In the dark and hidden backyards, factory halls, and lofts of the "Prenzlberg", as locals called their district, a dense network of independent galleries, theatres, coffee houses and intellectual discussion circles emerged. When, in the early 1980s, punks and other young drop-outs squatted a considerable number of virtually uninhabitable but vacant houses in this area, a colorful and vibrant street scene emerged that looked more like New York's East Village or West Berlin's Kreuzberg than your average socialist city in a country that was once called by writer Volker Braun "the most boring in the world."[18] But the Prenzlauer Berg also symbolizes that the "parallel culture" in East Germany was more like the Western ghettoized countercultures than the Eastern European repositories of national culture.

The Prenzlauer Berg became the home of East Germany's dissident scene as well as of a new "underground" literary scene that was socialized in the cultural stalemate of the post-Biermann era. Whereas the Biermann generation, now mostly in the West, had still sought the active political confrontation with the regime, these young writers and poets, most of them born after 1950, simply opted out of society. The best-known of them, the poet Sascha Anderson, who had grown up in an intellectual family in Weimar, stated laconically that the GDR "just [did] not interest" him.[19] This youngest generation of literary intellectuals had experienced socialism only as a "deformed reality" (Heiner Müller),[20] and consequently it was the first generation to give up the idea of reforming it. Young writers and poets like Sascha Anderson, Uwe Kolbe, or Bert Papenfuss sought refuge in an esoteric subculture of aestheticist experiment, whose touchstone was the latest word from Paris rather than the old-fashioned quest for the true socialism. Unable to be printed in the GDR, and too esoteric to find publishers in West Germany,[21] the postmodernist "word smashers" around Sascha Anderson developed their own media network with self-produced and self-distributed audio-tapes, anthologies, and samizdat journals.[22]

Despite their joint ghettoization and shared generational background, the political and literary opposition scenes of the Prenzlauer Berg failed to coalesce. To be sure, there were attempts to connect both. Since the early 1980s, there were several quasi-public "literary salons" where dissidents and writers would mingle to listen to and discuss poetry and prose. One such "salon" was the tiny flat of dissident Gerd Poppe, where sometimes hundreds of people would meet to listen to those outlawed writers who could not be printed in the GDR or elsewhere. Reflecting the attempt to build a public sphere, these meetings were not conspiratorial. "It was open house," Gerd Poppe recounts, "everybody was invited. Of course, also the Stasi."[23] But a Magic Lantern, the small Prague underground theatre that symbolized the close alliance between the cultural and political dissident scenes there, never existed on the Prenzlauer Berg. Due to their apolitical estrangement, the fixpoint of the Prenzlauer Berg poets was emigration, not reform. In 1986, Sascha Anderson emigrated to the West, and he was preceded or followed by the majority of the new literary avantgarde.[24] The writer Lutz Rathenow, who belongs to the Anderson generation but rejected its "compulsive apoliticity" (*krampfhafte Apolitizität*), aptly commented on the failure of political opposition and cultural avantgarde to coalesce: "The young literates of the Prenzlauer Berg sought to escape the GDR province through withdrawal and emigration. In contrast, the political opposition more or less happily accepted this province."[25]

The development of an own samizdat occurred rather late in the GDR, if compared with Eastern Europe. This points to a crucial hindrance to the rise of an independent "parallel culture" in the GDR: the fact that the West German electronic and print media served as a readily accessible ersatz public sphere. A critical turning-point in this regard was the founding of the Ecology Library in 1986, under the roof of East Berlin's Zion church. In fact, in a country where even typewriters were officially registered, not to mention that printers or photocopy machines were unavailable, church protection was instrumental to get a samizdat started. As in so many other cases, the approval of a friendly priest was instrumental to house the group of young people who would build up an astonishing collection of (forbidden) Western books and publications, the Ecology Library (*Umweltbibliothek*), in the vacant basement of the parish building. More than

just a collection of books, the Ecology Library became a
center of East Berlin's emerging "parallel culture," organizing literary readings and art exhibitions, and providing a
space for the various opposition groups in the capital.
Equipped with a primitive matrix-print machine that was
smuggled into the East by West German Green Party deputies,[26] the Ecology Library also printed the first political
samizdat journals of the GDR.

The first samizdat journal produced this way was the
Grenzfall, which was edited by the IFM and appeared from
1986 to early 1988 on a monthly basis with 900 copies.[27]
The average content of *Grenzfall* [28] mirrors the thematic concerns of IFM. One part of the journal was reserved for docu-
menting concrete human rights violations. The larger part,
however, was devoted to the documentation of dissident
activities in other Eastern European countries. A third focus was the raising of taboo issues, such as the Hitler-Stalin
Pact, which had been erased from the history books of the
"anti-fascist" GDR. While printed in the rooms and with the
facilities of the Ecology Library, the IFM-edited *Grenzfall* did
not enjoy church protection, and thus was completely illegal. Accordingly, it became a prime target of the security
police, whose huge crack-down on the Ecology Library in
November 1987 really aimed at the church-independent
editors of *Grenzfall.*

From 1987, the Ecology Library issued its own journal,
Umweltblätter (Ecology Papers), which was saved from the
grip of the security police by the innocent but essential cover
imprint "Only For Church-Internal Usage" (*Nur für den
innerkirchlichen Gebrauch*).[29] This imprint officially sanctioned
the *Umweltblätter,* like most other samizdat journals that pro-
liferated since the late 1980s,[30] as church-internal publications. But a polite church paper the *Umweltblätter* was certainly
not. While limited by the matrix-technique to appear in no
more than 1000 copies, the *Umweltblätter* became the most
widely read samizdat journal of the GDR, each exemplar
passing through many hands. As its name indicates, the
Umweltblätter addressed particularly the dismal state of the
environment in the GDR, but also covered the whole spectrum of dissident concerns, though from a decidedly anarchist perspective.

The new samizdat literature epitomizes the thrust of the emergent human rights opposition to act as if individual rights of free expression and assembly already existed. A declaration issued by IFM at the 1987 United Nation's Day of Human Rights states: "Our intention is to promote independent information and communication in this society, and to create a second sphere of culture (*zweite Ebene der Kultur*)" (quoted in Hirsch and Kopelew, 1989:VII). Given the many obstacles to do just that in East Germany, the results are impressive. But a repository of national culture and fountainhead of a civil society the "parallel culture" could not be.

STASI DEMONOLOGY

A major effect of *détente* and *Ostpolitik* was to transform the ways in which the party-state tried to hold down its opposition. Since the mid-1980s, arrests and imprisonments had become rare, and they were replaced by "political" forms of control.[31] This meant the systematic infiltration and manipulation of opposition groups by informers and agents provocateurs of the security police (Stasi). Gary Marx (1975) once argued that the undercover manipulation of movements by the state represented a "neglected category" in social movement research. With regard to the U.S., this neglect could be excused by the "rather amateurish" (ibid.) spying practices in a democratic state. The East German case, however, outstrips the wildest fantasies. Commenting on the high number of Stasi agents among the opposition groups, a founding member of the IFM even argued that "in a certain sense opposition and Stasi were one."[32] This may be exaggerated. But any account of regime opposition in the 1980s is incomplete that does not consider the active role of the security police in steering and manipulating its "opposition."

Among the most shocking post-unification revelations are the monstrous proportions of East Germany's security apparatus. The Ministry for State Security had 90 000 full-time employees;[33] the number of part-time informers is estimated at 300 000; 3000 operatives were deployed just to open mail and eavesdrop on telephone conversations; 5000 officers were permanently in use to follow people around. The Stasi was certainly "East Germany's biggest employer" (Worst, 1991:18). The Stasi archives contain six million individual dossiers, one for every second adult, on shelves that run 125 miles, each mile containing 17 million sheets of paper and weighing 50 tons (Kinzer, 1992:26). When the Stasi archives were opened in early 1992, a surreal world of trivia and tragedy was exposed. There are detailed reports about how often subjects took their garbage out and where they stored their ironing boards, but also reports of husbands spying on wives, of close friends and neighbours betraying one another, and of the engineered destruction of human life. Each individual was a potential subversive for its pathological leaders. But the lines between villain and victim become blurred if one considers that more than ten per cent of the populace actively collaborated with the Stasi.

After reviewing her file, dissident Bärbel Bohley mused "what a wonderful country this might have become if only its leaders had invested the same amount of energy into a dialogue with society."[34] Probably not. The Stasi corresponds to the logic of a Leninist regime, it is its caricature, not its aberration. Secrecy and subversion are constitutive of the "operational code" of Leninism (Selznick, 1952). Leninist ideology is in the first place a "negative ideology" that is directed "*against* dynamic evil forces rather than *for* an optimistic vision of the future" (ibid., 13). When *détente* and the inter-German "security partnership" removed the ethos of struggle and combat from overt political discourse, the combat disposition moved underground to puff up the ugly underbelly of a Leninist regime, its security police. Since *détente* was more clearly felt in East Germany than elsewhere, its security police had to be uglier than elsewhere. The security police became the refuge for the conspiratorial worldview that is constitutive of Leninist regimes. A recruitment manual of the Stasi states: "Committed to the historical mission of the working class, the Stasi's right and duty is to combat the enemy with patriotic forces – an enemy who tries to regain lost positions by means of subversion and conspiracy" (quoted in Kukutz and Havemann, 1990:88). If one holds the gargantuan spy apparatus of the Stasi against its main target, the two or three thousand dissidents scattered across the GDR,[35] the contrast baffles description. One is even inclined to agree with a victim's sarcastic guess that the Stasi nurtured the opposition in order to legitimize its existence.[36] "We all lived like rats in a laboratory," Wolf Biermann summarized the impact of the Stasi after reviewing his 40 000 page file.[37]

In the following, I will distinguish between "surveillance" and "manipulation" as the two *modi operandi* of the security police, and assess the impacts of these measures on the targeted opposition groups.

Surveillance

"The Stasi was always with us, always. We lived under permanent surveillance," says a former member of Women for Peace.[38] The Stasi's first objective was total information, and this implied the permanent observation of those who were considered the "fanatic hard core" of the regime opposition.[39] Surveillance was carried out by tapping telephone lines, installing cameras, opening mail, planting informers into the very heart of opposition groups, and permanent observation of key oppositionists by delegated officers. Such observation occurred quite openly, with the obvious purpose of intimidating. IFM co-founder Ralph Hirsch, a slender and inconspicuous man then in his twenties whom the Stasi considered an "incorrigible enemy of the state," remembers: "They were always in front of my house. It was ridiculous. Sometimes a grandmother would shout at them 'Get yourself a newspaper, then you look less conspicuous.' What a strange picture this was, twenty Stasi agents permanently at the heels of a small chap like me. It was ridiculous, but it was also intimidating." In fact, surveillance should convey the message of being under surveillance. A former dissident remembers that when returning home from work one day a stereo box was conspicuously missing to indicate that "they had been there," and quite often an official Notice to Appear would be found lying on the kitchen table.[40]

The almost comic aspect of all this was not lost on the observed dissidents, because imprisonment rarely followed. But surveillance was still received as a threat and a psychological burden. How did opposition groups respond to it?

One typical response was to behave as if surveillance did not exist. Indeed, a conspiratorial response would have violated the principles of openness and quasi-legality that guided particularly the human rights dissidents of IFM. Rejecting the Bolshevist notion of *virtuoso* activist, the IFM did not screen and examine its prospective members for "combat readiness."[41] While this helped the IFM evade the conspiratorial ways of its environment, it made the group also particularly vulnerable to infiltration by the security police – eight of IFM's 16 founding members were Stasi agents.[42]

Since complete openness would have been self-defeating, there were areas where secrecy was pivotal. Aware that the "firm" (as the Stasi was dubbed in mockery) was listening, the Women for Peace would scribble and pass around important information on the kitchen table, while continuing their innocent chat for the invisible intruders. Strategically important knowledge, for instance, about the location and usage of printing equipment, was confined to a few key activists – "not asking" about these matters was *de rigueur*, and too much interest was taken as a safe indicator of membership of the "firm". Contrary to all good intention, informal mechanisms of separating "us" from "them" inevitably did emerge. Each group would become stratified into layers of core and peripheral activists, with the strategically important decision-making and information-holding being confined to a small core of "trustworthy" key activists. The notorious fragmentation and personality rifts in East Berlin's dissident scene were also due to these self-protective measures in a hostile environment. Quite often to no avail. The "horror files," as the news-magazine *Der Spiegel* called the recently opened Stasi archives, reveal that even the most intimate opposition circles had been penetrated by Stasi agents.[43]

Manipulation

The astonishing feature of the Stasi was not so much its passive observation of opposition groups; secret services around the world do this, to varying degrees. Quite unique, however, was the Stasi's attempt to actively steer and manipulate the direction and agenda of opposition groups.[44]

This "political" form of control became internally referred to as *zersetzung*.[45] A Stasi ordinance from 1976 specifies the meaning of *zersetzung*: "Measures of *zersetzung* aim at provoking and enforcing internal conflicts and contradictions within hostile-negative forces that fragment, paralyse, disorganize, and isolate the latter" (Stasi, 1988:11). *Zersetzung* functioned both at the individual and group level. Among the "proved forms of *zersetzung*" the Stasi ordinance mentions the "systematic discrediting of public reputation," the "inducing of failures in professional and personal life," the "creation of distrust and rivalry within groups," and the "preoccupation of groups with themselves."

At the individual level, Stasi measures of *zersetzung* border upon the absurd and the pathological. Shortly after co-founding IFM, a leading dissident was confronted with the delivery of goods he had never ordered – half a ton of dog food one day, a horse the next day, followed by a truck-load of concrete; on a series of postcards from an unknown lady the married dissident was urged to pay for child support; an "Anne L." thanked for his alleged response to her contact ad – up to thirty or forty daily encounters of this sort turned the dissident's life into a nightmare, and, so figured the Stasi, would leave him with no time to conspire against socialism.[46] The Stasi's counter-subversive fantasy was boundless. In reviewing his 40-volume, 12 000 page file, IFM leader Gerd Poppe learned that a Stasi agent had targeted his wife for an extramarital affair, and that at school his son had been purposely turned against his own father. "It was criminal," the stunned veteran dissident indicts the Stasi, "Worse than that, it was evil" (quoted in Kinzer, 1992:42).

At the group level, *zersetzung* focused on blocking or delaying provocative action, fueling internal schism and rivalry, and preoccupying the respective group with internal procedure. For this purpose, the use of unrecognized "informal collaborators" (*informelle Mitarbeiter*, or IMs) was instrumental. "If you knew how many of you were IMs," a recently uncovered Stasi spy told her previous target group Women for Peace, "you would get sick" (quoted in Kukutz and Havemann, 1990:165). As a former IFM leader now knows, attempts by certain persons to engage the group in long and winding discussions about strategy and ideology, the relative merits of "reform or revolution", were deliberate attempts to keep the group from action. Also the wording of the various IFM appeals became the subject of endless debate – "they dickered about every word and phrase," says the same IFM leader with respect to Stasi collaborators, "just to tone down and soften all too irreverent phrases."[47] Whenever a small élite had "arbitrarily" rushed ahead with an action or an article, which *horribile dictu* even involved the Western media, the revenge of the grass-roots (*Basis*) was furious – and there certainly were no more passionate advocates of "grass-roots" values than "firm"-employees.

A favorite means to fuel group divisions was to plant rumors about alleged Stasi collaborators. Sometimes even the reverse attempt to uncover a real Stasi agent could be turned into a means of fuelling latent group tensions. When the Women for Peace, led by Bärbel Bohley, exposed a long-term core member as a Stasi spy, the latter skillfully denied the allegation and, in turn, put her accusers on trial – and she was believed.[48] A serious rift resulted in East Berlin's tiny dissident scene, just before the fall of 1989. Angered by her fellow dissidents in IFM, Bärbel Bohley left most of them out when she founded the New Forum, the central organization of the emergent citizen movement (*Bürgerbewegung*) of fall 1989. To be sure, this wasn't the only reason why East Germany's regime opposition entered this decisive period in fragmentation. But the attempts by the Stasi to manipulate the micro-dynamics of dissident politics cannot be ignored as an important factor.

Assessing the overall impact of the Stasi on opposition groups, IFM leader Wolfgang Templin still thinks that dissidents were "the actors..., the Stasi could only disturb and block."[49] This may be the case. But from a demonological point of view, such defensiveness corresponded to the Stasi calculus. As a Stasi instruction emphasizes, "informal collaborators must never appear as *initiators* of group activities" (Stasi, 1988:26).

The Case of IFM

Among East German opposition groups, the IFM became the Stasi's major target. The IFM comprised the "incorrigi-

ble hard core" of East German regime opposition. Moreover, its deliberate abandonment of church protection and
claim to be a "political" opposition group made the IFM a
thorny provocation to the party state. But most importantly,
IFM's tackling of the human rights issue touched the Achilles' heel of Leninist rule, and the anxious attempts by the
Stasi to destroy this particular group betray a keen awareness of this fact. "New social movement" issues such as peace
and ecology could be accommodated within a Leninist context. With regard to the peace issue, wasn't the GDR a "peace
state" itself? With regard to the ecology issue, the regime
set up the Society for Nature and Environment (*Gesellschaft
für Natur und Umwelt*) as a means to "integrate" independent ecology groups at the local level – here a limited "dialogue" between society and regime did indeed emerge.[50] Only
the issue of human rights could not be accommodated within
a Leninist framework. To insist on individual rights and
Rechtsstaatlichkeit (legal statehood) represented an intrusion
of "bourgeois ideology" that had to fire the conspiratorial
imagination of the "sword and shield of the party," the secret police. According to official wisdom, "the political underground is steered from the outside. It has no roots in
the existing socialist order" (Stasi, 1988:31). The IFM was
The Enemy personified, planted by foreign agents to sub-
vert socialism.[51]

From the beginning, the secret police had tried hard to
prevent the formation of a group that dealt with human
rights issues. Twice the Stasi intervened when, in 1985, a
Human Rights Seminar (IFM's direct precursor) sought to
constitute itself under the umbrella of the church, and the
church readily complied. When the move outside the church
made this form of institutional pressure ineffective, IFM
became the target of the full battery of *zersetzung*. Most interestingly, as internal Stasi documents reveal (Stasi, 1988:22–
25), the split of the original Human Rights Seminar into
two warring factions, the "bourgeois" IFM and the "socialist" Gegenstimmen (Counter-Voices), was, if not of conscious
Stasi design, at least in its best interest. A closer look at this
split reveals that the Stasi did not only smear and tear. It
also tried to neutralize the emergent human rights issue
on the ideological terrain, and even sought to provide an

distinguish between the profiles of the reformer, the cynic, and the true believer.[58]

The *reformer* is the most interesting type, because he is almost indistinguishable from the dissident. In his case, the line between opposition and collaboration is exceedingly difficult to draw. The reformist informer wanted what also the dissident wanted: the "dialogue" with the regime. Knud Wollenberger (IM "Donald"), who had been spying on his wife Vera (the prominent peace activist) throughout their ten-year marriage, saw this as an alternative way to achieve what his wife also wanted: the "great societal dialogue" with the state.[59] Dissident Vera, like most of her friends in the peace movement, also thought the SED state "could be re-formed and was worthy to be reformed." For Vera as well as for husband Knud, both privileged children of the GDR-*nomenklatura*, the GDR was the "better Germany." After re-viewing her shocking file, Vera was still embittered that this state considered her "hostile." Given this joint desire for "dialogue," why not go the direct way? And because its ante-rooms were evidently closed, why not approach the state through its backrooms, however filthy? The back rooms of the Stasi were the only place in this society where the state was indeed willing to hold this "dialogue:" the only place where "they" would listen, and where you could speak out and "risk a lip."[60]

For the reformist informer, there are no clear lines be-tween friend and foe, victim and villain, both in private and political regard. But wasn't this also true for the "loyal" peace activist who wanted to reform the state? Consequently, Knud Wollenberger deemed himself "not only the informer of the Stasi in the peace movement, but also the informer of the peace movement in the Stasi." Indeed, the Kafkaesque Stasi bureaucracy supported this double allegiance: for each col-laborator an additional file was held, where he was listed as a "hostile-negative force." So which file was the "real" file? This double allegiance is also evident in a second promi-nent spy case, that of Wolfgang Wolf (IM "Max") of Gegen-stimmen. This "senior of the Berlin peace movement" (Rüddenklau, 1992:53) had signed his "firm" contract al-ready in 1964. The leader of East Berlin's Ecology Library, and a close friend, finds Wolf's case "tragic" because he "was really in conflict with the SED and sought new perspectives in the peace movement" (ibid.). In fact, Stasi entries show that Trotskyist Wolf had become increasingly suspicuous as the author of "hostile-negative pamphlets." His friend of the Ecology Library expresses the typical dilemma of the reformist informer: "It is hard to say when Wolfgang Wolf worked for himself and when he worked for the Stasi" (ibid.).

The Stasi, East German communism's thinking man, was well aware of the fact that "dialogue" was what some of its collaborators and most of its victims wanted. But it knew the limits: "'Dialogue' means acknowledging each participant as equal. This, however, would entail bourgeois pluralism and undermine the existing power structures" (Stasi, 1989:17). Here you find what East German dissidents never found: the truth of Leninism.

A second type of informer, the *cynic*, is carved from different wood. The cynic does not aspire to reform or dialogue; he is the informer without conviction. The cynic opens a chilling window into the moral wasteland of a country surrounded by a wall. "If you grew up in East Germany, if you grew up after the wall, how... [are you] supposed to uphold any value," asks the young writer and Stasi informer Andreas Sinakowski, "How can you tell a guy who's in Sing Sing to behave like a human being?"[61] For the cynic, the GDR was indeed "the most boring country in the world," and he saw his morally dubious demeanor as a kind of adventure.[62] The cynic mirrored the "demoralization" that, according to Lutz Rathenow, characterized the last years of the GDR. "The GDR no longer needed people who believed. The one who still believed was a potential problem. The GDR needed cynics who functioned, not believers who held a flawed reality against its ideals."[63]

The cynical informer often had roots in the arts community. The cynical informer tasted the amoral "flowers of evil," he was the Rimbaudian "great criminal." Sascha Anderson, uncrowned king of the Prenzlauer Berg avantgarde, had been a Stasi collaborator for almost twenty years (IM "David Menzer"). And, as the documents show, he was one of the most compulsive and unscrupulous.[64] When asked if he had hoped to reform the East German system, he responds, "Of course not – no system, democracy or dictatorship, can be reformed" (quoted in Kinzer, 1992:50). While simply an "asshole" for Wolf Biermann, Anderson is described by others as "highly modern."[65] His was the play with identity, its loss and reassembly, life as an aesthetic experiment. "[I wanted] to lose my identity productively," Anderson excuses his betrayal of friends and fellow-artists. Not unlike the reformer, the cynic loses the sense for separating fantasy from reality. Both are products of East German communism's ultimate triumph, a triumph that struck the dissidents no less than the spies: of turning even its potential foes into its accomplices, of foreclosing "living in truth" even to those who did not comply.

The third category of informer, the *true believer*, is also communism's classic personality type. Arthur Koestler has enshrined it in his portrait of Nicolas Rubashov in *Darkness at Noon*. But if Rubashov had drowned sentimental "cricket morality" in the ice-water of "consequent logic," the true believer in communism's last hour had certainly lost the faculty of reason – the heroic credo *quia* absurdum shrank to the habitual credo *et* absurdum. Monika H., the notorious informer in East Berlin's dissident scene, relates to Rubashov as farce relates to tragedy. Like most other participants in the Stasi farce, Monika H. was the child of this GDR. But whereas many peace activists were the pampered flower-children of the élite, Monika H. had grown up as an orphan.[66] First the FDJ, later the Party, and finally the Stasi gave the emotionally troubled teenager and young adult the "family" she never had: "The Stasi gave roots to my life. There I felt secure. Day and night I could call Detlef, my contact officer, he was always there for me" (quoted in Kukutz and Havemann, 1990:145). Had she joined the Stasi voluntarily? "Of course, I thought this was the most important thing a Comrade could do" (ibid., 53). Whenever her mandate of *zersetzung* had been successful, she felt deep satisfaction: "I really have to admit that I felt joy if the group was divided, if we had split up the enemy" (ibid., 163).

But even the true believer was not immune from being drawn into the world of her targets. The closely knit dissident scene of East Berlin's Prenzlauer Berg also was a "family" that radiated warmth and could make you feel at home. "What you did," Monika H. told her previous objects of spying, "was also a part of me" (ibid., 85). For more than seven years, she lived with her victims, signed their petitions, plotted with them, partied with them. But still she remained faithful to her cause. One of her interviewers and former victims in Women for Peace expresses unmitigated anger about the betrayal: "How could someone pretend to be a friend, attend our meetings – 'lady's stuff and politics' – and then run straight to this Stasi officer to tell him everything? Maybe I understand her motivation better now. But my disgust about this falseness, this meanness, has not diminished. On the contrary, it all appears even more atrocious now."[67]

"VOICE" VERSUS "EXIT"

Why was the turn to human rights dissidence incomplete? The litmus test for human rights dissidence came with the rise of a phenomenon that would eventually cause the regime to collapse: the desire of increasing numbers of people to emigrate. Dissidents failed the test. While acknowledging that emigration was a basic human right, the human rights group IFM (as well as most other opposition groups) rejected adopting the emigrant quest for liberty: "The problem of emigration is a serious one. But it cannot become the focus of our work because we seek change *within* the society of the GDR."[68] This was a fateful decision, because it prevented opposition groups from overcoming their isolation and connecting with larger segments of society. It also indicated that East German dissidents remained dissidents *manqués*. As I outlined in Chapter 1, "dissidence" proper was activism by default, driven by a prepolitical impulse *not* to comply. By sharply separating the "political" case of reform from the merely "private" project of emigration, East German oppositionists professed their allegiance to the old model of virtuoso activism. Strictly speaking, East German oppositionists did not become "dissidents."

Albert Hirschman (1970), in his distinction between "voice" and "exit" as alternative responses to decline in firms, organizations and states, argued that voice was the political and exit the private mode of responding to a decline in performance. However, the distinguishing feature of dissidence proper is the blurring of the boundary between private and political. Considering the case of Charter 77, Jiri Wyatt (1984:7) argues that "dissent is [not] chosen as a political act" but springs from the impulse to rectify "moral integrity" under adverse conditions. A Czech dissident says similarly: "I am not a political person, and have never been a member of a political party. But I could live very happily in any society governed by the Universal Declaration of Human Rights and the Helsinki Accords" (ibid., p. 6).

In the German context, the "antipolitical" response to communist rule was to exit to West Germany, where civil liberties and citizenship rights were already in place. By their strict delimitation from the exit response, voice oppositionists remained caught in the logic of a regime that was itself based on the pretensions of virtuoso activism. As Michael Walzer (1970:229–38) indicates, the line between élite activism and "apparatchik tyranny" is a very thin one. Both imply the unfettered rule of the political virtuoso; both are subject to Oscar Wilde's objection that socialism would take too many evenings.

Exit Fever

Anniversaries always had a special meaning in the GDR. The 25th anniversary of the building of the Berlin Wall was a very special one. While the SED predictably passed it over in silence, this Wall anniversary unexpectedly revealed a growing uneasiness about physical confinement and curtailed liberties. On this occasion, IFM spoke out publicly for the "demolition of frontiers of every kind."[69] In a widely distributed appeal, an East Berlin church initiative took the Wall anniversary to denounce the "politics of delimitation." "Whoever rejects the principle of deterrence," the appeal says with a critical eye on the Protestant Church leadership, "must renounce the principle of delimitation" (quoted in Bickhardt, 1988:16). The taboo-breaking appeal, which a timid church leadership failed to accept at its synod in 1987, spoke out against the "narrowness" (*Enge*) in a society that restricted not only the free exchange of ideas and interests, but also the physical mobility of its members. What the appeal expressed in rather cautious clauses, its soft-spoken initiator now says more bluntly: "A self-appointed elite kept its own people as prisoners. *This* is the meaning of delimitation."[70]

As these two examples indicate, the GDR's constitutive symbol, the Wall, was no longer uncontested. In June 1987, a riotous crowd of rock fans, gathering at the Wall's eastern side to catch some sounds of an open-air concert just across the Spree river, struck a tone that hadn't been heard before: "The Wall Must Go."[71] This new tone was fed by a dramatic decline of positive regime identification, particularly among young workers and students, which surveys by the Leipzig Youth Institute had documented since the mid-1980s (Friedrich, 1990).

In the German context, however, the most direct expression of regime disaffection was not voice but exit fever. In 1986, the Church Synod in Erfurt stated that the number of exit applications had gone up in an "alarming and depressing way."[72] While official numbers were kept top secret, Western sources estimated that by 1986 between 400 000 and 500 000 East Germans had applied for legal emigration, a number that would even sharply rise in the following years.[73] What accounts for this society-wide regime disaffection and exit pressure?

Economic Decline
Most importantly, the economy no longer delivered. This undermined the implicit social contract in a post-mobilization regime, which consisted of the trading of economic well-being for political acquiescence. By 1988, East Germany had slipped from its earlier position as the world's tenth leading industrial power to twenty-sixth place (Ramet, 1991:59). Like all other socialist command economies, East Germany had missed the turn to advanced technologies and "flexible specialization" (Piore and Sabel, 1984). To be sure, East Germany had tried harder than others. But when, in 1988, the Robotron combine proudly introduced the first high-memory computer chip in communist lands, it was three generations behind comparable Western technology, at costs that had swallowed up more than one-third of annual industry investments (Maier, 1989). And the second major investment strategy of the 1980s, the replacement of Russian oil by domestic lignite, proved to be a fiasco (Uhlmann,

1989). In the early 1980s, the building of the necessary infrastructure had consumed almost 60 per cent of all industrial investments. Poor heating quality and the sharp drop of oil prices in the mid-1980s made this a thoroughly misguided and costly energy strategy, not to mention the vast ecological destruction brought by strip-mining and air pollution.

Since the mid-1980s, economic growth rates remained well below the projected size. Most fatefully, the austerity program, passed in the early 1980s to eradicate the foreign debt, led to a sharp reduction in investment and imports.[74] The result was aging factories, marred by obsolete machinery and frequent breakdowns. East Germany's products became increasingly unattractive on foreign markets. Since 1986, a narrow product range and quality problems had even led to a reduction in trade with West Germany, the GDR's most important trading partner in the West (Maier, 1989).

While the manipulation of data and statistics could cover the true extent of East Germany's looming economic disaster,[75] its impact on consumers was undeniable. Lagging investment led to a broad decay of the infrastructure – everything from railways and communication systems to housing, schools, and hospitals fell into a sorry state. For instance, in East Berlin, though trimmed as East Germany's show-case, the average wait for a telephone line was ten years, inner-city mail would take a week to reach its destination (Uhlmann, 1989). In East Germany's final hour, a Stasi officer reported to his Comrade Minister that the roof of Karl-Marx-Stadt's women's hospital was leaking, and this for the last ten years: "If it rains, the nurses run with buckets through the building" (quoted in Mitter and Wolle, 1990:132).

By the late 1980s, infrastructural decay was complemented by severe consumer shortages. Basic living goods, such as shoes, furniture, textiles, and children's wear, were no longer available in sufficient quantities.[76] At the same time, the prices for high-quality products were sharply raised to finance the (untouched) subventions for rents and basic consumer staples – if you could get them (Stinglwagner, 1989:132). Outside East Berlin, shortages were especially severe. No wonder provincial resentment turned against the pampered capital. In Dresden, stickers made the round in 1987 that showed a strangled bear (Berlin's symbol), and truck drivers reportedly refused to deliver their daily vegetable loads to the capital (Rüddenklau, 1992:94). Not by accident, Dresden was by then the city with the highest exit applications in the GDR.

Rejecting Glasnost
Reference to its "outstanding" economic performance was the GDR-leadership's initial way of rejecting political reforms, the second major factor behind the exit movement (Spittmann, 1987). Economic decline made this rejection of reforms even less palatable. In its last hour, the aging leadership rediscovered the virtues of a German road to communism, which took no heed of advice from Moscow. "Just because your neighbor changes his wall-paper," as chief-ideologue Kurt Hager's much-quoted statement goes, "would you feel compelled to do the same?"[77] In addition, the "special role" of the GDR at the borderline between East and West was cited, which would require unrepentant ideological struggle.[78] In this situation, the churches most clearly recognized the fateful relationship between the rejection of reforms and the increasing exit pressure. While trying to persuade would-be emigrants to stay, the churches also became the unambiguous advocates of political reforms. "Without perestroika things will not work any more," says church secretary Manfred Stolpe with obvious urgency.[79]

The church plea remained unheard. At a party congress in December 1988, Honecker terminally refused to "march into anarchy," and he dismissed the Soviet reforms as the "babble of mad philistines" (quoted in Kuppe, 1989:3). Indicating the strange revaluation of values in the age of glasnost, even Soviet magazines and literature became outlawed in the GDR. Since its frank discussion of the Hitler–Stalin pact and communist co-responsibility for the rise of Hitler, the popular journal *Sputnik* (which was issued in German language) could no longer be distributed legally.[80] To be sure, the party had good reason not to tinker with the creed of "anti-fascism." As Otto Reinhold, Rector of the Academy of Social Sciences, defended the Sputnik ban, it could not be tolerated to "relativize or excuse the crimes of German fascism" (ibid.). Questioning the "anti-fascism" formula would undercut the legitimacy of the GDR.

Indeed, the East German leadership well realized that political liberalization and economic restructuring threatened to reveal the GDR's core defect: its lack of a separate national identity. "What kind of right to exist would a capitalist GDR have alongside a capitalist Federal Republic?" asks Otto Reinhold in wary premonition of things to come. He rightly concluded that the GDR was "conceivable only as an antifascist, socialist alternative to the Federal Republic" (both quotes in Donovan, 1989:1). This is why reforms could not come about in East Germany.

Rising Expectations

While *détente* had initially helped the regime to stability, it now turned against it. Partial concessions, most notably the easing of travel restrictions, caused societal expectations to rise, the third factor behind the increasing exit pressure. Despite its rejection of glasnost, the regime was still in the grip of the German–German rapprochement. In fact, the regime was caught in a no-win situation: glasnost forced it to crack down, the German "coalition of reason" forced it to back down.[81] In a curious but logical counterpoint to its repudiation of reform, the regime pursued the politics of *détente* that had brought its leader international prestige and recognition. In August 1987, a joint resolution by SPD and SED pleaded for a "culture of dispute and controversial dialogue," the abandonment of old "enemy images" (*Feindbilder*), and the mutual recognition that both sides were "capable of peace" (*friedensfähig*).[82] One month later, Honecker's persistence as German peace leader was crowned with a state visit to Bonn. While the world was worrying that German unification was nigh, for Honecker the visit meant the opposite: finally the GDR had achieved a "basis of full equality" with West Germany.[83]

In the forefront of the long-aspired-to Bonn visit, the regime sought to present itself as reform-friendly – a general amnesty was declared, the death penalty was abolished, and the right to appeal was introduced in the judicial system (Fricke, 1987). Most importantly, since 1986 traveling had become easier. In 1985, the number of visitors below retirement age to West Germany was only 60 000. In 1986, the number was already up to 500 000. In 1987 and 1988, finally, the number of visitors had skyrocketed to 1.2 million and 1.3 million, respectively.[84] The impact of these visits to the West cannot be exaggerated. Millions of East Germans now saw the huge gap in quality of life that separated the two Germanies. It is hardly accidental that the exit movement took off when the other Germany had become a bit more accessible to many East Germans. Just when welfare social-ism reached its lowest point, invidious comparison with the West reached a new height. This was bound to fuel exit fever. As a high SED-functionary states, "traveling West is like a drug. If you did it once, you want ever more of it."[85] Since it had become a bit more penetrable, the Wall be-came a lot less acceptable. Why not cross it for good?

Exit Turns Political

The exit movement was not a "social movement" because it lacked organizational structure and a collective identity. Since exit was by definition an individual act, its constituency was almost impossible to organize collectively. This was com-pounded by the precarious situation of those who had taken the decisive step to file for legal emigration. These so-called *Ausreisewillige* (would-be emigrants) were the true pariahs of East German society, and they had to endure extraordinary hardship.[86] Filing for an exit application meant the step into isolation and despair which included the loss of job, friends and social life, and the prospect of years of endless waiting with no legal guidelines and protection whatsoever. Though a society-wide phenomenon in the 1980s, the exit movement was originally little more than the composite of atomized individuals carrying their lot in silent despair.

By the late 1980s, however, the general questioning of Wall and delimitation and the emergent human rights dis-cussion allowed would-be emigrants to tackle their plight from a political angle. A decisive step in this direction was the formation of the Berlin Citizenship Group (*Staatsbürgerschaftsgruppe*) in 1987. This was the first attempt to organize would-be emigrants, designed to provide moral support and legal counseling and to fight for the legaliza-tion of emigration. Its initiator, an unemployed theater di-rector who had applied for emigration the year before, admitted that he had been inspired by East Berlin's "peace and human rights movement" (Jeschonnek, 1988a). Consequently, he called his group a "human rights group" – without any "peace" prefix. But this human rights group soon had to find out that all its attempts to connect with East Berlin's opposition groups remained fruitless. "No group was willing to integrate us or work with us on common topics," remembers the founder of the Citizenship Group (ibid., 244). Why?

First, the social profiles of exit and voice constituencies differed. "They just looked different," says a member of the Ecology Library with respect to would-be emigrants.[87] The typical dissident, particularly in East Berlin's Prenzlauer Berg district, led a life at the fringes, with no career perspective or stake in "mainstream" society. By contrast, the typical would-be emigrant was a late breakaway of mainstream society, without previous involvement in opposition politics. The few surveys that exist found that emigrants were disproportionately young, male, and employed, with an above average education (Köhler and Ronge, 1984; see also Torpey, 1992). The typical would-be emigrant may be characterized as someone who had exhausted the modest career opportunities in a stagnant society and now was out for more (Fritze, 1990:47). In any case, for a member of the Ecology Library the would-be emigrants of the Citizenship Group were simply "too mainstream, we felt uncomfortable with them."[88]

Second, and in a curious counterpoint to the different social profiles of exit and voice constituencies, a hidden similarity at the individual level led dissidents to take a clear stance against would-be emigrants. Whether you were a dissident or not, "to stay or to leave" was a crucial dilemma that no one living in East Germany in the 1980s could escape; the boundary line between both was very thin for most (Rosenthal, 1988b).[89] "The fact that many left," says an East German theologist who did not leave, "forced you to re-think why you were still here."[90] Ironically, the decision by many to leave also turned staying into a decision. In fact, in facing the exit alternative, voice dissidents discovered that they were closer to the opposed regime than they had previously thought – as Albert Hirschman (1970) predicates, "loyalty" was the secret truth of voice. "There are enough reasons to stay," says a member of the Ecology Library, "and to make a bearable country a better one."[91] But those who left inflicted on those who stayed a feeling of loss and betrayal. "The predominant feeling," says the persistent theologist, "was one of injury and loss of own life chances, which increased with everyone who left."[92]

The third, and most explicit, reason for opposition groups to shun would-be emigrants was the obvious difference of goals. Dissidents wanted to change the regime; would-be emigrants just wanted out. Dissidents saw their cause as a "political" one, and they dismissed the motives of emigrants as "apolitical" and "egotistical." "They were just an interest group," the leader of the Ecology Library says of the Citizenship Group (Rüddenklau, 1992:176). Most opposition groups did not accept individuals who had filed for emigration, suspecting them of "instrumentalizing" the respective group for their individual departure. In fact, this charge cannot be lightly dismissed because political opposition was meanwhile known as the safest ticket to the West. A Leipzig dissident describes in credible terms the difficulties in cooperating with would-be emigrants: "The emigrants (*Ausreiser*) destroyed all substantial work. And one can understand them. They lived in an unreal situation. Their minds had already left, but their bodies were still there. For years they were sitting on packed suitcases. All activities then had to focus on this one theme: 'How can I speed my departure?' With this state of mind they entered our groups. Their impact had to be destructive."[93]

Finally, when exit turned political, a fourth motive of rejection emerged: competition. Politicized exit challenged the established meaning of regime opposition in the GDR. The founder of the Citizenship Group claims: "To say 'I'm not staying, I won't live this lie any longer, I'm leaving' – wasn't this more protest than that of the others?"[94] Since would-be emigrants had nothing left to lose, they dared more – "opposition", after all, could only speed their exit to the West. In fact, it was would-be emigrants, not dissidents, who staged the first open street protests in 1989. By contrast, voice had to be more restrained to avoid just what would-be emigrants tried to achieve: to be kicked out of the GDR. In addition, while opposition groups always failed to attract large numbers, the exit-oriented Citizenship Group underwent dramatic growth. This was obviously a galling sight for seasoned voice oppositionists whose mobilization efforts had never been granted similar success. At the first meeting of the Citizenship Group in September 1987, thirty local would-be emigrants participated. Only two months later, 300 would-be emigrants from all over the GDR would attend. But the eventual fate of the Citizenship Group also epitomizes the futility of self-organization among would-be emigrants: by early 1988, the group no longer existed because all of its members had landed in the West.

"Weak Revolutionaries"

The competition between voice and exit led to one of the most agonizing episodes of East German opposition politics. In early 1988, the Citizenship Group decided to participate at this year's official "Luxemburg–Liebknecht combat demonstration" (see Jeschonnek, 1988b). In order to enlist East Berlin's opposition groups, the Citizenship Group decided *not* to appear with slogans that addressed the emigration issue. Instead, it picked Rosa Luxemburg's own inconspicuous maxim that "freedom is always the freedom of those who dissent." This was an ingenious device that allowed emigrants and oppositionists to unite under one banner, and let the socialist heroine herself speak out against those who so obviously abused her name. But all East Berlin opposition groups refused to mingle with would-be emigrants. Wolfgang Templin, a true dissident he, who alone pleaded for a participation, tried in vain to convince his fellow oppositionists in IFM that human rights were "impartial," and that the causes of the emigrant and opposition plights were not so different: "It was the perversity of this system that you had to appear with a Luxemburg slogan on a Luxemburg demonstration in order to be thrown out of the country. My friends in IFM did not understand that."[95]

The secret police, who had long feared that exit and voice groups would merge, used this event to get rid of both at the same time. In a first strike, the unwanted participants in the official Luxemburg demonstration were arrested. Among them was the song-writer Stephan Krawczyk, who, like no one since Wolf Biermann, had become a popular symbol of regime opposition and was among the few oppositionists making common cause with would-be-emigrants. In a second and somewhat unrelated strike, the cream of East Berlin's opposition scene was rounded up and charged with "high treason" (*Landesverrat*) – including Wolfgang Templin, Freya Klier, Bärbel Bohley, Werner Fischer, and Ralf Hirsch.

The Luxemburg affair illustrates in minutiae the muddled picture of East Germany's opposition politics, once would-be emigrants had become players in their own right. The arrests spurred the biggest protest wave the country had seen since 1953. In more than forty cities solidarity committees were founded, protest resolutions were passed, and so-called *Fürbittandachten* (solidarity masses) were held in the churches. Again, the Protestant churches provided a roof for the protests, and never before had they so unambiguously sided with the foes of the regime. But these foes were now divided in two opposite camps with differing agendas. When opposition groups urged the church to work for the release of the arrested, exit advocates stepped in to prevent a release "into the false republic."[96]

While opposition groups were in charge of coordinating the church-based protests, it was mostly would-be emigrants who attended them. As an IFM pamphlet complains, "the meaning of the *Fürbittandachten* was increasingly distorted by the massive appearance of apolitical... would-be emigrants" (IFM, 1988:14). When the church leadership of Berlin-Brandenburg offered its contact telephone to be used by would-be emigrants too, the opposition group "Church from Below" cried out: "This means church protection for would-be emigrants, while progressive forces will be publicly suspected (of mingling with them)" (quoted in Rüddenklau, 1992:223) – note that in communist parlance "progressive" stood for "regime-loyal." Eager not to make common cause with exit constituencies, the voice-controlled Coordination Committee even cancelled its daily *Fürbittandachten* that meanwhile attracted thousands of people – alas, not the "right" ones.

But the nervously guarded boundaries between voice and exit were eventually eroded from above, by the arrested opposition leaders themselves. Faced with the alternative of stiff prison terms or leaving for the West, they all opted for the West.[97] After less than two weeks of imprisonment, the core leadership of the East German dissident movement found itself where it did not want to be – on the other side of the Wall. This caused a deep shock among those who stayed behind, and many fellow-oppositionists did not hide their bitterness. "The peace movement is now tainted with the odor of exit," wrote the samizdat journal *Umweltblätter*.[98] A leading Berlin peace activist delivered a fierce indictment that exposed all the elements of unreconstructed virtuoso activism. "Those were weak revolutionaries," he writes, "The wildfire of burning hearts and praying hands... was extinguished. Not by the all-powerful state, but by our own people... They had entered prison as political persons, but they left it as private ones."[99]

On the eve of 1989, the East German dissident movement presented itself in a sorry state of fragmentation and exhaustion. The forced exit of its leaders had practically extinguished the IFM. The Luxemburg episode further enforced the opposition groups' policy of non-cooperation with would-be emigrants, thus completing the self-inflicted separation of the virtuous élite of oppositionists from the greatest source of discontent in the GDR. "The opposition groups annoyed us, we did not feel threatened by them," says a member of the politburo (Schabowski, 1991:57). Indeed, exit, not voice, would be the nemesis of East German communism.

5 A German Revolution

Hannah Arendt, in her classic study of the American and French revolutions (1963), tied the modern notion of revolution to the pathos of a new beginning (*novus ordo saeclorum*) and the building of a constitution of liberty (*constitutio libertatis*). The revolution that swept communist Eastern Europe two centuries later certainly occurred in the name of liberty, the establishment of human rights and citizenship. But the Eastern European revolution of 1989 was peculiarly devoid of a pathos of novelty and it lacked grand utopian designs (Offe, 1991). "Not a single new idea has come out of Eastern Europe in 1989," says Francois Furet, the noted historian of the French revolution.[1] This was a paradoxical revolution indeed that undid a regime itself built upon an utopian-revolutionary design. It was a revolution that, as Furet (1990:61) argued to the point, "put an end to the revolutionary idea" as such. Not the utopian quest for a *novus ordo saeclorum*, but recovery, the return to history and "normality," is the true meaning of this epochal event – thus reinstating the original meaning of revolution as "restoration" (Münkler, 1989). If canvas-cleaning was the obsession of the communist revolution, the anti-communist revolution sought to retrieve the colours in which the real world is painted – which may explain why this was also the first non-violent revolution in modern times.[2]

The Eastern European revolution was a "dual revolution of citizenship and nationhood" (Vujacic, 1990), thus proving 1789, not 1917, to be the key break of modernity. As Jürgen Habermas's notion of the "catching-up revolution" (*nachholende Revolution*) conveys, "the spirit of the Occident finally caught up with the East" (Habermas, 1990:185).[3] While for Western observers the recovery of citizenship went without question, the resurgence of nations and nationalism appeared as one of the more puzzling and disconcerting aspects of 1989. But nationalism was the vehicle for resuming the historical continuities disrupted by communist rule, and in its civic form it aimed at restoring the nation-state that alone provides and guarantees individual rights and citizenship.[4]

Nowhere was the resumption of historical continuity and nation-building more visibly expressed than in Germany, where the fall of communism meant the regaining of national unity. But this outcome did not correspond to any conscious design. As Claus Offe (1990b) argues, "the dramatic and unexpected withering of the GDR cannot be understood in categories of `will' (and `intention'), but only in those of historical `contingency' and chain-reaction." This is in striking contrast to Eastern Europe, where the sudden and unexpected breakdown of communism has reasserted the role of agency and choice in history: "people make history."[5] Only in the German case, there was a peculiar disjunction between actors' intentions and outcomes. The movement that toppled the old regime in a mighty wave of mass demonstrations did not aim at national unity. Alone among Eastern European democracy movements, the East German movement remained under the spell of 1917; its motive was the reform, not the extinction, of communism. In a curious misreading of communism's terminal crisis, the movement saw its cause as one of "revolutionary renewal" (C. Wolf), while it inadvertently worked toward the dissolution of the communist regime. Also in East Germany, 1989 was the "year of truth," in which the "idea of normality," not the revisionist chimera of "socialism with a human face" prevailed (Ash, 1990a). But the movement which helped bring it about did not intend it this way.

Lamenting the disjunction between intention and outcome, some of the winners-turned-losers of 1989 reinvented the revisionist notion of the "revolution betrayed." Christa Wolf, who (like most of her fellow-intellectuals) set herself at the top of the democracy movement once it was under way, invoked this notion in her bitter reflections on the "movement of history" (*Gang der Geschichte*). "What is the movement of history?" she asks. "Certainly not the quiet and prudent movement (*Gang*) of the young people at the Gethsemane Church on October 7 and 8, who, with candles in their hands, defied the attacks by the security forces; not the courageous movement of the 100 000 in Leipzig on October 9; not the liberated, sovereign, almost insolent movement of Berliners on November 4. To be sure, these movements made history. But German history moves (*geht*) differently, I had almost forgotten it" (Wolf, 1990:7). Christa Wolf only alludes to the second, and decisive, part of the "revolution betrayed" formula. Her fellow-intellectual Stefan Heym (1990:71f) is more explicit: "The very same people who had just liberated themselves and seemed to be marching nobly into a promising future became suddenly a horde of frenzied shoppers, marching only to the Hertie and Bilka department stores on the hunt for glitzy trash" – easy prey for the West German "filibuster state" (Heym), which eventually blunted the project of a "humanized" socialism in its alleged quest for national aggrandizement.[6] Overwhelmed by the forces of unification, the democracy movement soon found itself in opposition to a regime it almost equally despised. "Only the powers (*Mächte*) have changed," as Christa Wolf (1990:168) sourly indicts the outcome of 1989.

The "revolution betrayed" formula epitomizes not only the élitist dissociation of East Germany's intellectuals from their society, which was without parallel in Eastern Europe. It also mis-states the actual forces of the regime breakdown. As I shall argue, exit, not voice, was the key force of the German revolution. Exit was the advocate of "normality" that would prevail also in East Germany. But because exit had to remain speechless and leaderless, it was voice that initially defined the situation and provided an organizational and ideological platform for the popular upheaval of fall 1989. However, this initial identification of voice and mass concerns turned out to be spurious. The crypto-nationalist motive of the exit movement, which first voted with their feet for liberty and reunification, reasserted itself at the ballot-box, when the majority of East Germans voted for the quick elimination of a separate socialist state. The exit movement proved to be both Demiurge and Nemesis of the GDR, first helping the regime to find its true, if tainted, identity in the Wall, and then being the decisive force in dismantling it.

Drawing a comparison with Czechoslovakia's fabled dissident movement, whose leader was voted president, John Torpey (1992:38) argues correctly that East Germany's less fortunate oppositionists were "like the foam that floats on top of the ocean, churned up by the primal forces of the deep but utterly powerless to control them." In the end, East Germany's, too, also was a dual revolution of citizenship and nationhood. But it was also a *German* revolution, whose complexity was realized by none of the involved actors.

EXODUS

Sebastian Haffner once argued prophetically that emigration was "the German form of revolution." While this dictum referred to the intellectual emigration of Karl Marx and Heinrich Heine, the non-intellectual emigration of thousands of East Germans would trigger the first successful German revolution that was not confined to the mind.

Voice being numbed by the disastrous Luxemburg affair of 1988, exit became ever more assertive as a political claim. In fact, for would-be emigrants the Luxemburg affair proved that public protest was a highly effective means of getting out of the GDR. In February 1988, 300 would-be emigrants joined a church rally in commemoration of the bombing of Dresden, but this time with their own slogans – "Don't Destroy Human Rights As Dresden Was Once Destroyed" being one of them.[7] One demonstrator said, "We were inspired and animated by Berlin," and another called out that this form of protest "must spread from city to city."[8] It did. One month later, 300 would-be emigrants staged a silent protest-march through the center of Leipzig, in the first cautious prelude to the Monday Demonstrations that would rock the GDR to doom in October 1989.[8] Similar exit protests occurred in East Berlin and Jena.

A reeling party leadership was unsure how to respond to the politicization of the exit movement. Voice could be muted by forcing its leaders to leave the GDR; exit, however, was further spurred by that same prospect. So the initial response was to crack down. In March 1988, more than 200 would-beemigrants suspected of political conspiracy were arrested *without* sending them to the West, and church services (meanwhile known to be platforms for would-be emigrants) were severely disrupted by security forces.[9] But the sheer magnitude of the exit wave rendered repression ineffective. Only one month later, the regime went over to a lenient response. In order to undercut public protest by exit groups, would-be emigrants were invited to individual "consultations" (*Aussprachen*), in which those who could not be won back were quietly assured that their exit plea would be granted.[10] At the same time, there was secret (if vain) hope that the "security partners" in the West would spring to the rescue – factions of the Social Democratic Party had long argued in favour of "respecting" the GDR citizenship,[11] and the recent exit pressure (surely a threat to "stability") reasserted their call to abandon the all-German citizenship, this bothersome "life-lie" (*Lebenslüge*) of the Federal Republic.[12]

A further easing of travel restrictions was the last desperate attempt by the regime to stem the exit tide. Introduced in December 1988, the new rules also provided the first legal framework for handling emigration requests, including the right to appeal (Böttger, 1989; Jeschonnek, 1989).[13] But the new rules necessarily fueled, rather than halted, the exit movement, because they established a quasi-legal basis to justify the exit claim.[14] Already in 1988, the number of legal emigrants had more than doubled, from 11 500 in 1987 to 28 000; and indicating the increasing urgency of the exit wish, the number of illegal refugees had almost doubled, too, from 7500 in 1987 to 12 000 (Gesamtdeutsches Institut, 1991).

As is well known, Hungary's opening of its border to Austria turned exit into exodus. Already before that decisive September 1989, the number of legal emigrants had skyrocketed to 60 000, more than in any year since 1961, and the number of refugees had reached 17 000, also a record since the building of the Wall (ibid.). After 10 September, when Hungary fully complied with the United Nations refugee statute, all floodgates were open. Scores of East Germans then vacationing in Hungary spontaneously decided not to return home; by early October, more than 45 000 new refugees were registered in West Germany's reception camps. As the GDR was approaching its 40th birthday, the West German embassies in Budapest, Warsaw, Prague, and East Berlin were filling up to the roof with East Germans seeking free passage to the West. In early October, the exodus reached a dramatic peak. Following complicated negotiations between Bonn and East Berlin, eight special trains with some 14 000 East German refugees were granted free passage from Prague to West Germany, via East Germany in a face-saving concession to East Berlin. The "concession" backfired. Thousands of East Germans flocked to the stations and junctions along the railroad line, in the hope of sneaking aboard. When the refugee trains reached Dresden, bloody street battles broke out between security forces and would-be emigrants, who tried to break into the forcibly emptied and sealed off terminal. A tumultuous crowd shouted "Freedom, Freedom" (was that word ever heard from dissidents?), one demonstrator was killed, police cars went up in flames.[16] By that time, all borders had been closed; East Germans could no longer leave their country. The GDR had reached its point of no return.

The mass exodus was particularly destructive for the GDR, because it consisted of the country's youth, and some of its best qualified at that. Over 80 per cent of those who fled the GDR in summer 1989 were under 40 years old, the majority of them being skilled workers and professionals (Hilmer and Köhler, 1989).[17] Most interestingly, and contrary to a typical allegation by voice oppositionists, the main concern of the 340 000 refugees and emigrants who left the GDR in 1989 was not consumption and welfare, but political freedom. Over 90 per cent indicated the general political conditions and the lack of civil liberties as the two major reasons for leaving (Voigt et al., 1990). Economic concerns, while important, were only one among several factors that motivated the exodus. As a comparison of two exile cohorts in 1984 and 1989 found, no clear line can be drawn between political and economic exit motives (Ronge, 1990). The desire for occupational and professional advancement was tightly linked with an uneasiness about political constraints and the lack of free expression. With regard to party preferences, about twice as many of those who left the GDR considered themselves supporters of the conservative CDU/CSU as supporters of the Social Democrats (SPD) (Voigt et al., 1990:746). This strikingly anticipated the outcome of the first free East German elections of March 1990, the unambiguous pro-unity vote. Indeed, the exit movement seemed to mirror true public opinion in the GDR. With the mass exodus, the script for national reunification was written on the wall. Few were able to read it then.

FROM DISSIDENT TO CITIZEN MOVEMENT

Applying his exit-voice scheme to the East German revolution, Albert Hirschman (1993) argues that the mass exodus created a situation in which exit and voice were no longer "antagonists" but "confederates." Whereas previously exit had forever undermined the stabilization of a voice opposition, the drama of a whole society leaving had to be a boost for political protest. The previous "seesaw" of exit and voice turned into a "joint grave-digging act" (ibid., 186).

Voice oppositionists tend to portray the revolution of 1989 as the logical culmination of an opposition movement that had grown and matured over the years.[18] This interpretation, which brackets the exit component in the regime breakdown, is misleading. For the established opposition groups, 1989 had begun as a "completely normal year" (Rüddenklau, 1992:259). To be sure, after a year of stagnation there was a notable urge to coordinate the fragmented protest scene and to escape the church confines toward a more political form of opposition. But the outcome was small. At the annual Peace Concrete (*Frieden Konkret*) meeting in February, the attempt by some opposition leaders to found a party-like "political association" failed miserably.[19] In March, a parallel call by the decimated IFM for a GDR-wide coordination of opposition groups yielded no response.[20] The only success was a well-organized "supervision" of the communal elections on 7 May, which revealed a large-scale falsification of the election results. This was no small thing. As the leader of the Ecology Library says, "for the first time the opposition tackled a concern that was widely shared by the population" (Rüddenklau, 1992:288). But tellingly, even the election fraud did not help opposition groups to break through their isolation. A noted Berlin church oppositionist recounts the lack of a popular response: "On 7 June, one month after the election fraud, we tried to hold a rally near the Sophien Church. It did not work. Only 250 people showed up, plus 1,000 Stasi agents. But the *Volk* (people) we did not reach."[21] Like every year, most opposition groups went into their usual "summer recess" (*Sommerpause*), intent on resuming activities in the fall. Nothing seemed to point to a break in routine, let alone a "revolution."

It took the exodus to shake up the opposition. For those who were left behind, the situation became unbearable. In an interview with West German radio in early October, Christa Wolf (1990:77) described her reaction to the television images of the mass flight: "I was shattered, sad, and disconcerted. Why did these young people leave, so easily and with a smile on their face?... During the last four or five weeks we in the GDR were all dominated by these images, couldn't sleep, were in despair."[22] Things were aggravated by an insensitive and hardened party leadership that did not grasp the seriousness of the situation. Until late September, the only response to the exodus was Honecker's caustic remark that "one should not shed a tear" for those who left – rounding off a series of hair-raising statements that included warm words for Beijing's Tiananmen Square massacre in June.

The opposition quickly sensed that the exit crisis opened up a window of opportunity. A long-term dissident and later member of the New Forum remembers: "We sat together in the countryside that summer, and said `more, more, more have to leave'. Of course, we cried when we watched how these people lifted their babies over the fence in Prague. And still we said, `This has to go on, because otherwise nothing will ever change.' But we also knew that if *we* did not step forward, this country would flow into the Federal Republic. And *this* we did not want."[23] The step forward was taken with the formation of the New Forum (*Neues Forum*) in early September. Only a few days earlier, an IFM leader had deplored the lack of a "public sphere" (*Öffentlichkeit*) for the discussion of reform alternatives: "What is missing is the contact with society."[24] The New Forum provided just that. This was the first step out of the dissident ghetto, and the starting-point for the broad "citizen movement" (*Bürgerbewegung*) that would topple the regime in a mighty wave of mass unrest. The initiator of the New Forum, long-time dissident Bärbel Bohley, had even minimized the involvement of fellow-dissidents. The group of hand-picked founding members, which convened in secrecy on 10 September in Robert Havemann's old country-house in Grünheide near East Berlin, was representative of a wide cross-section of the GDR-population. Bärbel Bohley explains her rationale: "I wanted to transcend the narrow church and dissident circles and appeal to the broader population. So I invited a group of people of various ages and professions from all over the GDR. No one declined. My idea had struck a nerve."[25]

It had indeed. In a complete surprise to its initiators, the New Forum quickly gathered over 200 000 signatures for its founding manifesto, which was copied (often by hand) and distributed throughout the GDR, soliciting enthusiastic responses even in the most provincial and inconspicuous backwaters. "New Forum! New Forum!" would become a key slogan of the Monday Demonstrations in Leipzig. The New Forum presented itself as a deliberately unprogrammatic call for dialogue. Its founding manifesto states: "In our country the communication between state and society is obviously disturbed ... We need a democratic dialogue about the reform of state, economy, and culture ... The time is ripe" (New Forum, 1989:1f). Aware of its bad press, the drafters did not mention the word "socialism" (which actually caused some leading intellectuals not to sign the manifesto).[26] But they did not have to mention it, because the polite tone could hardly be mistaken for antisocialist rhetoric. In fact, the founding manifesto of the New Forum was also a manifestation of the revisionism that still characterized regime opposition in East Germany.[27] Its odd warning against a "degenerated elbow-society" left no doubt that Western-style democracy and capitalism was not on its mind. While the manifesto is replete with notions such as democracy, justice, and peace, the word "freedom" does not appear even once. This should not diminish its provocative edge. In fact, the New Forum was designed as a party-like "association" (*Vereinigung*), and from the start its initiators tried to put it on a legal basis. "We wanted to act legally – revolutionaries who first buy a platform ticket," New Forum co-founder Jens Reich notes with irony (1991:187). But even this modest request, if implemented, would have implied the end of communist one-party rule.

The foundation of the New Forum, which was received in opposition circles with some surprise, kicked off the feverish foundation of similar political groups and platforms.[28] Only two days after the New Forum had emerged, a group of theologians, church-based oppositionists and IFM members founded "Democracy Now" (*Demokratie Jetzt*). The most intellectual and programmatic in outlook, Democracy Now introduced the word that would identify all the new groups: *Bürgerbewegung* (citizen movement). A co-founder of Democracy Now indicates that he had initially been unaware of the "Western dimension" of the notion of citizen: "Our model was the democratic decision-making process within the church."[29] A similar church-influenced new group was the small "Democratic Awakening" (*Demokratischer Aufbruch*), which was founded in early October by a group of noted dissident-theologians. The fourth new group was the only one to claim explicit party status, the "Social Democratic Party" (SDP), which was formed in late September. All new groups were almost identical in their "dialogue" orientation, prosocialist programmatic, and church background. None of them, however, could match the mass appeal of the New Forum.

The new citizen movement was dominated by a new type of participant who epitomized the opening up of the dissident ghetto. For this new type of dissident, Lutz Rathenow coined the notion of "corridor dissident."[30] The corridor dissident had hibernated in a professional niche or within the party apparatus itself, waiting in vain for Gorbachev-style reforms from above. The New Forum, polite and reformist as it was, offered her the chance to come out. A New Forum member introduces himself with the typical slant of this dissident-of-late: "I spent the time in the GDR in the academic niche, and never had to suffer much under the old system."[31]

The two principal authors of New Forum's foundation manifesto, Rolf Henrich and Jens Reich, represent typical yet contrasting profiles of the corridor dissident. Rolf Henrich became known in early 1989 for his Bahro-style analysis and indictment of bureaucratic socialism, *Der vormundtschaftliche*

Staat (The Paternalistic State), for which he was expelled from the SED. The book was explicitly addressed to his fellow party members, and it advocated a "reform of German state socialism" (Henrich, 1989:316). Why did he step out of the apparatus so late? "Unconsciously I preferred to be with the power and the majority," the lawyer oddly admits (ibid.). As in the Henrich case, the New Forum would be the platform of reform-minded defectors from the ruling SED.

Jens Reich, the intellectual leader of the New Forum and maybe the freshest new voice to emerge in fall 1989, represents a contrasting, but no less typical, version of the corridor dissident. The soft-spoken physician and biophysicist at the Academy of Sciences had shelved his literary ambitions and picked a scientific career in order not to compromise himself ideologically. "I was unpolitical," the dissident professor describes himself, adding in self-mockery that he wasn't exactly attracted "by the unkempt manners and the bad German of the oppositionists" (Reich, 1991:30). In a "niche profession", as at the Academy, one could survive comfortably, "as long as you shut up, your desires were modest, and you were not plagued by career ambitions."[32] Parallel to this, all interest was channeled into the private sphere. For almost 20 years, Jens Reich was a member of the informal Friday Circle, a small group of like-minded colleagues and friends, who read and discussed philosophy, literature, theatre, politics and everything that crosses the mind. "Jacobin Club" (*Jakobinerclub*) is Reich's ironic name for it, "long on words, short on action" (ibid., 174). "We thought that dozens, even hundreds of such circles had to exist," Reich remembers, "but we did not know about them because of the lack of a public sphere, self-imposed insulation, and the simple fact that no more than twenty tea-drinking and smoking men and women would fit into one living room" (ibid., 172). For corridor dissident Reich, private salons like this were the "preschool to the non-violent upheaval." Indeed, in fall 1989 the whole Friday Circle refashioned itself as a subgroup of the New Forum.

The New Forum and the other new political groups provided identification and a reference point for the spontaneous mass demonstrations of fall 1989; in no way did they organize or steer them. Their leaders deliberately stayed clear of open protest, intervention being limited to pleas for non-violence.[33] A leader of Democratic Awakening admits: "Of course, we did not *make* the revolution. But there was no one else to *talk*."[34]

LEIPZIG – CITY OF THE REVOLUTION

The revolution was *made* in Leipzig. East Berlin provided the organizational and thematic platforms of the emergent citizen movement; Leipzig was the actual site in which the "demos" stood up against the old regime. Considering East Berlin's leading role as political and intellectual capital, this inversion of capital roles might come as a surprise. But, as I shall argue, it was not accidental. In Leipzig, as throughout East Germany's depressed south, the exit movement was stronger and more politicized than elsewhere. And only in Leipzig a voice opposition existed that did not shy from making common cause with would-be emigrants. Exit led the way to mass-based public protest; voice picked up the message and offered the organizational clues. Only in Leipzig, exit and voice were "confederates" (Hirschman, 1993) not just in a metaphorical sense, ready to launch the "joint grave-digging act" (ibid.) out of which the German revolution was made.

More than East Berlin, Leipzig felt the decay of East Germany's welfare socialism. Strip-mining and smoke-stack industries had turned East Germany's second largest city into one of the most polluted spots of Europe. In Leipzig "you can see what you breathe," runs the local sarcasm (Unterberg, 1991:21). Just when East Berlin experienced a frenzy of new building projects, Leipzig's long-neglected infrastructure reached a point of near-collapse. Walking through Leipzig's historic downtown at Grimmaische Strasse, the merry site of Goethe's Faust saga, one could still see, in 1991, the craters and ruins left by the nights of bombing some forty years previously. A substantial portion of the old housing in the inner city had become virtually uninhabitable, its residents being relocated to hastily constructed and shabby satellite cities at the periphery. Lignite strip-mining had already drawn

near to the city's outskirts, raiding whole historic neigh-
borhoods. Only twice a year, during the international trade
and industry fairs in March and September, the empty shelves
in Leipzig's grocery stores would miraculously fill up,
and more than cabbage and potatoes could be had.
So grim were the living conditions in Saxony's former
metropolis that since 1970 the city's population had
shrunk by more than ten per cent (Hofmann and Rink,
1990:117f). Defeatism and despair were widespread – in the
1989 communal elections, an estimated 20 per cent of voters rejected the unity list of the National Front (Rein,
1989:180). For Leipzig's workers, once the proud core of
Germany's socialist working-class movement and still representing 40 per cent of the city's workforce, socialism had
long gone to the dogs. In fact, together with Dresden, Leipzig
had the GDR's strongest exit movement. In the first half of
1989, Leipzig scored the second highest number of legal
emigrants and illegal refugees in the GDR (Mitter and Wolle,
1989:91f).

Opposition Groups

Since 1988 Leipzig had also overtaken East Berlin as a center
of political opposition. When the Luxemburg fiasco had left
East Berlin's dissident movement in disarray, the fresher and
younger dissident groups of Leipzig moved to the fore. Indicative of this, in early 1988 the GDR-wide coordination of
approximately 50 opposition groups in 20 cities moved from
East Berlin to Leipzig. With the shift in regional focus came
a shift in the themes and forms of protest. Reflecting the
disillusioned environment of a rotting city and the strong
exit pressure, human rights advocacy was more unambiguous in Leipzig than in East Berlin. This opened up the
possibility of exit–voice coalitions, something East Berlin had
never seen. Exposed to the uninhibited and risk-prone exit
constituencies, Leipzig's opposition groups became more
action-oriented than those in East Berlin, exploring and
anticipating the forms of public protest that became the
hallmark of fall 1989.

This is not to deny that Leipzig's opposition scene was as
marginal and fragmented as that in East Berlin. Less than

300 oppositionists were scattered over some 20 ecology, peace and human rights groups, many of them living as young drop-outs in squatted houses in Leipzig's dark and deserted East End section (Findeis, 1990). But the two most important of these groups, the *Initiativgruppe Leben* (IGL) and the *Arbeitskreis Gerechtigkeit* (AKG), displayed some altogether new features. First, the average age of the members of both groups, which were formed only in late 1987, was well below twenty-five years (Unterberg, 1991:75). Whereas East Berlin's more mature opposition leaders had a memory that often stretched back to Prague 1968 and the Biermann-Havemann era, the young oppositionists in Leipzig were completely devoid of any ties to preceding protest generations. They represented a new generation that had never accepted the claims, let alone the reality, of the socialist state.[36] A co-founder of IGL, a soft-spoken drifter in his early twenties, says: "I never had a relationship to this society, I mean other than a negative one... I was part of a new generation without role models, which either fell silent or tried out something new. All I wanted was tolerance and to live an individual life, and this was quite difficult in this society."[37] Asked how his group dealt with would-be emigrants, he responds with shrugging shoulders: "This was no issue for us. Of course we had would-be emigrants in our group. We did not think much about it. This was a human right, so what the heck... I myself might have left for the West, if all my friends would have left with me."[38] Because of its daring and uncompromising activism, the IGL acquired some fame in East German opposition circles as the *Himmelfahrtskommando* (Rüddenklau, 1992:181), many of whose members ended up in the West, if they wished to or not. It was the IGL which put Leipzig on the map of East German opposition politics through a series of small but well publicized protest actions, including the two Pleisse Memorial Marches in 1988 and 1989 (which branded the pollution of the small Pleisse river), and a Luxemburg-Liebknecht follow-up demonstration in January 1989.

The *Arbeitskreis Gerechtigkeit* (AKG), Leipzig's major human rights group, was more tightly organized and less action-prone. AKG was founded in December 1987 by a group of former theology students and draft resisters from the University of Leipzig. Like IGL, the AKG was not tied to a certain parish, thus freeing the group from the constraints of direct church supervision.[39] In contrast to East Berlin's Initiative for Peace and Human Rights (IFM), to which it had close ties, the AKG did not camouflage itself as a friendly "peace" group. Instead, it made its position plain as an "opposition group" that tackled definite human rights violations, showing no ideological scruples to use the Western media for its purposes. Efficient and adept in organizing, the AKG soon coordinated the activities of 25 human rights groups throughout East Germany's south.

AKG's most crucial innovation was to take up the concerns of would-be emigrants. A member of AKG strikes a tone rarely heard in East Berlin: "The desire to leave the GDR was based on the same causes as our desire for change. Many did not see this connection, or did not *want* to see it."[40] And dissidents could even profit from enlisting would-be emigrants. "They were less intimidated, because of this one decisive step not to stay," a young female member of AKG says, "and they were also an enormous intelligence potential."[41] But in order to contain the risk of fluctuation and prevent the loss of public legitimacy, the AKG imposed tight organizational restrictions on its members and subgroups. The would-be emigrants, who formed the Working Group Emigration (*Arbeitsgruppe Ausreise*), were denied representation in AKG's elected leadership (*Sprecherkreis*). This leadership made all relevant decisions, and even ordered the themes to be addressed by the emigrant group. "Who did not comply had to go," the resolute *spiritus rector* of AKG says.[42] While this smacked of "politburo" for some,[43] the outcome was extraordinarily effective. With the help of the ten to twelve members of the emigrant group (most of them academics and professionals), AKG gathered meticulous information about the dismal living conditions of would-be emigrants in the GDR, including a mail survey with over 2000 respondents. Through its exit-connection, the AKG could mobilize a considerable mass of people that other opposition groups could only dream of. An example is the GDR-wide petition (*Eingabe*) to the People's Congress after Berlin's Luxemburg arrests in 1988, in which some 5000 would-be emigrants mockingly inquired why one had to become a "state traitor" (*Landesverräter*) before being allowed to leave the GDR.[44] In sum, this exit-voice collaboration, which remained the exception in the GDR, was mutually beneficial: voice could tap a premier source of societal discontent and protest potential, while exit was given an opportunity to get organized and articulate itself politically.

The Peace Prayers

The exit-voice collaboration was forged at the famous Peace Prayers (*Friedensgebete*), which were held in Leipzig's St. Nikolai Church almost every Monday from 1982. Until 1988, the Peace Prayers had been a little-noticed affair of church-based opposition groups, which rarely attracted more than thirty participants.[45] This changed with the Luxemburg events in East Berlin, when would-be emigrants discovered the church as a platform for their concerns. Suddenly up to a thousand and more people would attend the Peace Prayers every Monday. From now on, the Peace Prayers were no longer a sleepy backwater for marginal peaceniks, but a highly political forum that offered opposition groups the chance to escape the ghetto. Whereas East Berlin's dissidents stalled and withdrew in view of the exit challenge, Leipzig's dissidents saw it as an opportunity to grow. Ironically, the same Luxemburg affair that paralyzed East Berlin's opposition thus injected new life into Leipzig's opposition.

In response to the increased audience, the content of the Peace Prayers became more political. The local church leadership, which was traditionally more conservative than that in East Berlin, showed little tolerance of this. Already in March 1988, it denounced the enlarged Peace Prayers as a "mass meeting" (*Grossveranstaltung*) that was to be put back under church supervision.[46] In August 1988, the church leadership even banned the opposition groups from active participation in the Peace Prayers. Leipzig's church superintendent Friedrich Magirius left no doubt that the real target of this measure was the would-be emigrants: "Most participants are not interested in the prayers as such..., but they expect that the church will help them with their personal problems."[47] The church attempt to exclude would-be emigrants became the first test case for the exit–voice collaboration. In a joint protest note, the opposition groups re-taliated: "For the state the recently enlarged parish represents a potential threat...With your intended exclusion of would-be emigrants, you take sides with those who deny that the parish has an honest interest in the content of the Peace Prayers."[48]

Though conditioned by Saxony's conservative church, this solidarity between voice and exit groups was still unprecedented. Most importantly, it helped voice groups become more activist and public-oriented. After their exclusion from the Peace Prayers, the focus of attention shifted from the church hall to the outside churchyard. Here the opposition groups now read the protest notes, passed the resolutions, and discussed the issues that no longer had a place inside the church. A few bricks and planks were quickly arranged to install a podium, and suddenly a public space had constituted itself outside the church. A member of AKG assesses this small but significant surprise invention: "This was new in the GDR. We had a real 'speaker's corner', everyone could get on the podium and speak his mind, completely free and without censorship. We even handed out candles and un-rolled banners." And this oppositionist was well aware who had made this possible: "Without the would-be emigrants the shift to the public would not have been possible. They were our audience. Through surrounding us, they also served as our protection."[49]

Gradually, the Peace Prayers were perceived as mere preludes to action. A participant remembers that the prayers were now followed with less attention, "because one waited for the action outside" (quoted in Unterberg, 1991:142). Exit groups then used these churchyard meetings, which were growing in size from week to week, as starting-points for furthergoing protests. Already during the Spring Fair in March 1988, exit groups had staged the first silent protest march following Peace Prayers. Since fall 1988, the weekly churchyard meetings became the occasion for similar marches. It is important to notice that exit groups were the driving force of these demonstrations, which took on an increasingly urgent and self-confident character. Particularly the Mondays during the Trade and Industry Fairs in March and September soon became known as the traditional dates of "exit demonstrations" (*Ausreiserdemonstrationen*). This was the only time in the year when Western journalists were present in the city, and exit groups quickly learned to use them as protection and amplifier of their cause. At the exit demonstration during the Spring Fair in 1989, many participants carried black berets with white cords, which symbolized the number of years that had passed since filing the exit application.[50] When the secret police tried to intervene, this was no longer a silent march – "We Want Out!" could be heard for the first time.[51]

Throughout this time, exit groups dominated the themes at the weekly churchyard meetings and pushed ahead with ever more daring forms of public protest, particularly during the biannual Leipzig fairs.[52] A member of AKG has no illusion about the pivotal role of exit groups: "Of course, these demonstrations were made by would-be emigrants. But for us they were also an opportunity to speak out and reach a public that was normally closed to us."[53] After the exit demonstration in March 1989, there was almost no week in which the Monday Peace Prayers were not followed by similar rallies.[54] Under the obvious impact of exit, voice also became increasingly assertive. In May, the falsification of the communal elections was responded to with a spontaneous rally in front of Leipzig's Municipal Hall; in June, opposition groups held a music festival in the pedestrian zone, which was brutally dissolved by security forces under the disapproving eyes of the public; in July, the exclusion of opposition groups from that year's GDR-wide Church Convention (*Kirchentag*) became the pretext to hold a protest march through the inner city. If Döhnert and Rummel (1990:147) concluded that since 1989 "opposition groups in Leipzig were ever more inclined to resort to public protest," there can be no doubt that the exit model had shown the way.

The Monday Demonstrations

Referring to the hailing of Leipzig as the "hero city" of the revolution,[55] Hofmann and Rink (1990) rightly aver that would-be emigrants were the first to deserve the title of hero: "Their break with the existing conditions was radical, and

their courage was the catalyst for the revolutionary change"
(p.114). Opposition groups only occupied and adapted the
forms of public protest first ventured by exit groups. Nowhere was this more evident than in the famous Monday
Demonstrations of fall 1989.

By September 1989, the opening of the Hungarian border had fundamentally transformed the exit–voice conjunction.[56] Because exit now had the opportunity to leave, there
was no point in continuing demonstrating. For its part, voice
(like everyone else) was hard pressed to justify staying, thus
becoming increasingly assertive.[57] The changing exit–voice
conjunction was already visible at the first Peace Prayers after
the summerbreak on 4 September. Twelve hundred people
had crowded the St. Nikolai Church in downtown Leipzig
that day, more than ever before, and sermons were the last
thing they wanted. It was also the Monday of the Fall Fair,
the traditional date of the exit demonstration. But for the
first time, opposition groups tried to make it *their* demonstration. When the crowd was about to leave the churchyard, members of IG Leben suddenly set themselves in the
lead, unfurling banners such as "For an Open Country with
Free People" or "Freedom to Travel Not Mass Flight" – evidently concerns that were shared jointly by voice and exit
groups.[58] But after the banners had been quickly taken away
by the secret police, the few leading oppositionists discovered
that no one had followed them. The would-be emigrants
had stayed in the churchyard, where Western television was
posted, shouting their "We Want Out" into the cameras.
The defiant "We Stay Here" of the oppositionists was returned with hisses. Western journalists later reported that
would-be emigrants and dissidents had "marched separately"
that day[59] – missing the essential point that dissidents had
tried to take over the traditional exit demonstration. Some
of the frustrated dissidents later met at the Reformed Church,
where the noted theologian Friedrich Schorlemmer, one of
the later founders of Democratic Awakening, was spreading
the reformist gospel of the emergent citizen movement: would-
be emigrants should please stay away, because "we have
nothing helpful to say to one another." "The reforms," stated
the hopeful theologian, "have to be made with the leading
party."[60]

Two weeks later, the "We Stay Here" of the oppositionists already drowned the opposite call of the would-be emigrants – no wonder, because by then Hungary had fully opened its border to Austria. As Döhnert and Rummel (1990) report, the border opening abruptly changed the character of the Peace Prayers: "It was like a signal of hope in the midst of the huge psychological pressure put on those who stayed" (p.149f). "From now on," a participant says, "the issue was to change the GDR" (Wielepp, 1990:74). On 25 September, opposition groups used the Peace Prayers to brand the brutish beatings and arrests which had occurred in the previous weeks. After the prayers, more than 5000 people marched unhindered through the inner city, shouting "We Stay Here" and "Freedom, Equality, Solidarity." This was the first of the famous Monday Demonstrations that catalyzed the fall of the communist regime. At the second Monday Demonstration on 2 October the number of participants had skyrocketed to 25000. In the biggest demonstration the GDR had seen so far, the people of Leipzig were on the brink of reclaiming their city. Several times the demonstrators could break through the police cordons set up to seal off the inner city. The specter of a violent confrontation loomed.

By that time, all eyes in East and West were fixed on Leipzig. Everyone knew that the third Monday Demonstration on 9 October had to be a turning-point. In fact, the week between 2 and 9 October saw East German communism's endgame. The battle at Dresden's train station on 5 October was followed two days later by the most serious clash so far in East Berlin, when demonstrators tried to interrupt the official anniversary celebration of the GDR. Gorbachev's obvious scorn of the petrified GDR leadership made clear that Soviet bayonets would no longer jump to their rescue (Gedmin, 1992:97–100). But they still had their own bayonets. Party chief Honecker himself had given a shoot-to-kill order for the next Monday Demonstration. In obvious preparation for a massacre, troops were deployed around Leipzig in large numbers; hospitals were advised to increase their blood supplies and to be prepared for gunshot wounds; arrest lists for an internment camp were compiled. In the *Leipziger Volkszeitung,* the chief of the local factory militia announced that "law and order would be restored, if necessary by force" (quoted in Wielepp, 1990:75). On the eve of 9 October, a police officer advised his troops: "Comrades, today it's class struggle. The situation is as serious as on 17 June 1953. Now it will be decided: us or them. Be class-vigilant (*klassenwachsam*). If the club is not enough, use your guns" (quoted in Unterberg, 1991:92).

Today we still do not know why Leipzig was spared a Tiananmen-style massacre on this dramatic October day. But until the early evening the situation was tense and uncertain. Opposition groups, now already joined by the New Forum, issued an appeal to demonstrators to refrain from violence, and they nervously negotiated with moderate local party officials to press for a change of orders from East Berlin.[61] All shops and offices had closed by midday, and heavily armed troops roamed the city. Already by afternoon the downtown churches had filled up, and the Saxon Bishop Hempel appeared in person to advise the people to go home. No one did. A last-minute initiative by a group of local SED-functionaries and Kurt Masur, the music director of the Gewandhaus orchestra, resulted in a call for "peaceful dialogue," which was broadcast several times by Leipzig's radio stations.[62] While this may have reassured the 70000 demonstrators, it remains doubtful that a local cabal could have revoked a shoot-to-kill order by the state leader himself. In any case, when the demonstration took off, shouting "No Violence!", it met no resistance, and all troops suddenly withdrew.

The Monday Demonstration on 9 October was the most important turning-point of the East German revolution. As Robert Darnton (1991:99) assesses its impact, "the 'demos' demonstrated that the people could defy the state." Not by accident, on this day the central slogan of the East German revolution was born: "We Are The People." Two days later, the politburo declared itself ready to discuss political and social change, and the news service ADN referred to demonstrators no longer as "rowdies" but as "citizens."[63] At the fourth Monday Demonstration on 16 October, the factual right to demonstrate was no longer in question, and the number of participants had increased to 150000. Leipzig was out of control, but the maxim "No Violence!" was at no time broken. Next day, party chief Erich Honecker and two other hardliners in the politburo resigned. But as if to indicate that this wasn't enough, and distrustful of the swift "dialogue" protestations from above, the Monday Demonstrations continued to grow. On 23 and 30 October, over 300 000 people attended the rallies, which were now carried live on television. "From that time forward," writes Timothy Garton Ash (1990d:68f), "the people acted and the Party reacted." Twenty more Monday Demonstrations would be held, pushing the East German revolution with irresistible force to its final stage, German unity. The people had stood up, not to be put down again.

BREACHING THE WALL

The breaching of the Wall turned the East German revolution into a German revolution. In retrospect, it seems clear: the Wall had helped the GDR to independent statehood; once it disappeared, so did the state that was built in its shadow. But with the Wall passed also the dissident movement's moment in time. As long as the 'demos' confronted the old regime, Leipzig-style, the front-line was stark and clear. The street call for free elections and against one-party rule easily resonated with the intellectual reform socialism of the New Forum. After the opening of the Wall, this unity fell apart. Now the issue was not to put "the D for Democratic into the GDR" (Ash, 1990d:69), but whether the GDR should continue to exist at all. The dissident movement said yes; the majority of the people said no. This led to a curious redrawing of the front-lines. Dissidents found themselves uneasy but inevitable bedfellows of the retreating communist party. They conjoined to "save the GDR" against a growing movement for national unity, which now dominated the streets of Leipzig and elsewhere.

As everywhere in Eastern Europe, the anti-communist revolution reinstated the principle of national self-determination. In divided Germany, this meant the recovery of national unity and the disappearance of a separate communist state. Ulrich Beck (1991:24) has put it well: "Poland minus communism is still Poland. The GDR without communism is – the Federal Republic." As clear as it seems in retrospect, none of the actors initially realized the national implications of the communist breakdown. Shortly before the Wall was broken, a leading member of the New Forum brushed off the national question: "We really have other problems now" (quoted in Rein, 1989:25). This proved to be a fateful neglect. But there was also little choice. Whether addressed or not, the national question locked East Germany's dissidents into a no-win situation. In its most sympathetic reading, the dissident project of social self-determination worked from the bottom up, whereas the logic of national unification was top–down, with the established political actors of West Germany in charge. As Timothy Garton Ash (1990d:74) recognizes, East Germany's dissidents were destined to be tragic losers because "the boundaries of social self-determination and national self-determination were not the same." The dissidents remained prisoners of the Wall even after helping to dismantle it.

The Moment of Civil Society

The period preceding the Wall break was the emphatic moment of society's self-liberation. Demonstrations spread from city to city; between 16 October and 5 November, the Stasi counted almost 400 demonstrations with more than two million participants (Mitter and Wolle, 1990:234,249). "Dialogue," that notorious watchword of East German intellectual regime opposition since 1953, finally came about. Over night, the monotonous language and ossified rituals of Leninist *apparatchik* rule broke down. All across the country, discussion rounds were established between party reformers, intellectuals and citizens, such as East Berlin's Sunday Talks ("Open Doors – Open Words"), Dresden's Municipal Talk (chaired by mayor Wolfgang Berghofer, an early reform advocate), or the weekly public meetings in Leipzig's Gewandhaus (initiated by conductor Kurt Masur). The media stripped off censorship and refashioned themselves as critical voices of reform at breathtaking speed – including the party newspaper *Neues Deutschland*, the former bastion of communist orthodoxy. The populace, previously lethargic and accustomed to the cynical art of doublespeak, was reborn as an active citizenry.

Dissidents would later look back at this period as their moment in time. A long-time dissident and leader of Democracy Now remembers: "The mood was fantastic. Everybody was politicized. There was an exuberance, an awakening in the population. People who had previously been apathetic and silent turned into brilliant speakers, people with ideas and initiative. Our dreams had come true."[64] Christa Wolf even saw herself in a play by Brecht: "How excited the people were, how irreverent and disobedient. Strangers in the street would smile at you, salespersons in the supermarket would draw you into discussions about politics, as if you were in Brecht's play on the Parisian Commune. One almost began to take this for normal" (Wolf, 1990:15). The dissident movement finally seemed to have reached the people. Was there better proof than the weekly cheers for the New Forum at Leipzig's Monday Demonstrations? A participant of a Monday Demonstration in late October reports: "While they were few in numbers, the New Forum was thoroughly in charge. Whenever the words 'Here Speaks the New Forum' were uttered through the megaphone, the people cheered loudly and gathered around the speaker."[65]

But if one looked close enough, the role of the dissident opposition was riddled with ambiguity from the start. While the public voice of Leipzig was an unmistakable call for an end to one-party rule, a leader of the New Forum found this an "unrealistic" and even "questionable" goal: "We must make the reform with the Comrades."[66] The demonstrations also worried the New Forum: "We look at these demonstrations with a very critical eye. They have no form and contours. This worries the security forces and we well understand their concerns."[67] Was this so different from the party newspaper *Neues Deutschland,* which wrote that "we need dialogue, not screaming (*Gebrüll*) and unrest"?[68] Indeed, "dialogue" and "reform" was also the mantra of the new party leadership under Egon Krenz, which tried to set itself on top of the movement for change (or the *Wende* [turnaround], as the October upheaval was officially dubbed).[69]

In the blurred landscape of East German reform communism, where there was no genuinely *anti*-communist opposition, the line between reform rhetoric from above and reform pressure from below was difficult to draw. Consider the so-called *Umbaupapier* (Reconstruction Paper) of Humboldt University's Project Group "Theory of Socialism", one of the hottest reform tickets at the time. This proposal by a group of leading academics called for a set of sweeping political and social reforms, which was almost indistinguishable from the demands of the New Forum, only more detailed and elaborate. But in a typical demonstration of East German academia's kowtow to the powers that be, the proposal called upon "our party" to "put itself in the lead of the inevitable renewal," adding that "opposition against socialism must not be allowed" (Land, 1990:155).

While the questioning of the leadership status of the communist party was probably the touchstone of genuine opposition, there was considerable hesitation on all sides to do just this. Note how a workers' collective affiliated with the citizen movement justifies its call to cancel the notorious Article 1 of the GDR constitution, which enshrines the leadership role of the communist party: "We think that all GDR citizens are grown-up (*mündig*) enough to resist nationalist and fascist tendencies."[70] Despite its obvious irony, this statement also invokes the GDR's "antifascist" foundation myth and acknowledges the initial legitimacy of the Party as an educator of the *unmündig* accomplices of Hitler. A leader of Democracy Now, the theologian Wolfgang Ullmann, is more explicit: "With regard to the antifascist orientation (*Grundentscheidung*), I always knew myself [to be] on the side of the communists."[71] For the dissident leaders, the issue was renewal, not revocation. They almost seemed to aspire to the pedagogical mandate for which the party was no longer deemed qualified.

Ambiguity also best characterizes the role of the intellectual élite, which jumped on the revolutionary bandwagon once it was under-way. The numerous platforms, resolutions and public appearances of intellectuals in October and November had this one purpose: to deliver a wake-up call to the party leadership.[72] The demonstration of 500 000 on 4 November in East Berlin, organized by the Writers' and

Artists' Unions, struck a tone that was remarkably different from the unruly Monday Demonstrations of Leipzig. What has been celebrated as the "brilliant zenith" of the East German revolution (Reich, 1991:196) bore more resemblance to a new solemn state ritual than to a protest rally. As Lutz Rathenow says, "this was a mixture of opposition and almost a new *raison d'état*."[73] Indeed, this was the most definite attempt to stamp the October upheaval as one of "revolutionary renewal" (C.Wolf). Whereas the Leipzig demonstrations were spontaneous and unorganized, the Berlin rally had been officially licensed by the authorities;[74] all schools were closed, and the event was carried live for several hours on East German television. Among the speakers were not only the cream of East Germany's literary intellectuals, including Stefan Heym, Christa Wolf, and Christoph Hein, but also politburo member Günter Schabowski and the former Stasi General Markus Wolf. Christa Wolf herself provided the core motif repeated by speaker after speaker: "Imagine it's socialism and nobody leaves" (ibid., 120). Christa Wolf later elevated this event into a "voice" cosmology of the East German revolution· "4 November on East Berlin's Alexanderplatz was the point of greatest possible approximation between artists, intellectuals, and the people; and it did not happen by chance. This was the culmination of a long joint effort by writers, artists, and peace and other groups under the roof of the church" (ibid., 159). Cleansed of the nasty exit component, the revolution appears here as the work of a long-standing opposition movement, with the intellectual élite in the lead – no small feat of intellectual *escamotage*.

Two days later, an unruly crowd at Leipzig's Monday Demonstration set a striking contrast to East Berlin's intellectual dreamland. Here was little interest in a "revolutionary renewal." By contrast, insufficiently relaxed travel rules aroused the passions of the 200000 who defied biting cold and rain on Leipzig's Karl-Marx-Platz. When a local party reformer, appearing side by side with members of the New Forum, admonished the crowd that "the tender new plant of reform must not be trampled on," he harvested an outburst of fury: "Too late, too late," "The SED Must Go!", "Resign!" the angry crowd retaliated. An observer compares the different moods of Berlin and Leipzig: "Whereas the demonstration in East Berlin tried to fill the old socialist formulas with new meaning, in Leipzig it's finished with 'dialectic'. The rotting, ruined 'hero city' wants everything and now."[76] More than a sour counterpoint, Leipzig continued to be the inexorable pacemaker of East Germany's revolution.

After the Wall

It is sometimes overlooked that the Wall had already become obsolete before its official breaching on 9 November. The new travel rules that angered Leipzig as still too restrictive also contained the implicit end of the Wall: not only had the border with Czechoslovakia been reopened, but East Germans were free to move on from there directly to West Germany. As a West German official interpreted the impact of the new rules, the Wall "is just going to be superfluous."[77] The following days saw the biggest exodus East Germany had ever seen; between 3 and 8 November, 48 177 East Germans headed West (Baumann et al., 1990:142). To stem this tide, only one solution seemed possible: to open the Wall itself. Again, it was the exit movement that had pushed the East German revolution to its next stage. While the opening of the Wall on 9 November was little more than a formality, it was the event that shook the world.

The fall of the Berlin Wall and the dancing of exuberant Berliners on that monstrous and seemingly unmovable shrine of the Cold War order became emblematic of the revolutionary changes that swept Eastern Europe in 1989. But what the world celebrated as a victory of liberty, East German dissidents took more like a disaster. A veteran dissident and member of the New Forum describes her emotional response: "I was sick for three days, lying down with a terrible headache, and I couldn't be glad. I took it as an outrageous betrayal (*unerhörter Beschiss*). For years one had been imprisoned, and then they snapped their fingers, the Wall was open, and everybody could pass through. To be sure, this was only *one* response. The other response was to dance on the Wall."[78] Bärbel Bohley, by then celebrated as "Mother of the Revolution", expressed her anger in one blunt sentence: "The people are crazy, and the government has lost its mind" (quoted in *TAZ Journal*, 1990a:126).

These responses, as extreme and emotional as the times in which they were made, express a keen foreboding that with the arrival of liberty the dissident movement had lost its case for a socialist renewal. It became clear that the reform socialism of the month after 9 October shared the GDR's birth defect – both needed the Wall. This was the dissident movement's core dilemma: Its project of democratization "from below" needed the independent statehood of the GDR,[79] but this was inexorably coupled to the existence of the Wall, the symbol of the illegitimacy of communist rule. Few went as far as Friedrich Schorlemmer of Democracy Now, who insisted that "the Wall should stay for a while" (quoted in *TAZ Journal*, 1990a:126); but this was the logical consequence of the dissident position. From this point on, the former dissidents of SED rule would tune in to the official campaign to "save the GDR", in which the lines between opposition and regime became virtually indistinguishable. When party chief Egon Krenz combined the opening of the Wall with the hope that a new socialism was in the making that would be "democratic ... and turn to the people in everything," a dissident could not have put it differently. But it was West Germany's foreign minister, addressing a cheering crowd of Berliners at the Rathaus Schöneberg, who anticipated the inevitable outcome: "There is no capitalist and there is no socialist Germany, but only one German nation in unity and peace."[80]

Ralf Dahrendorf (1990:40f) noted that not capitalism but the open society was the true winner of 1989. East German dissidents, however, continued to divide the world into capitalist and socialist halves. Consequentially, the breaching of the Wall meant not liberty but the imminent sell-out to capitalism. As Friedrich Schorlemmer put it, the "rule by ideology" was about to be replaced by "the rule of big foreign money" (quoted in *TAZ Journal*, 1990a:133). Already in 1961, most intellectuals and oppositionists had tacitly accepted the building of the Wall as a "chance" to build the true socialism – as if to admit that Utopia was "of necessity a closed society" (Dahrendorf, 1990:61).[81] By 1989, this attitude had not changed much. Still, there was the utopian hope of a complete alternative, a thoroughly politicized society of the virtuous citizen-activist. Therefore the fear of a leader of the New Forum that the "small amount of national identity" forged since October would be drowned in "West Berlin chocolate": "Now that they can travel they will stay out of politics."[82]

The first public statement of the New Forum after the opening of the Wall, though designed as a damage control to Bärbel Bohley's frank but disastrous indictment of the people flocking into the West, still suggests that one had been better off *with* the Wall: "We don't want a society of profiteers and elbow-types. You are the heroes of a political revolution. Don't succumb to the temptation of traveling and consumption" (New Forum, 1989:20). The louder the calls became for reunification, the more desperate the attempt to conjure up the loyalty to "our country." But what was "our country" – the "socialist state of workers and peasants" as stipulated in the GDR constitution? Because the October revolution had obviously been too short and fickle to produce a positive "GDR-identity," as some had hoped, the only resort left was the "antifascist" foundation myth. Christa Wolf's "For Our Country" initiative of 26 November, though highly contested within the dissident scene, was the logical culmination of the post-Wall shock. It drew a stark contrast between the "solidaristic society" of an independent GDR and the "sell-out of our material and moral values" and subsequent "annexation" by West Germany: "We still have a chance if we return to the antifascist and humanist ideals from which we had once started."[83] Tellingly, the "For Our Country" appeal was printed prominently in *Neues Deutschland* and among its first signatories were not only some noted dissident leaders, but also party chief Egon Krenz and the new Prime Minister Hans Modrow.

Power Vacuum

After the Wall, East German opposition groups faced a problem that all Eastern European dissident movements faced once the first strike against the old regime had succeeded: to provide feasible political alternatives. As Ralf Dahrendorf put it (1990:12), "we the people" can rise against an auto-cratic regime; but "we the people" cannot govern. "Now we needed concrete programs to rebuild society (*Gesellschaftsmodelle*), including an economic reform program," says New Forum leader Sebastian Pflugbeil, "But we had none."[84] In early October, the New Forum still rejected the presentation of a concrete reform proposal, trusting that one would emerge in "comprehensive discussion" (New Forum, 1989:3). This evasiveness combined with vague socialist rhetoric no longer sufficed. When the old regime was dwindling toward the abyss, a disoriented public found the New Forum and the other opposition groups locked in sectarian rivalry and quib-bling about internal procedure that was painfully reminis-cent of the party versus movement debate in the early phases of the West German Green Party. A participant at an oppo-sition meeting in late November in Leipzig noted with sur-prise that "the country [was] falling apart and they were talking about statutes" (quoted in *TAZ Journal*, 1990a:153). Internal divisions, the absence of effective organizational struc-tures, and the lack of competent leadership prevented op-position groups, such as the New Forum, from assuming a more prominent role in the post-Wall turmoil.[85]

The turn West and reunification may have been inevitable in the long run. But in the short run this was no foregone conclusion. The reunification debate only gained ground when the disintegration of the old regime became unstoppable, with no opposition in sight to prevent the ship of state from running aground. By late November, the winds of change had become rougher. The first reliable data of the economic slump, combined with shocking revelations about widespread corruption and the sumptuous life-style of the old élite, moved anti-communist sentiments into high gear. The hunting lodges and bungalows of Wandlitz cer-tainly looked paltry to Western eyes; for East Germans, they epitomized the hypocrisy of the élite that had preached "de-limitation" from the West while going there for shopping sprees. As Robert Darnton (1991:94) put it nicely, the hunting lodges doomed the communists "just as...Marie Antoinette's diamond necklace brought down the monarch in France." By then, politburo members were not just ousted but ar-rested; criminal charges were filed against Erich Honecker himself, who was put under house arrest "like Louis XVI in the Tuileries" (ibid.). The last sympathies for a socialist renewal melted away once the rotten backstage of communist rule had come into view.

In late November, when the rebellious party basis of the SED ousted Egon Krenz and the last holdovers of the old *nomenklatura*, the GDR threatened to slip into anarchy. "Power is up for grabs, yet no one picks it up," said the mayor of Dresden, Wolfgang Berghofer.[86] On the Leipzig Monday Demonstration of 18 November (the first to be officially organized by the New Forum), not "Germany United Fatherland" but "New Forum to Power!" was the dominant call. But a local leader of the New Forum rejected the popular request in revealing terms: "An organization that is just two months old cannot run a country. We have slept during the last ten or twenty years, and we have failed to build up an opposition competent enough to seize power. At best, we might consider to *participate* in power in order to *control* it" (quoted in Schulz, 1991:24). Reflecting the logic of a grass-roots movement, the speaker of the New Forum added that it was more important to build the "basis" than to mingle in high politics.

But it was the "basis" itself, particularly in the disillusioned and impatient south of the GDR, that continued to press the dissident leadership to take action. In early December, local New Forum groups throughout Saxony urged the leadership in East Berlin to support a call for a general strike, a strategy that had just carried the Czech Civic Forum to state power. New Forum leader Jens Reich admits that there was an "overwhelming" readiness for a general strike in the southern province that was blunted by the dissident leadership: "Several delegations of workers approached us to support their strike call. But we tried to calm them down. Our goal was not to usurp power, but to push for elections. 'Democratic legitimation' was our key concern, not power. In the end, the Thermidor would have caught up with us anyway. Yet we missed the opportunity, we ducked in the decisive moment."[87]

The ensuing political vacuum nourished the call for national reunification. Because they had missed the moment when bold initiative might have turned the tide, the opposition groups soon found themselves on the defensive and forced to react to developments outside their control. The growing reunification sentiment made it self-defeating to stick to the socialist reform rhetoric and to insist on East Germany's independent statehood. Moreover, a refashioned SED, which had given itself a new name (Party for Democratic Socialism, or PDS) and a young dynamic leader (the lawyer Gregor Gysi), visibly occupied the "third path" terrain of a socialism beyond Leninism and capitalism. Because their pro-socialist disposition was always counteracted by a strong instinct not to make common cause with their former oppressors, the opposition groups reset their agenda. By late November, the very notion of socialism disappeared from the platforms of most opposition groups. Erhart Neubert, a leader of Democratic Awakening remembers: "Still in October, our democratic socialism flyers were torn out of our hands with enthusiasm. In November, the same people would throw them away in anger, exclaiming that 'we are no guinea-pigs.' So we replaced the notion of democratic socialism with social democracy."[88]

The toning down of the socialist rhetoric was also conditioned by a second wave of activists that transformed the opposition groups from within (see Schulz, 1991). Initially, the New Forum and all the other opposition groups were small, Berlin-centered initiatives of long-standing dissidents with distinctively intellectual profiles. By November, the New Forum was a mass-member organization with several hundred local branches. The local activists, well represented in the regional and state-wide steering committees, increasingly pushed the intellectual leadership aside. Particularly the New Forum branches in Saxony, the industrial heartland of the GDR, took on a "conservative" pro-unity and pro-market profile. The old "leftist" leadership around Bärbel Bohley and Jens Reich soon found itself in the minority position, and, as the faction *Aufbruch '89* (the title of the initial founding manifesto), it repeatedly threatened to split off from the New Forum. At the official founding congress of the New Forum in January, the conservative rank-and-file majority even committed the New Forum to an official pro-unity course.[89]

In the Democratic Awakening also, a conservative basis

pushed aside the intellectual leadership. Though (in contrast to the other groups) the Democratic Awakening had
aspired to become a party from the outset, it had initially
been a small élite of leftist reform theologians that prided
itself on not dodging the notion of socialism, as the New
Forum had done. "The word 'socialism' still sounds good
to us," said the Erfurt-based theologian Edelbert Richter in
an obvious sneer at the New Forum.[90] Not for long. In mid-
December, at the official founding congress of Democratic
Awakening in Leipzig, the conservative party basis, supported
by Reverend Rainer Eppelmann and Stasi-lawyer Wolfgang
Schnur, led the party to abandon its socialism goal and to
adopt an unconditional pro-unity and pro-market course
instead. When the refashioned Democratic Awakening even
joined Chancellor Helmut Kohl's pro-unity "Alliance for
Germany," the entire old leadership left the group in angry
protest.[91]

Nationalism

National symbols and sentiments fueled and accompanied
the victorious revolutions in Eastern Europe. When the German flag appeared in the streets of Leipzig, the East German revolution had reached its inglorious end – or so it
seemed to the leaders of the citizen movement. Why? In
post-war Germany, the Nazi legacy and the genocides committed in the name of "race purity" had thoroughly discredited
any positive national identity. This anti-national disposition
was particularly strong among the intellectuals. West German intellectuals hoped to replace the ethnic and cultural
bases of nationhood with a post-national commitment to
constitutional principles. Jürgen Habermas (1990:149–75) and
Rainer Lepsius (1989:255) called this a "patriotism of the
constitution." East German intellectuals committed themselves
to the redemptive utopia of socialism. In the words of Stefan
Heym (1990:75), East Germany had set out as "a community
that conspired to build a new world in which there is justice" (see Chapter 6).

In contrast to Eastern Europe, East German opposition
politics thus could not draw upon nationalist motives. When
Polish dissidents and Czech Chartists, most notably in the

Prague Appeal of 19`85, argued for a unified and neutral Germany, East German oppositionists were less than enthusiastic. "A unified Germany was in the interest of the Eastern Europeans because it would bring them closer to Europe," IFM leader Gerd Poppe says, "But for us this was anathema. We only argued in terms of a democratized GDR."[92] In fact, East German dissidents had to eschew a national orientation, not only because it was delegitimized, but also because it conflicted with the project of democratization from below. Ludwig Mehlhorn of Democracy Now, one of the most perceptive and "Eastern European" of East Germany's dissidents, crisply articulates the conflict between the "national" and "civic" paradigms in the East German revolution: "We renounced the national paradigm. If we had not done so, the civic aspect of our project, democratization and societal renewal, would have been lost. And democratization was indeed our priority. Of course, we wanted a Western-style legal state [*Rechtsstaat*] and democracy. But not as a ready-made imposition from above. *Klar, Romantik.*"[93]

Because the dissidents refused to take on the national paradigm, other groups would do so. Obviously angered that after the breaching of the Wall it was no longer priests and intellectuals who set the agenda, Friedrich Schorlemmer complained that "the primitive German petit bourgeois [*Kleinbürger*] has occupied the political scene, and you'd better not say it to him." Indeed, since late November the tone at the Leipzig Monday Demonstrations had changed remarkably. Not only had the anger about corruption, privilege and Stasi turned against anything that smacked of the old ways, but the call for national reunification had become dominant. As surveys show, this change of orientation coincided with a change of participants (Mühler and Wilsdorf, 1990, 1991; Förster and Roski, 1990:159–70). While in the first Monday Demonstrations students and the young intelligentsia had been overrepresented, later it was workers and the older generation who formed the majority of participants, most of them being pro-unity. In late February, the deputy chair of the refounded SPD of Leipzig even publicly announced the "withdrawal of the democratic forces" from the Monday Demonstrations: "Considering the changed character of the Monday Demonstrations in Leipzig, in which a nationalist pathos now predominates, it is the consensus of all new democratic forces to withdraw from these demonstrations."[95]

As the "democratic forces" overlooked, the 200 000 that raised the first loud call for national unity on the Monday Demonstration of 22 November *also* fell into absolute silence when asked to commemorate the victims of the Prague upheaval.[96] This was hardly the German nationalism of old. Moreover, the alleged "nationalist pathos" expressed itself in inconspicuous symbols. It was not the notorious first part of the West German anthem, but the "Germany United Fatherland" verse of the GDR hymn that was chanted by the demonstrators; Johannes R. Becher, the first minister of culture of the GDR, had written the text that became outlawed once the German component was to be eradicated from the "socialist nation." Moreover, the German tricolor, which now dominated the streets of Leipzig, had never been the banner of Wilhelminian Imperialism, let alone of Nazism, but of the *Wartburgfest* and the (aborted) democratic revolution of 1848. Throughout Eastern Europe, the victory over communism was symbolized by cutting out the hammer and sickle emblem from the national banners. As irony would have it, once you did this with the East German flag, you had the West German flag, and with it a powerful symbol of national unity.

Claus Offe (1990b) has argued that the nationalist turn of the East German revolution was more the result of Western élite design than of Eastern mass pressure. This interpretation has two weaknesses. On the one hand, it overestimates the flexibility and perceptiveness of the West German political élite, which by then had become accustomed to the German division and abhorred any questioning of the status quo as a threat to "stability" (see McAdams, 1993:175–226). Even Chancellor Kohl's ten-point plan of November 1989, which was widely interpreted as the first call for reunification, mentions only the creation of "confederal structures" between the two Germanies. On the other hand, Offe's claim of élite nationalism ignores the internal development in the East, particularly the pace-setting role of Leipzig's Monday Demonstrations. Long before the Western élites became involved, national slogans had filled the vacuum left by a collapsing old regime and an opposition hovering in indecision.[97] But Offe's observation contains a grain of truth. Like the civic nationalisms of East Central Europe, this nationalism was not an affirmation of ethnic Germanness but a mere vehicle to express the desire for a "normal society" and a "return to history" (see Kocka, 1990). As Timothy Garton Ash (1990d:72) put it nicely, the voices for reunification were not so much driven by the "power of nationalism" as by the "power of common sense." After the breaching of the Wall, the people had seen West Germany, and it worked. Jürgen Habermas's notion of "DM Nationalism", though a polemic hint that material needs were less important than immaterial ones, is strikingly accurate. The desire to close the huge quality-of-life gap between East and West, not the exalted pathos of nationalism, led the way from the "social" into the "national" phase of the East German revolution (see Walser Smith, 1991).[98]

The GDR had always been compulsively fixated on the West, and failed to produce an identity in itself. The regime-breakdown only ratified the implications of this. The GDR was not Austria, as some had argued in defence of a separate GDR, because the GDR lacked an indigenous historical tradition and had never subjected itself to the test of popular consent (see Kocka, 1990:492f fn.4). In subverted ways, many East Germans had already "lived" in the West long before they had the actual choice, from the nightly escape via Western television, the purchase of Western goods in the Intershops and Delikat-Läden, to the reading habits of the intellectuals, whose bookshelves were filled with Suhrkamp, Fischer, and Luchterhand paperbacks. Whereas in West Germany the national division had been gradually accepted over the years, particularly among the younger generations (Jansen, 1989), this division was always more difficult to accept in the East. This was not only because of the obvious inequity of life chances in East and West, but also because of unevenly distributed kinship contacts: roughly two-thirds of East Germans had family members in the West, whereas only one-third of West Germans had relatives in the East (Niethammer, 1990:277). These observations suggest that in everyday life the idea of national unity remained more relevant in the East than in the West. Certainly no cynical strategy of Western *conquistadores* was needed to make the idea of unity palatable to the East Germans, as Claus Offe (1990b) seems to imply.

THE ROUND TABLE

As throughout East Central Europe, a Round Table between opposition and old regime guided the transition to democracy.[99] But whereas in Poland or Hungary the Round Tables were laying the fundaments of institutional renewal, East Germany's Round Table would preside over the state's self-extinction. The Round Table was also the logical culmination of East Germany's regime opposition. "Considering our history," says dissident Gerd Poppe, "it was logical to come to this Round Table."[100] The Round Table finally established what the opposition had wanted all along: the "dialogue" with the regime. By the same token, the East German Round Table was not, like the Polish one, a means to hand over power to the democratic opposition, but an expression of the opposition's *refusal* of power. This refusal of power, which distinguishes East German oppositionists from their less scrupulous Eastern European counterparts, partially reflected the Protestant church environs of most dissidents. "We were deeply distrustful of power," admits a shivering dissident theologian who had helped instal the Round Table, "this was something abominable to us."[101] In addition, as cut off from society as the dissidents were, their claim to power would have been putschist and devoid of democratic legitimacy indeed. But most essential was a basic allegiance to the leading party, which was chided more for its bad leadership than for its continued existence.[102] "Now that the SED had maneuvered the cart into the mud," a Round Table participant describes the dominant attitude, "we said 'so please pull it out yourselves.'"[103] Whatever led the opposition there, the Round Table would draw the latter into the maelstrom of the declining regime. The Round Table became the most telling symbol that both, the regime and its opposition, had to perish together.

Contrary to other reports, the initiative to set up the Round Table came from the opposition groups.[104] The Contact Group of the new opposition groups, which had met clandestinely since early October to coordinate their activities, first proposed the idea in early November (Thaysen, 1990:30).[105] Since the Contact Group understood itself as the nucleus of an electoral alliance against the SED, it targeted the SED and the other parties of the National Front as its opposites. This proved to be a grave strategic error. By early December, when the first Round Table convened, the center of power had already shifted from the party to the cabinet under the new Prime Minister Hans Modrow. In fact, the separation of party and state was the first major reform step taken by the communist leadership. If not of its design, the Round Table was thus in the regime's best interest. First, by being included in the Round Table, the old bloc parties of the National Front, the notorious satraps of communist one-party rule, were revalorized in public view (or, to use the pertinent phrase, 'whitewashed'). They also were made attractive to the Western parties who were then beginning to look for "partners" in the East. Second, by leaving out the actual government, the Round Table allowed Prime Minister Hans Modrow to bind the opposition into an attention-getting but ineffectual side-show, while having free room to maneuver for himself.[106] "The Czech Civic Forum was smarter," a Round Table participant deplores in retrospect, "they would only negotiate with the government."[107] Indeed, the Round Table experience introduced a new proverb into German everyday language: "to pull over the table" (*über den Tisch ziehen*).

Old versus New Forces

The first Round Table, which convened in early December in Berlin-Niederschönhausen, still looked like an opposition dream come true. Strict parity between "old" and "new forces" had been negotiated,[108] and three churchmen functioned as non-voting moderators.[109] Though designed as a passive instrument of public control without explicit veto-right, the Round Table seemed like an ironic echo of the Leninist "dual power" strategy in which old authority is undermined while new authority is created (see Selznick, 1952:ch.4). The first Round Table meeting determined 6 May as the date of the first free and secret elections; a committee was formed to work out a new constitution; and – reflecting the opposition's most urgent concern – the Modrow government was requested to dissolve the secret police and abandon its plan to create an Office for National Security, a barely disguised follow-up organization to the Stasi.

But, as the opposition groups soon noticed, the Modrow government stubbornly ignored most Round Table resolutions.[110] The Prime Minister even launched a silent but effective attempt to stabilize the old forces, or at least to wipe out their most incriminating traces (especially with regard to the hated Stasi). "We simply slept through these developments," Round Table participant Gerd Poppe remembers.[111] Parallel to this, a rejuvenated SED-PDS, led by the young and energetic Gregor Gysi, tried to enlist the opposition forces into a noisily constructed "Front Against Fascism," which conjured up the need for unity against a recent wave of juvenile right-wing extremism. On 3 January, a pompous "anti-fascist combat demonstration" was held at the Soviet War Monument in Berlin-Treptow, where party chair Gysi called for a "unity front against neonazism, neofascism, racism, and xenophobia" (Baumann et al., 1990:202) – the old package wrapped up anew.[112] In addition, wild rumors of an imminent Stasi putsch made the round.[113] Not yet quite beaten, the communist hydra seemed to rear an ugly new head.

In this critical situation, the Round Table opposition proved that the "save the GDR" rhetoric of the time had not yet muted its critical instincts. When repeated calls on Modrow to cancel his plans for a new security police and to comment on the putsch rumors had not found any response, the Round Table, in a rather dramatic two-hour ultimatum on 8 January, ordered the Prime Minister to appear in person.[114] Modrow had just departed for a state visit, and thus was unable to come. But the public reaction to this determined move left no doubt that on the Stasi issue the opposition was still in line with public sentiments. In fact, Leipzig's Monday Demonstration on the same day was one angry call to stop communism's clumsy comeback attempt: "Down With the SED!" was the unconditional demand of the day (Döhnert and Rummel, 1990:157). Three days later, East Berlin construction workers interrupted their work to march to the People's Chamber, where Modrow was presenting his plan for the new security police – "Opposition at the Round Table, We Construction Workers Are Supporting You" was their slogan. On what other issue had workers and dissidents ever agreed? "Distrusted on almost every other issue, the opposition still had legitimacy with regard to the Stasi issue," says Lutz Rathenow.[115] The Stasi issue was the unfailing litmus test of authentic regime opposition – no wonder, because the dissidents had been the Stasi's prime victims. As in their later demand to open the Stasi files, dissidents insisted that the past must be confronted rather than repressed, and that the villains must be identified and put on trial. With regard to the painful exercise of *Vergangenheitsbewältigung*, dissidents loom large as the unimpeachable voice of communism's victims.

In the larger picture of East Germany's breakdown, the Round Table's January ultimatum seems small and unimportant. But it restored the dignity of the opposition, whose contours had become ever less distinguishable from the old regime forces. And it showed how effective a determined move could be. At the next Round Table meeting on 15 January, Hans Modrow appeared, to deliver the "oath of manifestation" that the opposition had so far been waiting for in vain. Not only did Modrow abandon his plan to revive the secret police, but he asked the opposition to enter into a coalition government with the old forces.[116] "Pick the ministries you like to have," Modrow later underlined the urgency of his plea, "so that you don't think I am choosing" (quoted in Thaysen, 1990:82). After Leipzig's Monday Demonstration of 9 October and the opening of the Berlin Wall one month later, the East German revolution reached its third and final round.

In the very moment when Modrow declared his bankruptcy at the Round Table, a rally called by the New Forum resulted in the dramatic storming of the Stasi headquarter in East Berlin's Normannenstrasse. Afraid that the long-avoided violence had finally arrived, the Round Table immediately broke off its meeting and rushed with the Prime Minister to the center of unrest. "This was a ghostly convoy that moved under police sirens through the wet and dimming streets of East Berlin," participant observer Uwe Thaysen (1990:66f) remembers, "The former victims of the Stasi were summoned up to protect the Stasi from the mob." Though the details of the event are still unclear,[117] the Stasi rampage on 15 January was East Germany's storming of the Bastille. The deeply shaken government even deemed the country on the brink of civil war, and in a countrywide broadcast appeal the populace was called upon "to stay calm and collected in this critical hour" (quoted in Darnton, 1991:121). From now on, there was no tinkering with the dissolution of the Stasi. With the loss of its "shield and sword," the communist party also lost its main bastion of power. After 15 January, no doubt was allowed that the SED was on the way out. The party had already shrunk from its previous membership of two million to just 1.2 million. But now even the party reformers considered the party incapable of reform. In late January, led by Dresden's Wolfgang Berghofer, a group of prominent reformers left the SED, blaming the party for "having ruined the GDR in an irresponsible and shameless way," and chiding it for "lacking the political will" to reform itself (quoted in Baumann et al., 1990:222). At the same time, the exit movement reached a new peak. Since the opening of the Wall, close to 140 000 more people had left the GDR. By January an unprecedented 2000 people were leaving the GDR every day, amounting to the record number of 73 700 at the month's end (Gesamtdeutsches Institut, 1991).

Changing Front Lines

For the besieged Modrow government the coalition offer was the *ultima ratio* to prevent the country from sinking into anarchy. For the opposition groups, however, the Prime Minister's offer posed a serious dilemma. With the spring 1990 elections forthcoming, a mingling with the old regime would taint the opposition groups with the air of collaboration and defeat. By that time, the unity train had inevitably departed, and it was clear that the election campaign would be oriented to, and influenced by, the West. The GDR-internal front line between "old" and "new forces" was no longer. The CDU prepared itself for a fusion with the West CDU by leaving the National Front and ousting the old leadership. At its founding congress on 13 January, which was attended by Willy Brandt, the SDP pioneered the *Anschluss* in renaming itself SPD, making the "unity of the German nation" its top priority (Baumann et al., 1990:215). The Democratic Awakening also left the opposition camp, seeking ties with the West CDU (also because all other Western parties were already "committed" by that time). On 1 February, after Gorbachev's *d'accord*, Prime Minister Modrow himself jumped aboard the unity train by declaring that Germany should become "the united fatherland of all citizens of the German nation" (ibid., 229).

The opposition groups eventually bowed to the pressure to take over political responsibility, sending eight of their leaders into the new "Government of National Responsibility." By the same token, the Round Table became East Germany's central steering instrument. But this meant little by then, because "government" had become a mere bridging institution until the forthcoming elections. To secure the participation of the SPD, which showed little enthusiasm for spoiling its bright election prospects, Modrow moved the election date forward to 18 March [118] This left the opposition groups without Western support at a great disadvantage. Because there was not even time to restructure the ministries, the eight ministers delegated by the Round Table opposition were left without a firm resort – "a grave mistake," as Ludwig Mehlhorn of Democracy Now thinks, because the accord provided the old forces with new legitimacy, while the opposition could not effectively control any of the key government operations (including, as we now know, the frantic destruction of incriminating evidence and the "whitewashing" of the old apparatus). "We only legitimized the government," says the perceptive dissident, "without being able to change anything."[119]

In its last breath, the GDR offered the odd, yet consequent, picture of the dissident opposition stubbornly aboard the sinking ship of state, while the people had long jumped into the life-boat of unification. The biggest street actions by then were not the dwindling Leipzig demonstrations, but the campaign rallies of Chancellor Helmut Kohl and SPD chief Willy Brandt. In the Government of National Responsibility, opposition and old regime became joint advocates of "GDR interests" against the pending Western takeover, thus foreshadowing the newest cleavage line in German politics. This became clear during Modrow's humiliating Bonn visit in February, with his eight dissident ministers in tow. In a foretaste to the rough winds of electoral politics, Modrow's team did not receive the "solidarity contribution" it had asked for, and, taken *überhaupt,* no one in Bonn liked to mingle with the certain losers of the forthcoming elections. What government in the world would have filled the pockets of nose-diving communists with a check of $10 billion? "We also have something to offer," says an offended dissident minister, "we are no small *Michels*" (quoted in Thaysen, 1990:139). Alas, in the new world of electoral politics, they were, cruel as that may be.

The last activities of the Round Table were all addressed to Bonn. Though meanwhile tainted by irrelevance, the Round Table prepared a programmatic package for the forthcoming unity negotiations. If the GDR had to be "sold," then at the highest possible price. A Social Charter sought to preserve the so-called "social achievements" (*soziale Errungenschaften*) of the GDR, and it included a list of legal provisions guaranteeing the equality of women, free abortion, health care, education, and workplace protection. Most importantly, the Round Table presented the outline of a new constitution. Though closely resembling the Western Basic Law, the constitution outline stressed the component of social rights (including the right to work), and it included a strong plebiscitarian element that payed tribute to society's self-liberation from communist rule (see Preuss, 1990). The new constitution should allow the GDR to unify with West Germany on an equal basis, because a simple annexation would "violate... the dignity of our people" (quoted in Thaysen, 1990:146). Noble as these efforts were, they lacked one crucial element: democratic legitimation.[120]

The last meeting of the Round Table, on 12 March 1990, which might have been the crowning ceremony of what some called a "School of Democracy," was a sad demonstration of how little it mattered four days before the elections. At 6 pm, East German television (which had carried all previous meetings at full length) said good-bye to the Round Table – the children wanted to see their *Sandmännchen.*

Electing Another Republic

After the June Uprising in 1953, a sarcastic Berthold Brecht suggested that "the government dissolve the people and elect another." In the elections of 18 March 1990, the people dissolved the state and chose another.[121] The election campaign had one theme: not if, but how quickly unification should come. The outcome included three surprises. First, the huge win for the conservative Alliance for Germany (48 per cent of the vote) and the parallel loss of the Social Democratic Party (the distant second with 22 per cent). How can we explain this success of the conservatives? The Alliance for Germany led by Chancellor Kohl promised the quickest road to unity via a swift monetary union, and it profited from the fact that during East Germany's grim endgame even Social Democracy smacked of Socialism. And, after 50 years of dictatorship and state imposed opportunism, many may have felt like the deserter from Democracy Now who "wanted to be with the strongest party and the majority."[122]

The second surprise was the blasting defeat of the citizen movement (whose Alliance 90 got a bare 2.9 per cent of the vote) and the impressive showing of the PDS, the successor to the communist party (16 per cent). To be sure, the decline of the citizen movement had been in the making since the Wall was opened. In early March, a disappointed Jens Reich (1991:214) noted that his New Forum chapter of Berlin-Pankow, which in the glorious days of October had easily filled a church with 600 people, now attracted no more than 25 people. How can we explain this defeat of the citizen movement? Chided by some for their short memory, voters were only repaying the evasive refusal of power politics by the opposition groups. The New Forum, Democracy Now, and the Initiative for Peace and Human Rights (IFM), which constituted the Alliance 90, all refused to adopt formal party status, clinging instead to the hypostasized label of "citizen movement" (*Bürgerbewegung*). How should voters deal with groups that wanted to be "neither government nor opposition" but "conscience of the nation" and "pioneer of the communal, multicultural society of the 21st century" (quoted in Schulz, 1991:42)? The more they became entangled with electoral politics, the more the opposition groups resembled the quagmire of the West German Green Party and the new social movement, with their paradoxical claim to be the "included excluded third," a parasite in the interpretation of Michel Serres (see Luhmann, 1989:121–6). Moreover, the relatively good showing of the ex-communists indicated yet another dilemma for the "new forces" of the East German revolution. Since both "old" and "new forces" competed for the same slot of advocating "GDR interests," their boundary lines became blurred. But if voters succumbed to GDR nostalgia, the heirs of the old party seemed the more credible address.

The third election surprise was the exceptional status of East Berlin (see Glässner, 1991:126–35). In East Berlin, the conservative Alliance for Germany had its weakest showing with a bare 20 per cent of the vote, while the PDS achieved a triumphant 30 per cent, making it the strongest party there. In the south of East Germany, however, the PDS did poorly, while the Alliance averaged an impressive 60 per cent. Ironically, the walled city that symbolized to the world the brutality of the Cold War divide wanted unity least. By contrast, the south, including the ruined "hero city" of the revolution, wanted unity most. The revolution, which had started with the "we want out" of Leipzig's exit movement, thus came full circle, reinstating the forces that had set it off in the first place.

The winners-turned-losers of the East German revolution had to say "Adieu GDR," some with bitterness, some with melancholy. Ludwig Mehlhorn of Democracy Now reminded them all that a "dictatorship" had been dismantled and buried: "Not more, but also not less."[123]

AFTER UNITY

With reunification under way, East German dissident politics resumed its original shape of a "politics of minorities for minorities" (Poppe, 1991:81). After the March elections, the further steps toward national reunification, such as the monetary and social union in July and political unity in October, were mere formalities, with the outmaneuvered opposition groups watching the process from the sidelines. Their defeat was ratified by the modalities of reunification. On 3 October, the GDR ceased to exist, by simply "joining" (*beitreten*) the Bonn Republic via Article 23 of the Basic Law, thus bypassing the Article 146 that had called for a new constitutional assembly (see Beyme, 1991). For the opposition groups, which had favoured reunification on the equal basis of a new constitution, this amounted to the GDR's "annexation" by the West, retroactively devaluing the societal self-liberation of fall 1989. More appropriately, however, the opposition groups remained hostage to an illegitimate state. How could the remains of this state ever hope to deal on equal terms with a legitimate state, which certainly showed no sign of collapse?[124] Again, the German situation exposed more clearly than elsewhere the shocking truth of the communist experience, which Eastern European dissidents faced with less sentimentality: "A kind of unnatural hole in the historical process, an empty time, a total break in continuity, a sheer waste" (Kolakowski, 1992:56).

After withdrawing from the stage of history, East German dissident groups could finally become what they had always been at heart: a new social movement dealing with issues of ecology, peace, and minority rights. In the new democratic context, the remains of the dissident movement even replicated the notorious debate over accepting, or rejecting, the rules of representative democracy that had plagued the Western new social movements since the early 1980s. But this party-versus-movement debate was also shaped by a unique history, which kept East German dissidents at a distance from their Green counterparts in the West, and which made the transition to a new world of conflict and differentiated spheres and functions particularly difficult.

Four major elections in 1990 made the adjustment to the new political context an urgent necessity. From the beginning, the opposition groups realized that complete abstinence from electoral politics would be self-defeating. But the ensuing debate over forming electoral coalitions and eventually building a joint party led to a bitter schism among the opposition groups. A hypostasized "basis" resisted the compromises and organizational structures entailed by the involvement in electoral politics. Ironically, the leadership of the New Forum became the most outspoken advocate of "basis" values. For Bärbel Bohley, playing by the rules of electoral politics was no less than a "betrayal" of the "idea of the citizen movement."[125] "If there was anything new in the Revolution of 1989," says the irreverent founder of the New Forum, "it was the refusal of power."[126] According to this "politics from below," the "basis" always knows what is right: "Only the basis knows its forces, desires and problems. The basis always makes the right decisions."[127] To be sure, this populism did not go uncontested. Particularly those former dissidents who had accepted political office and mandate from early on rebuffed the "basis ideology" as a smokescreen for the rule of the committed activist. Konrad Weiss of Democracy Now, a prominent advocate of party-building, says it clearly: "If the citizen movement refuses to say 'yes' to power it is bound to degenerate into a memory club of the Revolution."[128]

The conflict between organizational efficiency and participatory ideology is a general dilemma of left-wing grass-roots movements.[129] The specific East German context, however, brought additional factors into play. It was mostly the New Forum that blocked the process of party-building and refused to abandon its organizational autonomy. In fact, in size and public recognition the New Forum far outweighed the other opposition groups, such as Democracy Now or the Initiative for Peace and Human Rights. In late 1990, the New Forum had local chapters in 80 per cent of the eastern municipal districts (*Kreise*), and its membership was estimated at 10 000. By contrast, the other groups hardly stretched beyond East Berlin and had at best a total of a few hundred members (Enbergs, 1990). No wonder that the New Forum showed little enthusiasm for abandoning its emblematic name and merging with the other groups, which on their part had less to lose and more to gain from party-building. The result, however, was a nasty quibble over names and statutes, just when the sad conditions of post-communist eastern Germany called for programs and action. At the state (*Landtag*) elections in October 1990, for instance, the citizen movement presented itself in chaotic fragmentation – in Saxony as the New Forum–Alliance–Greens, in Thuringia as the Alliance 90–The Greens, in Saxony-Anhalt as Green List–New Forum, and so on.[130] In Mecklenburg-Vorpommern, the citizen movement was split in no less than three separate lists, which received a combined nine per cent of the vote, but failed to enter the state parliament because each list remained well below the five per cent hurdle.

The most serious obstacle to adjusting to the post-unity conditions arose from a stubborn commitment to a politics of consensus, which echoed both the Rousseauian underpinnings of communist ideology and the old German dislike of liberalism. A pamphlet of Democracy Now reflects the genuine enthusiasm about newly gained democratic rights, but also expresses a characteristic uneasiness about interest conflict: "Democratic argumentation is precise, parsimonious, and lean... It is not based on merely partial interests, because tackling an issue without the consent of the opponents would only bring harm. Instead, democratic argumentation is interested in truth."[131] From this angle, secular party conflict and parliamentary debate was certain to be received with distaste. A deputy of the New Forum recounts his experience in Berlin's state parliament (*Senat*): "We reject these parliamentary mud battles, this conflict for the sake of conflict, where everything is predetermined by party dictate, and where true discussion does not take place."[132] Instead, the citizen movement tried to stay aloof from party antagonisms, presenting itself as a party-transcendent force of "Citizens for Citizens."[133] As a leader of the New Forum put it, the citizen movement was more like an "umpire" than a "party," and it spoke to all those who disliked the "party quarrels."[134]

Therefore, it cannot surprise that the Round Table of the transition period was retroactively elevated into the "hour of authentic democracy."[135] Here the search for consensus had overridden divisions of interest. So great was the mystique of the Round Table as a platform of cooperation and consensus that a leader of Democracy Now even called for a refashioning of the citizen movement as an all-German

Initiative Movement 'Round Tables'.[136] Along these lines, some Berlin dissident leaders founded, in August 1990, the Round Table From Below, which claimed to represent all those who were "socially disadvantaged" by German reunification. Bärbel Bohley defended this initiative in revealing terms: "At the Round Table, people cooperate. Here the focus is on the issues, not on power."[137]

There was yet another reason for Round Table nostalgia. The Round Table symbolized the personalized power structures of a Leninist regime, which the opposition groups had learned to cope with and which even had lent them a certain importance that they now lacked.[138] In the old regime, dissidents knew their opponents, and the repression showed them indirectly that opposition mattered. In the new liberal democratic context, power no longer had recognizable names and faces, and no one took notice of those who did not comply with the official rules. "Now we can do what we want," says a frustrated co-founder of the New Forum, "but nobody cares. Now as before there are rulers who do things we do not like. But they are harder to identify and to grasp, they forever slip through our fingers."[139]

These adjustment problems should not conceal the fact that the rejection of *realpolitik* remained confined to a dwindling, if vocal, minority in the citizen movement. In the long run, the remains of the opposition groups of fall 1989 will hardly escape the fate of the West German Greens, and adjust to the exigencies of electoral politics. Not surprisingly, the push for *realpolitik* originated from the elected deputies of the citizen movement, most notably the small Bundestag faction of the Alliance 90. And where the adjustment was made, the results are respectable. In the eastern state of Brandenburg, for instance, which until recently was governed by a coalition of SPD, FDP and Alliance 90, certain elements of the Round Table's Social Charter and Constitution Outline were incorporated in the state's constitution, and the two ministers of the Alliance 90 have left clear imprints on their education and environment resorts. The Alliance 90, which attained formal party status in October 1991 and officially merged with the Green Party in January 1993, has been keenly aware that its refusal to do so would have spelled the end of even the last remains of the citizen movement (see Wiegols, 1993). And considering that right-wing extremists and Neo-Nazis have now taken over the torch of regime opposition in Germany's east, the virtues of an uncompromising "politics from below" are increasingly difficult to see. In view of burned-down asylum shelters and a raging street mob, the "basis" might turn out to be not democracy's friend, but its foe.

6 Why Was There No "Dissidence" in East Germany?

In Eastern Europe, intellectuals were at the forefront of the revolutionary changes of 1989. This is ironic, because intellectuals had played a leading role in creating the regime they later helped to demolish. Since communism was ultimately based on ideas ("logocracy" says Milosz), the abandonment of these ideas by intellectuals-turned-dissidents was a critical factor in the regime's demise. As Daniel Chirot (1991:20) emphasizes, more than from its economic malaise or the pressure of organized opposition movements, communism died from ideological exhaustion and "utter moral rot."[1] The dissident intellectuals, powerless as they seemed to be, delivered the decisive blow by denouncing the regime's underlying ideology as ritualized lies out of touch with reality.

When intellectuals in Eastern Europe adopted the role of dissidents, they also fundamentally revised the political role played by intellectuals since their first appearance as a corporate group in the age of the French revolution. Tocqueville (1955:140) noted that the "men of letters" who had taken the political lead during the last phase of the ancien regime tended to "indulge in abstract theories and generalizations" and to be "quite out of touch with practical politics."[2] Ever since, and dramatized by 1917, the "intellectual mode" had been "proselytism, moral mission, and cultural crusade" (Bauman, 1987:174), that is, to make the world safe for abstract reason.[3] In this light, the renunciation of utopia by Eastern European intellectuals was also an extraordinary act of self-denial. In Michael Walzer's (1988) terms, Eastern European intellectuals abandoned the role of the "stereotypical leftist critic" who cuts himself off from his society to discover truth and universal values. Instead, they adopted the role of the "national-popular" critic, who remains grounded in his society and, like Hamlet's glass, turns his society's eyes into its very soul. This conversion prepared the "heroic comeback" of the intellectuals in 1989 (Lepenies, 1990:12).

In abrogating utopia and shedding the pretensions of virtuoso activism and privileged access to truth, Eastern European dissidents moved out of the doctrinary orbit of communism. As Elemer Hankiss (1990:273) put it, the "freedom" so achieved was an "ironical" one, and it consisted of a new-won capability to "think in alternatives." To be sure, any alternative to communist regimes, with their disregard for civil liberties and national self-determination, could not but aspire to the model of the constitutional regimes of the West, with their stress on the rule of law and political pluralism. This led to the ironic yet consequent result that dissidents adopted a language which in the West was used by the political center to calm down an agitated periphery: the open society was held against the straitjacket of utopianism; defensive antipolitics took the place of virtuoso activism; and the personal should not be political but be rescued from politics. To put it with Gyorgi Konrad, the alternative to communism was to obtain "what the West already [had]" (quoted in Kennedy, 1992:63).[4]

The turn from revisionism to dissidence as premier mode of communist opposition politics also implied the invocation of national discourse, thus tapping the most powerful resource in the exit from communist rule. Without national discourse the dissident quest for human rights and citizenship was bound to lack political concretion; the collectivity had to be defined in which these rights and citizenship were to be effective. In a world of "bounded citizenries" (Brubaker, 1992), the concept of nation forms the logical complement to the concept of citizenship rights, because nations are the collectivities within which these rights are actualized. The nation is individual self-determination transposed to the level of the collectivity: it is the "self" if self-determination is to have a political sense (see Bubner, 1991:15). Nationalism so understood permitted the bundling of the grievances of society under communism, such as the forced disruption of tradition and cultural identity: nationalism was the memory that withstood the force of organized forgetting.

Compared with Eastern European intellectuals, the fate of East German intellectuals has been less fortunate. As Wolf Lepenies (1990:13) states, "the heroes of the (East German) revolution ... were not intellectuals." In East Germany, intellectuals did not become dissidents in the Eastern European sense. In fact, the resulting lack of an indigenous counter-élite with popular legitimacy facilitated the rapid extinction of East Germany's statehood. Why did East German intellectuals remain basically loyal to the communist regime, and why did even the existing opposition groups not turn to the "ironical freedom" of dissidence? It must be noted that East German exceptionalism does *not* consist in the numerical weakness and societal insulation of regime opposition, which East Germany shares with Hungary or Czechoslovakia. Instead, East Germany was different because the decisive step from revisionism to dissidence as premier mode of communist opposition politics was not taken.

A common explanation of East German exceptionalism refers to geopolitical factors, such as East Germany's "front state" status, which would make less polite forms of regime opposition self-defeating. But if revisionist rhetoric was only "tactically" motivated (Philipsen, 1993:88), why was it not simply dropped once the geopolitical environment had radically changed in 1989? A more sophisticated rational-actor account, which also stresses East Germany's geopolitical location, operates with Albert Hirschman's ingenious exit-voice model.[5] According to this model, the available option to "exit" to West Germany has forever undermined the consolidation of a "voice" opposition in East Germany: "Exit tends to undermine voice, particularly ... when exit deprives the potential carriers of voice of their most articulate and influential members" (Hirschman, 1993:176). This explanation has some undeniable plausibility. The exit-conditioned leadership fluctuation has prevented the continuities and cumulative learning experiences that helped stabilize regime oppositions in Eastern European countries. We must not forget that most prominent Eastern European dissidents, from Sakharov to Michnik, had started as socialists, and that only the repeated disappointment of reform hopes turned them away from socialism. This continuous experience was not available in East Germany, where the regime even deliberately used the exit valve to hold down its domestic opposition. While the exit-voice model helps explain the organizational fragmentation and numerical weakness of opposition, and – as demonstrated above – is helpful to analyze the dynamics of the regime-breakdown in 1989, it still falls short of explaining the peculiar *mode* of regime opposition in East Germany: the maintenance of socialist revisionism. For instance, the exit-voice model is insensitive to the fact that most "articulate and influential" voice oppositionists lost through exit became "dissidents" proper only *after* their expulsion from the GDR, when the "capitalism" verdict acquired in the East melted away in the light of new-won rights and opportunities.

If we want to explain why revisionism prevailed in East German opposition politics, we must move beyond the formalistic exit-voice model to an appreciation of the historical and cultural context that made East Germany different. As already intimated throughout, East Germany was different in that national discourse[6] could not be mobilized against communist rule. Thus there was no language for oppositionists to "think in alternatives." The historical separation of the German concept of nation from civic principles of liberty and democracy, which was completed by Nazism, made a "national" opposition to communism impossible; the divided post-war nation became couched in a Manichaean dualism of capitalism versus socialism that proved immune to revision and even secured the GDR an irredeemable advantage. The Hungarian dissident Miklos Haraszti (1987:160) once argued that the opposition in his country was helped by the fact that Hungarian communism did not exist *sui generis*: "Communism... was imposed upon us by an invading and then occupying foreign army. Dissent, however feeble, can at least draw upon a democratic past" (p. 160). This it could not do in East Germany, where all reference to the past became overshadowed by Nazism. Nazism even obliterated the fact that the GDR was an occupied country. As oppositionist Bärbel Bohley put it, "we always thought (the occupation) serves us right. Why did we have to start WW II?"[7] In turn, in its "antifascist" clothing East German communism was *sui generis* like nowhere else in Eastern Europe – at least in the view of most intellectuals. Communism meant redemption from the sins of the past: organized forgetting was welcomed here. Against this backdrop, regime opposition had to be a paradoxical "opposition against the own consent," as the playwright Heiner Müller (1990:93) aptly put it.

The following sections further explore why "dissidence" could not occur in East Germany. I explain this outcome in reference to both "push" and "pull" factors. On the "pull" side, there was no legitimate national discourse that could be mobilized against the communist regime. On the "push" side, socialism had indigenous roots in German culture, which could be uniquely preserved in a society that defined itself as socialist, and which made it particularly difficult for intellectuals to abandon it. In historical analysis, single-factor explanations are always incomplete, as would be an account of East German exceptionalism that brackets its *German* component.

THE DELEGITIMIZATION OF NATIONAL DISCOURSE

In her imposing study of Soviet dissent, Ludmilla Alexeyeva (1987:451) gets to the core of the meaning of "dissidence." Dissidence, she argues, abandons existing ideological schemes and "start(s) from the very beginning;" it is grounded in a basic "social instinct" to escape lies and manipulation, and operates in moral rather than political terms, "so that righteous persons and not politicians emerged" (ibid.). Interesting are some of the comparisons she draws, such as Gandhi's opposition to British rule in India, the resistance of the early Christians in the Roman Empire, or the black civil rights movement in the United States. Obviously, demands for rights and liberty are always raised by, or in the name of, a bounded collectivity. In Eastern Europe, this collectivity has been the "nation." In East Germany, there could be no dissidence proper because no unambiguous "nation" existed in which it could be grounded. For historical reasons, recourse to the German nation had become inconceivable for democratic movements; and if one accepted the regime's definition of membership, as most opposition groups indeed did, one was caught in the socialist self-definition of the "GDR."

The German Concept of Nation

In the modern world, it is inconceivable not to be the member of a nation. As Ernest Gellner (1983:6) put it, "a man must have a nationality as he must have a nose and two ears." While nations always present themselves in the "primordial" form of language, ethnicity or history (Smith, 1986), they are also constructed and thus amenable to reconstruction and change. Following Pierre Bourdieu, it is useful to conceive of the nation not as a fixed entity or thing but as a discursive "field of struggles," in which competing forces try to define and redefine its content and boundary.[8] Along these lines, Katherine Verdery (1993:41) sees "nation as a construct, whose meaning is never stable but shifts with the changing balance of social forces." Such a "constructivist" view of the nation allows one to see the shifting meaning of nation over time, and to look at these shifts as the outcome of social struggles. But there are certain parameters within which the struggle over the meaning of nation occurs. In substantial regard, there is a general tension in the concept of nation between the civic component of plurality and the ethnic component of unity; in temporal regard, past outcomes successively narrow down the possible range of future revision.

One may reconstruct the development of the German concept of nation as the successive depletion of its civic component, culminating in the assault of the ethno-racial *Volksgemeinschaft* on the civic *Weltgesellschaft*. This is ironic, because the modern concept of nation was born under the civic premises of citizenship and democracy. But since its inception in the romantic reaction to the Enlightenment, the German concept of nation presented itself as an ethnic countermodel to the civic nations of the West (see Greenfeld,1992:ch.4). Friedrich Meinecke's (1970) classic distinction of "state nation" (*Staatsnation*) and "cultural nation" (*Kulturnation*) is still helpful to make sense of this essential difference. In the nation-states of the West, the processes of state- and nation-building coincided, so that the nation became defined through the political principles of constitution and citizenship. In Germany, where for historical and geopolitical reasons the process of state-building occurred belatedly and remained incomplete, the nation became defined as a prepolitical community of culture, language and ethnicity. While itself a historical outcome conditioned by Germany's relative backwardness *vis-à-vis* its Western neighbors, this ethno-cultural notion of nationhood became perpetuated over time, and it planted the seeds for the xenophobia and racial exclusivism with which the meaning of "German" has remained associated ever since (see Hoffmann, 1990). When German nationalism first emerged under liberal premises in the Napoleonic period, it was already the "anti-French" cause, thus putting the ethnic over the civic component. Heinrich Heine, himself an exponent of liberal nationalism, noticed this ethnic bias early on when he compared the cosmopolitan patriotism of the French with the parochial patriotism of the German, "who hates all that is foreign, and no longer wants to be a citizen of the world or a European, but only a narrow German."[9]

While the ethnocultural component was dominant from the outset, the meaning and boundary of the nation was still subject to conflict and change. The changing face of German nationalism represents *in extremis* the development of European nationalism in the nineteenth and early twentieth centuries.[10] One may differentiate between an early "liberal" phase, which culminated in the aborted revolution of 1848, and in which the concept of nation stood for the democratic transformation of the feudal order; a conservative middle-phase of "official nationalism," which became dominant with the foundation of the German Reich in 1871, and in which traditional élites used national rhetoric to repress the democratic opposition at home while fostering military aggression abroad; and a militant third phase of "integral nationalism," which peaked with the Nazi movement, and in which the nation became a weapon in the struggle of the extremist right against the liberal-democratic order of the Weimar Republic. At the endpoint of this development the notions of nation and democracy had become antithetical.

Since the foundation of the first German nation-state under Bismarck, democratic reform movements in Germany not only could not invoke national discourse, but were even denounced by the established élites as "antinational" forces. As is well known, one of the characteristics of German pol-

itical development is the intertwining of nation-state building and the rise of the socialist working-class movement (see
Conze and Groh, 1966). The initial alliance between liberal
bourgeoisie and socialist working-class for a democratic nation-state was blunted by Bismarck's "revolution from above,"
with the result of turning the bourgeoisie into an appendix
of the autocratic order, and excluding the Social Democrats
as *Reichsfeinde* (enemies of the Reich) from the first German nation-state. This was a crucial historical juncture, because national unity, which had previously been associated
with democratic emancipation, could be reached only under
non-democratic premises. The "nation" now lost all democratic connotations, and turned into a particularistic "status
ideology" (Mommsen, 1990:13) of the traditional élites allied with Bismarck. Conze and Groh (1966:115) rightly argue that it was more an "excess" than a "deficit" of "national
energies" that prevented the socialist working-class movement from identifying with the first German nation-state.
But the delicate distinction between national patriotism and
state opposition proved difficult to maintain, and the working-class movement now redirected its "national energies"
into Marxist internationalism.

At this historical juncture, the German concept of nation
took on some lasting characteristics which made it unsuit-
able as an asset in democratic struggles. First, the meaning
of nation became devoid of a civic creed. "To be German,"
argues Helmut Plessner (1959:33), "was and is simply the
expression of a reality." There is no "golden era," no foundation myth, no common symbols that could bind all groups
and classes and inspire civic action across time; as it were,
the reference to Germanness is less an argument to stand
up against despotism than an explanation why despotism
was possible. An East German dissident expresses this lack
of a civic creed very clearly: "The history of our nation offers little occasion for celebration... There's no reason to
be a German other than that one already is one."[11] In lieu
of a civic creed, the instrumental values of economic success and power-political aggrandizement gave German national identity the necessary sense of direction.[12] Second,
following the ethnic "us" versus "them" code, the German
nation has primarily constituted itself *ex negativo*, through

an act of delimitation: externally in the wars against France, internally in the exclusion of certain groups such as the Social Democrats, the Catholics, or the Jews. The German concept of nation thus became more like a weapon than a unifying symbol, the property of some, but not of others. General de Gaulle once refused to arrest a heretical Sartre because he was "also France." This would be difficult to imagine in Germany, where the great heretics from Heine and Marx to Rosa Luxemburg were never acknowledged as *national* heroes, but instead were forced into emigration or murdered (see Greiffenhagen, 1986:105). This leads to the third, and decisive, point that since the late nineteenth century the nation had been the property of the political right. This became evident in the fate of the Weimar Republic, which offered the nominal chance to reconcile nation and democracy. But a host of militant new movements, which were inspired by the World War I experience and absorbed impulses of the antimodernist youth movements of the time, and of which the Nazi movement was only one, succeeded in turning national discourse into a weapon against the first German democracy. The antidemocratic "new" nationalism of the Weimar period differed from its Wilhelminian precursor in its chiliastic militancy and anti-bourgeois radicalism.[13] Its reduction of nation to blood-affiliated *Volk* carried the ethnic streak of the German concept of nation to its racist extreme, an extreme through which the latter has remained tainted ever since.

The Legacy of Nazism

While the aversion of democratic movements to the nation has deep historical roots, only the experience of Nazism lastingly excluded nationalism as a counter-discourse to communism. The German defeat in 1945 marked the deepest caesura ever experienced by a modern nation. This was the "zero hour" (*Stunde Null*) in which all historical continuities were shattered, and "renewal" was the unanimous imperative of the day. If there ever had been a common reference point in German national consciousness, it was provided by the Holocaust and the crimes of the Nazi regime. Only, this was a negative reference point which made any positive national identification impossible. Anti-nationalism became a dominant habitus, especially among the intellectuals, the category that had previously conducted and crafted national discourse in its liberal and less liberal shades. Even Chancellor Adenauer denounced nationalism as the "cancerous sore of Europe" (in Alter, 1992:164) – these were new words for a German state leader to utter. Because the old political right was destroyed and discredited, national discourse was open to restructuring. This led to interesting new conjunctions. In West Germany, the conservative CDU under Chancellor Adenauer *de facto* abandoned the ideal of national unity in favor of tying the Bonn Republic firmly into the Western alliance – never before had German conservatives sacrificed "national" goals for the sake of liberty. In turn, the Social Democratic Party under Kurt Schumacher, and later Willy Brandt, became a protagonist of national unity, even though the reentry of the left into national discourse remained cautious and incomplete. In East Germany, the Comintern Popular Front strategy moved the communists also in a national direction; but – as demonstrated above – the need for socialist self-definition eventually required all national rhetoric to be dropped. While the division of Germany naturally made the "national question" a perennial issue, the very meaning of German remained peculiarly untouched, and political ersatz identification was sought in new ideas such as European integration, socialism, or the fierce opposition to it in terms of "anticommunism."

The central problem for both German post-war states was how to demarcate themselves from the Nazi past. Identity had to be built on a delicate balance of continuity and discontinuity. A radical break with the past was needed, because otherwise no moral and political renewal was possible. On the other hand, without a basic national continuity no mastery of the past was possible, because the subject of guilt and remembrance had vanished; the complete denial of continuity would amount to exculpation. The German successor states to the Nazi regime went in opposite directions to solve this dilemma, and the strategies they chose decisively influenced the shape of opposition movements in both societies. West Germany tended toward the pole of continuity. This expressed itself in its self-understanding as the "legal successor" (*Rechtsnachfolger*) to the German Reich of 1871, and in its attempt to restore and rebuild the democratic fundaments of the Weimar Republic. This is not to deny that the need for a "total renewal" (A.Andersch) was felt as urgently in the West as in the East. But a secular regime had to abrogate utopia in favour of Popperian "piecemeal engineering." "Paradise exists only in utopian novels," said Theodor Heuss, West Germany's first president, "We shall be happy without Paradise if only we get back to the firm ground of a free life" (quoted in Alter, 1992:159). East Germany, by contrast, opted for the radical break and utopia. As Andrzej Szcypiorski puts it, the GDR was designed as a "purification from the sin of fascism" and "founded on the principles of expiation and absolution."[14] Here the task of confronting the past was not, as in West Germany, left to the moral discretion of the individual, but was elevated to the central program of state and society. Programmatic continuity was limited to the "progressive" strands in German history and culture, which the GDR claimed to inherit.[15]

Both options, the one for continuity as well as the one for a radical break, were riddled with ambiguity. *Continuity* meant the shouldering of the political and moral responsibility for the Nazi past, whose most famous symbol may be Chancellor Willy Brandt's humble bowing to the victims of the Warsaw Ghetto. No other successor state to the German Reich went through similar exercises – indeed agonies – of mastering the past, from the student movement to the Historians' Struggle. But continuity also implied the permanent suspicion that the Nazi past was not really over. Reflecting a deplorable leniency in the prosecution of Nazi criminals and a propensity to repress the immediate Nazi past,[16] the charge that "reconstruction" (*Wiederaufbau*) really meant "restoration" was raised from early on by concerned intellectuals (for example, Dirks, 1950). West Germany's radical protest culture of later years, with its peculiar proclivity to *Totalkritik* and violence, could not be understood without the ever-present Nazism-charge against the élites in society and state – "this is the generation of Auschwitz," said terrorist Gudrun Ensslin, "you cannot argue with them."[17]

Radical break meant more symbolic efforts to make a clean

severance from the past, as expressed in more rigorous measures to identify and persecute Nazi criminals. Tellingly, East German regime oppositionists have never been tempted to draw unfriendly parallels between the Nazi and communist leaderships, even though both were certainly dictatorships. On the contrary, the anti-fascism formula provided an unshakable bond between regime and opposition, up to the "For Our Country" initiative of November 1989. But behind the façade, "radical break" meant exculpation. Since anti-fascism was elevated to an official state doctrine, the whole society was automatically absolved from responsibility for the past. As Peter Bender (1989:48) notes sarcastically, "Hitler had obviously been a West German." In East German parlance, May 1945 was referred to not as "breakdown," as in the West, but as "liberation."[18] The secret truth of "radical break" was thus to exempt from responsibility and guilt. Accordingly, East Germany's communist leaders ignored Israel's claims to be compensated for the Jewish victims of the Holocaust, and they felt free to participate in military action against Czechoslovakia in 1968, and to recommend such action against Poland in 1081, the two first victims of Nazi Germany's crusade for world domination.

Regime and protest movements are thus inversely related to one another in both German post-war states. In West Germany, the relationship is a centrifugal one: the ever-present Nazism charge caused the polarization between regime and opposition, with left-wing terrorism as its most extreme, yet consequent, expression. In East Germany, the relationship is centripetal: the myth of the radical break created a basic consensus between regime and opposition. If West Germany's radical protest culture may be interpreted as belated and apocryphal resistance to Nazism, such "catching-up resistance" (Trommler, 1991) was redundant where card-carrying "anti-fascists" were the leaders of the state. When Christa Wolf was asked why a broad democracy movement had emerged only so late, she touched the core problem of regime opposition in East Germany: "This has to do with the fascist past and the partition of Germany. As very young people who had grown up under fascism, we suffered from guilt feelings. [The communists] helped us out of this. These were antifascists and communists who had returned from concentration camps, prisons, and emigration and, more than in the Federal Republic, dominated the political life in the GDR. We felt a strong inhibition to oppose people who had sat in concentration camps during the Nazi period" (Wolf, 1990:135f).

Its programmatic "antifascism" and utopian promise of redemption made East Germany the obvious choice of the intellectuals, particularly those who had been forced to flee Hitler. This was *their* state, a state devoted to a moral vision and not just the cold proceduralism of market capitalism and representative democracy. A prevalent motif at the time was that "total defeat" offered the chance of "total renewal" (see Mommsen, 1990:16). The departure to socialist utopia corresponded to this hope more intimately than the restoration of capitalism. The intellectuals operated on a basic consensus and loyalty to the communist regime, which was modified by successive generations, but never given up. Ernest Renan once remarked that part of being a nation is getting one's history wrong. The one success of East German "nation"-building was the firm and unshakable acceptance, and perpetuation, of the GDR's founding myth by the intellectuals.[19] Hans Mayer, an exile intellectual of the first hour who was also one of the first to flee the GDR, still remained convinced, in 1991, that "the bad end does not refute a – possibly – good beginning" (Mayer, 1991:15f).

While all intellectuals accepted the GDR's "antifascist" founding myth, the modalities of this acceptance differed, particularly over time and generations. For the Weimar generation of exile intellectuals, regime loyalty was the most genuine and unconditional. Anna Seghers, returning from her exile in Mexico via Frankfurt am Main, recounts that she "travelled into the eastern zone [*Ostzone*], because I was sure that my work... was needed and welcomed there in the struggle for the new society" (quoted in Franke, 1971:13). The "antifascism" of the Weimar intellectuals was genuine in that it resulted from personal experience of persecution and struggle, not from the adoption of an already established doctrine. Indeed, these intellectuals helped cement the official founding myth, often from privileged positions in the emergent cultural institutions, such as the *Kulturbund* (see Pike, 1992). For them the GDR was a chiliastic community of antifascists who had set out to "build a new world in which there is justice", as Stefan Heym (1990:75) put it. To leave this Zion of the Persecuted was out of the question. In his autobiography, Stefan Heym – maybe the most irreverent intellectual of the exile generation – admits the "fear ... of being expelled from the warmth of community, however flawed this community may be" (quoted in Noll, 1991:62).

The modalities of acceptance shifted for later generations of intellectuals. Those who had experienced war and Nazism in young age adopted the founding myth often via conversion, guilt, or submission to quasi-paternal authority. The writer Franz Fühmann, who had been drafted into Hitler's army as a high-school student, indicated that "Auschwitz" had converted him to "the other society".[20] The element of guilt and authoritarian submission is unsparingly revealed by Christa Wolf, who had been a member of *Bund deutscher Mädchen*, the Nazi female youth organization: "My generation ... has a tendency to follow authority and a compulsive need to conform, and it fears conflict with the majority and exclusion from the community. We had difficulties in growing up, in becoming independent, and standing on our own two feet".[21] For those who had been too young to be responsible for Nazism but old enough to carry a memory of involvement and guilt, the "antifascist" communist leaders represented the lost father generation. Characteristically, Christa Wolf argues that the decay from the "good beginning" set in when a "small group of anti-fascists, who ruled the country... in the conviction of being the 'victors of history', failed to explicate the... intricacies of Nazism to *their children*".[22]

Over time, the intellectual syndrome of "critical loyalty" (Domdey, 1993) shifted ever more toward the "critical" component. But "loyalty" was maintained nevertheless. The literary imagination continued to conjure up the founding myth, even though one began to realize that the "dream" had meanwhile turned into a "nightmare" (Müller, 1992:363). In the 1980s, Volker Braun compared the failing socialist project to a small iron cart turned into the uncontrollable "locomotive of history": "It was a ... small and uncomfortable cart, which we pulled out of a rotten barn near the city, and on which we climbed. We: a few down-and-outs who had barely survived, but who knew the way." Yet the "small cart" turned out to be the "locomotive of history": "The machine kept me tight ... I could not escape ... The cart would be my mausoleum, my grave".[23] This remarkable metaphor, though intended as a critique, still left the founding myth intact; the author, who was six years old in 1945, even imagines himself as a member of the heroic founding élite. The metaphor also conveys the complete absence of an alternative, which forced one – almost by fate – to stick to the once-chosen path. In his autobiographical reflections, Heiner Müller (1992:359) accepts the criticism that the "critical solidarity" displayed by the intellectuals *vis-à-vis* the regime "fed the illusion that a reform of the system was possible." But he adds: "The problem was, in my view, the lack of an alternative (*Alternativlosigkeit der Alternative*)" (ibid.). Why was there no alternative?

There was no alternative because of the German division. It perpetuated the absence of national discourse, thus burying the alternative that East German intellectuals could not find. The loyalty of intellectuals was based not only on the positive acceptance of the founding myth, but also on the negative demarcation from the other German state. Peter Brückner (1978:150) has cogently argued that in post-war Germany "the one nation became decoupled into society and its counter-society." The notion of German became peculiarly repressed, or "homeless" (ibid.,7), which was convenient because of its association with Nazism. In intellectual discourse, the dualism of capitalism and socialism came to signify both half-Germanies. Because it was fused with the problem of national identity, this dualism proved immune to revision, and it accounts for some peculiarities of intellectual culture in East *and* West Germany.

In early post-war West Germany, a virulent anti-communism provided a dearly needed ersatz identity, particularly for the political élite, which also allowed the immediate Nazi past to be repressed. When the student movement criticized the legitimizing function of official anti-communism, its critique had to be couched in "anti-anticommunist" terms (Dubiel, 1991b).[24] Peter Schneider (1993) has characterized the ensuing mindset as "thinking in the opposite" (*Denken aus dem Gegenteil*). It prevented West German intellectuals from recognizing the totalitarian aspects of the East German regime, because this was the abhorred turf of conservative anti-communism.[25] Accordingly, the Gulag Archipelago debate, which converted a great part of the French intelligentsia from Marxism to liberalism in the mid-1970s, failed to appear in West Germany. Criticizing socialism forever smacked of exculpating Nazism, and any deviation from the Manichaean socialism versus capitalism scheme would lead one into the repressed abyss of national identity. So it was more convenient to ignore Solzhenitsyn's trenchant exposure of communist terror because of the author's "nationalism", or to rail against the "Catholic-reactionary" nature of the Polish Solidarity movement (see Markovits, 1992:178f). National opposition to communism was simply unacceptable for German intellectuals, in or outside of Germany. Because the national option was excluded, the GDR always retained its socialist bonus.

Similarly, the capitalism-socialism duality muted the critical impulses of East German intellectuals. There was no alternative to the socialist regime, paradoxically, because it already existed in form of the capitalist West. This "alternative" was taboo, because it revoked the "radical break" with the German past that was seen as the GDR's decisive advantage.[26] From this angle, the preoccupation of intellectuals with the Nazi past fulfilled important legitimizing functions in the GDR, even if the results are as subtle as Christa Wolf's novel *Kindheitsmuster* of 1976. In striking similarity to the official line, intellectuals continued to portray the West as always threatened by a rebirth of Nazism. "In this way one could bear the GDR," Heiner Müller admits today (1992:312). On the opposite side, when the regime started to expatriate its opponents, as it did with Wolf Biermann in 1976, none of the protesting intellectuals drew the obvious comparison with the Nazi regime, which had pioneered this inhumane practice. This association was simply not thinkable within the capitalism-socialism scheme, because Nazism was confined to the "other" side.

The prevalence of the capitalism-socialism duality also prevented the intellectuals from recognizing the national implications of East Germany's revolution. Within this scheme, there was only the alternative of a "revolutionary renewal" (C.Wolf) or a fall-back to capitalism. "Renewal" was thus the initial enthusiastic reading of the intellectuals. In striking contrast to Eastern Europe, the enthusiasm of East German intellectuals was not about freedom from dictatorship, but about the final arrival of utopia. Christa Wolf, for instance, compared the East German upheaval to the uprising of the Paris Commune, and this through the lense of Brecht's pedagogical drama (Wolf, 1990:15). Helga Königsdorf praised the "moment of beauty, in which utopia was near": "For a moment we were so sick with happiness that we poured into the streets to turn reality into our work of art."[27] When the people abandoned the script, the intellectuals faulted the people instead of questioning their own writing. Leipzig's pro-unity demonstrations now appeared to them as the "tyranny of the bawling mass" (Fritze, 1991:561), or even as "Nazi parades" (Hörnigk, 1990:140). Devoid of a national language to tie them to their society (Offe, 1991:26), the intellectuals remained isolated from the popular forces that *intuitively* grasped the national implication of the anti-communist revolution.

Because the concept of national self-determination did not exist for German intellectuals, the extinction of the socialist GDR was perceived as the simple victory of capitalism. Agnes Heller (1990:14) argued that the image of capitalism as a "closed totality encompassing every aspect of life" was a product of "adversarial imagination." This Eastern European insight could not take hold in Germany. For a young East German intellectual, the new "capital democracy" imported from the West was "not the smaller but the other evil."[28] In a similar vein, Stefan Heym (1990:77) conjured up the rise of a "new *Grossdeutschland* dominated by Daimler-Messerschmitt-Bölkow-Blohm and the Deutsche Bank." To the imagery of a "colonizing" capitalism was added the one of Nazism reborn: the polemic notion of *Anschluss* (annexation) of East Germany to the West suggests an analogy to Nazi Germany's annexation of Austria in 1938. Andreas Hyssen (1991:122) noted in his balanced account of the heated unification debate that the "discourse of colonization" betrayed a "lack of understanding, if not contempt, for Western style democratic institutions." But it was indeed the only "discourse" available because no legitimate discourse of nationhood existed.

As the reunification debate also revealed, the political division of Germany, which was originally the contingent result of geopolitics, had tacitly turned into a moral imperative. Already in 1960, Karl Jaspers demanded the abandonment of the goal of national unity, because the principle of the nation-state was the "disaster of Europe" (Jaspers, 1960:53). He added that Germans in particular were called upon to spread the word, thus inaugurating the peculiar habitus of "negative nationalism" among contemporary German intellectuals (Reese-Schäfer, 1991). Along these lines, Günter Grass argued that Auschwitz forever prohibited the recovery of national unity: "The place of horror precludes a future German nation-state".[29] In a similar way, Jürgen Habermas argued that the break of continuity brought by Auschwitz made it impossible to conceive of the nation in ethnic terms: "With this monstrous break of continuity the Germans have lost the possibility to ground their political identity in anything other than universalistic citizenship principles" (Habermas, 1990:219f). Reunification undermined the postnational "patriotism of the constitution" (Habermas), on which Western intellectuals tried to ground the political self-understanding of Germany after Nazism. While this moral objection to reunification remained specific to the West, it epitomizes how much the legacy of Nazism had turned German intellectuals into covert or overt supporters of the second German state.

The Dilemma of Opposition

But weren't there dissidents in East Germany? What about the indefatigable activists of the peace and human rights movement of the 1980s, who displayed no less courage than the Eastern European dissidents in speaking out against repression at great personal risk? This movement was carried by a younger generation of peculiarly nameless intellectuals, who had been socialized in the post-war period and whose key experiences had been the Western student upheaval and the Prague Spring of 1968. To distinguish these younger peace and human rights activists from the established literary intellectuals, John Torpey (1993a:150) introduced the useful category of "blocked ascendents." It points to the greater disillusionment and distance of the young dissidents from the official institutions of party and state. One must note, however, that ascendence was blocked precisely because of a greater propensity to carry risk – which is altogether difficult to categorize.[30] As in Eastern Europe, the annals of the GDR opposition are not short on careers broken and life-chances forfeited. As a result of the shared experience of marginalization, a distinct dissident milieu emerged, particularly in the 1980s, which proved that more consequent forms of opposition were possible than the "critical solidarity" of the literary intellectuals.

While the elevation of opposition into a life-form separates these younger dissidents from the established intellectuals, they still did not revoke the basic loyalty to the regime. Yet their loyalty was not so much the result of a positive "antifascist" commitment as of a negative lack of alternatives. "The opposition was operating on the basis of this [antifascist] consensus," says one of the most perceptive East German dissidents, "for the simple reason that you could not abolish what you wanted to reform."[31] These dissidents had not known anything but the GDR, and they took its existence simply for granted – as did almost everybody else, including the political élites, in both Germanies at that time. Moreover, they had come of age in the era of *détente*, when the regime had systematically purged its ethnic-national component and tried to elevate socialism into a quasi-national identity. "The so-called 'national question'", says a young dissident, "was neither negatively nor positively discussed; it was taboo" (Rüddenklau, 1992:13).

Due to the lack of a national alternative, these young dissidents became caught in the regime's socialist self-definition. Their opposition to the regime was genuine, yet marred by the artificiality of the opposed regime. Even if one limited oneself to the "antipolitical" defense of elementary human rights, as particularly the Initiative for Peace and Human Rights (IFM) set out to do, one still had to define the bounded collectivity on whose behalf this defense was made. Who was this collectivity? Obviously the "East Germans," or "GDR-citizens" (*DDR-Bürger*). The German term is more fitting here, because it indicates that one was "a GDR-citizen" only by virtue of the regime's socialist self-definition. Otherwise one was simply a German. But *this* the dissidents could not even *think*, because no legitimate national discourse existed. A perceptive dissident explicates the dilemma of opposition in East Germany: "We always had a broken relationship to the concept of nation. In contrast to the opposition movements in Eastern Europe, we could not ground our opposition in the nation, but had to resort to socialist ideology instead. Therefore we were not 'against' but 'for' socialism ... One could almost believe that we became the Fifth Column of the SED."[32]

The dilemma of opposition was that without national discourse no genuine opposition to communism was possible. If one accepted the regime's definition of membership, even intentionally genuine opposition had to turn into an unintentional collusion with the regime. This "implicit loyalty to the rulers" (Rüddenklau, 1992:12) characterized even the most outspoken of all East German opposition groups, the Initiative for Peace and Human Rights (IFM). The IFM went as far in the direction of Eastern European human-rights dissidence as was possible in the GDR. Yet when confronted with the massive movement of exit petitioners, IFM experienced the limits of such opposition. Because political opposition was premised on rejecting the exit alternative, it was consequent not to make common cause with would-be emigrants. But in doing so, IFM undermined its own claim of unconditional human rights advocacy, and implicitly sided with the regime that it so adamantly opposed. Startling examples of such collusion abound. When it broke the taboo of convening with the conservative Christian Democratic Party (CDU), the IFM still rejected any Western critique of the human rights situation in the GDR, admonishing the CDU and "other state-carrying parties" to "concentrate on the improvement of the human rights situation in the Federal Republic."[33]

Though unparalleled in their fearless and outspoken opposition to the iron claw of SED-rule, the peace and human rights activists of the 1980s thus continued the collusion with the regime that had characterized the stance of East German intellectuals since 1953. Wolfgang Rüddenklau

(1992:13), no meek oppositionist he, now mocks at his and his fellow-oppositionists' "inappropriate (*verfehlte*) loyalty, about which at best a few Stasi officers may have giggled." These oppositionists are the tragic victims of the East German regime's ultimate triumph: to impose socialism as a quasi-national imperative even on its most courageous opponents.

As its quick evaporation after 1989 testifies, the socialist rhetoric in East Germany's dissident movement was at least as much the result of political context as of inherent idealism. To a certain degree even the rejection of national unification sprang from a rational perception that the "civic" and "national" dimensions of the East German revolution did not coincide. Influenced by the "new social movements" of the West, East German dissidents were committed to the civic principle of grass-roots democracy, which was at odds with the top-down imposition of the established political institutions of the West. Yet, once again, the modeling of East German regime opposition on the Western-style new social movements proved inadequate for the particular context of (post)communism. A characteristic of new social movements is their "self-limitation"; they complement rather than replace market and state (Cohen and Arato, 1992). The East German regime breakdown generated the inevitable illusion that grass-roots democracy could be more than institutional corrective and *replace* the process of institution-building. The capitalism versus socialism rhetoric nurtured by the established intellectuals obscured the real duality at work here, which was one between "civic" grass-roots democracy and "national" market- and state-building. It must be stressed that shrewd grassroots dissidents like IFM-leaders Wolfgang Templin and Gerd Poppe were quick to abandon the illusions of yesterday, and to carve out a niche for their "civic" cause in the new nation-state. While the more established intellectuals still deplore the death of "GDR culture," the marginalized and persecuted one-time dissidents are mostly free of such nostalgia, and readily admit the "many new opportunities" that exist in a liberal democracy.[34]

In an implicit attempt to destroy the image of past collusion, the former dissidents are now at the forefront of "coming to terms" with the East German past, and of drawing stark lines between "victims" and "perpetrators" (see Torpey, 1993b). In an unusual alliance with conservative anti-communists, former dissidents pressed for the opening of the Stasi files; demanded unrelenting punishment for those who, for whatever reason and in whatever position, had collaborated with the Stasi;[35] and supported the formation of the parliamentary "Commission of Inquiry into the History and Consequences of the SED Dictatorship in Germany", which seeks to reestablish the previously much-chided totalitarianism paradigm in GDR-research. In a statement entitled "Theses on the Clearing-Up [*Aufklärung*] of the Past," a group of former dissidents and Western politicians sharply rejected the campaign by the left-liberal establishment to close the painful investigation of the Stasi past: "The Germans in the West must learn that even in a dictatorship civic courage and resistance were possible."[36] When had dissidents ever called the still-existing SED regime a "dictatorship"? This new posture is evidently not free of a certain distortion of their own dissident past. Vaclav Havel argued in his dissident manifesto *The Power of the Powerless* that no neat distinction between victims and perpetrators in "post-totalitarian communism" was possible, and that everyone was "both a victim and a supporter of the system."[37] It is ironic that East Germany's dissidents, whose collusion with the old regime was unique in Eastern Europe, are now so insistent on a clear distinction of victim and perpetrator. But it reflects their marginal status in the new Germany and the understandable desire to find retroactive meaning in the now apparently quixotic quest for the true socialism.[38]

This post-festum presentation of resolute "resistance" cannot hide the fact that, as long as the GDR still existed, the dissident reality, too, was painted in grey, not in black and white. Here it is important to point out a schism between the domestic dissidents, who remained committed to the socialist project, and the exiled dissidents, who tended to overthink old positions. For instance, in his West Berlin exile the Jena peace veteran Roland Jahn realized that the ominous split between dissident groups and would-be emigrants had to be overcome if opposition was to become more effective. In turn, East Berlin's opposition leaders jealously declined such outside intervention (Rüddenklau, 1992:172f).

If East Germany had generated "dissidents" in the Eastern European sense of the word it was the ones who had forcibly or voluntarily left the GDR, even though this conversion occurred only after the fact. The exiled dissidents were *personae non gratae* in Eastern and Western intellectual opposition circles alike. From the Eastern perspective, the ones who left "betrayed" the ones who were left behind.[39] Reiner Kunze, who was expatriated in 1977, says with bitterness that "those who stayed expatriated us once more with their silence" (quoted in Anz, 1991:12). Only, "silence" was not the worst response. A leading East Berlin peace activist indicted the freshly exiled song-writer Stephan Krawczyk for his lack of interest in the "political prisoners in the FRG", thus drawing a strange parallel between Western terrorists and Eastern oppositionists.[40] And the Western reception of exiled dissidents was less than warm. The latter were tainted by the stigma of anticommunism. Consequently, the exiled dissidents were kept out when Eastern and Western writers exercised their ghostly peace ceremonies in the early 1980s, and a post-Wall reunion of Eastern and Western writers in Potsdam included the former minister of censorship, but not the "revanchist" exiled dissident writers.[41]

The exiled dissidents were the only intellectuals who could emancipate themselves from "thinking in the opposite" (P.Schneider), the mindset that a truth was not a truth if the political opponent also held it. Accordingly, exiled dissidents, no rightists they, did not hesitate to use conservative newspapers, such as *Die Welt* or *Frankfurter Allgemeine Zeitung*, as platforms for their views. What is the reason for this relaxed attitude? Those who had left the GDR, whether voluntarily or not, simply discovered that they had not changed the country. Hans-Joachim Schädlich, who had moved from East to West Berlin in 1977, explains: "I have not changed the country, not even the city; I have only changed the political system".[42] In fact, most exiled dissidents rejected the very notion of exile; even Wolf Biermann, who initially had claimed that a "violent deportation to Moscow" would have been "less of an exile" for him, later changed his mind (see Serke, 1985:35-53). However grudgingly, exiled dissidents realized that West Germany was not just capitalism but a democracy that offered some advantages over the regime that had forced them out. At the same time, they began to look at communist regimes with unsentimental eyes – as "simple dictatorship" (J.Fuchs) or "pedagogical prison" (W.Biermann).[43] Czeslaw Milosz, that quintessential dissident, once admitted that in the West too there was pressure to conform: "The difference is that in the West one may resist such pressure without being held guilty of a mortal sin" (Milosz, 1953:XIII). In Germany, this simple truth, which is inaccessible within the capitalism-socialism scheme, was open only to the exiled dissidents. Who but an exiled dissident, such as Jürgen Fuchs (1990:75), would admit that a "pluralist democracy" was preferable to "dictatorship, whether right or pseudoleft"?[44] Only exiled dissidents managed to reconcile what remained separate for the rest: nationhood and democracy.[45]

GERMAN CONTINUITIES

As Gordon A.Craig demonstrated with much success in his panoramic reflections on *The Germans*, historical analysis in general, and of Germany in particular, is necessarily a "balancing act" between the "contesting claims of change and continuity" (Craig, 1982:11). So far, this account of East German exceptionalism has stressed the discontinuities, or "pull" factors, which kept East German dissidents within the orbit of communism – most notably the lack of a legitimate national discourse. But there are, in addition, important continuities of German culture, or "push" factors, which contributed to this outcome. Archie Brown and Jack Gray (1977) have argued in their seminal work on political culture in communism that communist regimes, contrary to their intention, have not succeeded in extinguishing the national cultural traits of their host societies. On the contrary, these authors observed that the "official" communist culture and the "dominant" national cultures have remained "mutually antagonistic" (ibid.,257). Applied to the German case, this statement is both true and untrue. It is true in the sense that East Germany, in contrast to the "Westernized" Federal Republic, has remained in many ways traditionally "German." In fact, the peculiar GDR nostalgia of some West German intellectuals stems from an infatuation with the "slower speed of life" (Grass, 1990:17), if not the rediscovery of one's own "lost soul" (Bender, 1989:120f) in a society that has remained largely untouched by the winds of modernization. In the late 1970s, when the Western ennui with progress and consumption had reached a peak, a typical visitor to the GDR would be struck by "this first, deep feeling of once-upon-a-time" (Krüger, 1977:244); the romantically minded could find his *fremde heimat* there.

Yet in one important regard Brown and Gray's observation does not fit the German case: communism and national culture are not entirely "antagonistic" in Germany. Why should one be surprised that German intellectuals have been unwilling to abandon Marxist socialism, which is, after all, a German tradition? In a provocative analysis, Liah Greenfeld (1992:ch.4) has demonstrated that Marxist socialism inherits key motifs of German romantic nationalism. Both share the anti-Western thrust (transmuted as "anti-capitalism" in Marxism), both subordinate the individual and her liberties to the collective requirements of *volk* or class, both depict the modern individual as alienated from her true nature but awaiting complete transformation in a perfect society that is yet to come, and, finally, both accord the intellectuals a cardinal role in this transformation (ibid.,386f). If one studies the peculiar affection of German intellectuals for the experiment of socialism on earth, and particularly their fierce resistance to abandoning this experiment after 1989, one cannot help but conclude that subterranean "push" factors are at work here that have deep roots in German culture.

The "third way" rhetoric in the unification debate, particularly, may be looked at as an implicit continuation of the German *sonderweg* between east and west.[46] It is sometimes overlooked that the notion of *sonderweg* was not invented by historians, but originally referred to the conscious self-delimitation of German intellectual culture from the West.[47] The roots of this self-delimitation go back to the romantic reaction to the Enlightenment. In a resentiment-laden "transvaluation of values", the intellectuals of backward Germany transformed the values of the developed West, such as progress, reason and individualism, into the evils of mechanization, calculation and egotism (Greenfeld, 1985:159). At the same time, they introduced organicist and collectivist conceptions of individual and society, and looked at history not as universal progress but as the realization of national *besonderheit.* The self-proclaimed difference between Germany and the West became enshrined in the dualism of "culture" and "civilization."[48] In his *Reflections of an Unpolitical,* Thomas Mann delivered the classic formulation of this dualism: "The difference of spirit and politics includes the difference of culture and civilization, soul and society, freedom and the right to vote, art and literature; and Germanness is culture, soul, freedom, art, and *not* civilization, society, the right to vote, and literature" (Mann, 1988:23).

As in Thomas Mann's classic statement of the German *sonderweg,* the rejection of the West is coupled with a peculiar rejection of politics as secular interest conflict. Because both motifs became expressed in the defense of a separate GDR, it is useful to further illuminate their historical background. In contrast to Britain or France, where intellectuals were integrated into the world of democratic politics early on, German intellectuals, after the defeat of their democratic aspirations in 1848, turned away from politics.[49] In the shadow of the autocratic state, which often employed them as teachers, bureaucrats or priests, the intellectuals developed into a self-conscious "mandarin élite" (Ringer, 1969) that combined a strong distaste for interest politics with a penchant for impractical learning (*Bildung*) and the refinement of the spirit. Thomas Mann, now distancing himself from his earlier diatribe against the West, characterized the ensuing intellectual habitus as one of "power-protected inwardness" (*machtgeschützte Innerlichkeit*). It drew a sharp distinction between *geist* and *macht,* the inward realm of artistic creativity and scholastic learning, and the outward realm of pure power and *realpolitik.* This habitus nourished a pessimistic attitude toward modern social conditions – the genre of *zivilisationskritik* and the pessimism of modern German sociology have their origins here (Hughes, 1958). The aversion to market and politics, which also reflected the provincial closure of the German "home towns" in which most mandarin intellectuals lived (see Craig, 1982:24), made them receptive to utopian fantasies, such as *völkisch* nationalism.

The infamous "ideas of 1914" were mandarin ideas: the death of politics, the triumph of ultimate, apolitical objectives over short-range interests, and the reassertion of moral cohesion and social unity against the "materialism" of Wilhelminian modernity (Ringer, 1969:180f).

Jürgen Habermas (1986) pointed out that the mandarin duality of spirit and power left no room for the institution-alization of the role of the modern intellectual, who is situ-ated in the space *between* spirit and power. Indeed, in the world of mandarins the intellectual was a despised figure who stood for the shallow rationalism of the West. For young Thomas Mann, an intellectual was "someone who fights on the side of civilization against the 'sword', that is, Germany" (Mann, 1988:51). When in *fin-de-siècle* France *les intellectuels* forcefully entered the political scene in defense of the Jew-ish General Dreyfus, in Germany there were only counter-intellectuals – no intellectuals. As Martin Greiffenhagen (1986:107) noted, political impotence generated the syndrome of "bourgeois self-hatred"; German intellectuals denied them-selves *as* intellectuals. Most paradoxically of all, their noisy withdrawal from politics went along with a moral elevation above all politics, which was itself presented in distinctively political terms – as in Mann's anti-French propaganda trea-tise entitled *Reflections of an Unpolitical*.

Only in post-war Germany, where right-wing thinking was thoroughly discredited, could intellectuals achieve a recog-nized status in society: in the West, after 1968, as French-style critics of power; in the East, from the start, as actual participants in power, ambitiously claiming to have overcome the mandarin duality of spirit and power. These obvious discontinuities could obscure the fact that central motifs of mandarin culture remained alive, only migrating from the right to the left wing of the political spectrum. Utopianism, the flip-side of the unpolitical tradition, was even subterraneously reanimated by the defeat of Nazism. In the West, a left-Catholic intellectual argued that the meaning of the "second republic," originally nothing but a military occupation regime, lay in the future, not the present, and that this meaning had to be found via "productive utopia" (Dirks, 1946:15). But the true place of utopia was the East. Still in 1989, intellectuals would depict the GDR in the dual terms of *traum* (dream) and *alptraum* (nightmare): "*Traum* stands against *alptraum*", says Günter Grass (1991:37) in his defense of a "third way"; "a *traum* which history has turned into an *alptraum*", says Heiner Müller (1992:363) about the late GDR; "the GDR was an utopia ... [A] German possibility went to ruin here", Hans Mayer similarly concludes (1991:258). Nazism, or the capitalist West as its successor, figures as the negative reference point, the *alptraum*, against which the *traum* unfolds. In Christa Wolf's defense of the Warsaw Pact invasion of Czechoslovakia, socialism appeared as "the solution" (*die Lösung*) that had to be defended against its enemies (quoted in Domdey, 1993:165). In all these accounts, the GDR figures as an unpolitical republic of the spirit, always at risk of being swallowed by a predatory West. Irritated by the elusive search for a "third way" in the unification debate, a perceptive American observer diagnosed the continued longing of German intellectuals "for the all-encompassing solution, the total transformation of politics and economics, the definitive answer, the new – and completely moral – human being" (Markovits, 1992:185).

One of the most obvious continuations of mandarin motifs is the pessimistic genre of *zivilisationskritik*, which likewise migrated from the right to the left side of the political spectrum. The apocalyptic visions of the ecology and peace movements, combined with startling anti-Western (particularly anti-American) and crypto-nationalist rhetoric, have some similarities with the beliefs of the right-wing movements of the Weimar Republic, such as the "conservative revolution".[50] In East Germany, the cultural pessimism of the peace movement and its intellectual allies helped obscure the *specific* shortcomings of the communist regime. The discontent with "real socialism" was broadened into an all-out attack on "industrialism." The disenchantment with growth and progress could even be turned into a new legitimacy for the communist regime. Now that the image of progress had exhausted itself and the economic superiority of the West could no longer be challenged, the GDR could still be defended as a refuge of slowness and contemplation amid the catastrophic self-destruction of Western civilization. The later work of East German literary intellectuals like Heiner Müller or Christa Wolf borrowed typical motifs of German *zivilisationskritik* to demarcate an idyllic and communal GDR from a materialistic West. As two literary critics observed in an analysis of this work, "the tradition of antifascism as legitimacy of socialism is transformed into an antirationalism as legitimacy for the opposition to Westernization" (Herzinger and Preusser, 1991:199). Christa Wolf, for instance, now saw herself "standing aghast before the objectified dreams of that instrumental thinking which still calls itself reason", nevertheless detecting an "utopian rest, never quite illuminated (*aufgeklärt*)" (in Emmerich, 1989:270,275). If the main problem in communism was not the lack of civil rights and democracy, but the "pure utilitarianism (*blanker Nützlichkeitswahn*) of the industrial age" (C.Wolf, in ibid.,270), the communist regime was exculpated.

In historical perspective, the "third way" rhetoric, which was so innocently used in the opposition to unification, has rather dubious precursors (see Jesse, 1992). When Fritz Stern (1961:254) observed a German penchant for "thinking in thirds", of course he meant the reactionary "politics of cultural despair" that had foreshadowed Nazism. Möller van den Bruck, the proto-fascist ideologue of the "conservative revolution," had first popularized the notion of third way in his option for a "Germanic socialism," which was corporatist and anti-modernist. Indeed, National Socialism may be looked at as the other "blossom" of the "Blue Flower" of German romanticism (Greenfeld, 1992:386–95), and the familiar juxtaposition of Marxism and a conveniently anonymized "fascism" in German intellectual discourse helps obscure the common roots of both. The multiple discontinuities in modern German history have prevented an awareness of such cultural affinities. But one of East German communism's most secret sources of stability was its exploitation of cultural traits that had also made Nazism possible: the deep German affront against western "civilization" and its "formal" democracy.[51]

While such cultural continuities are hard to deny, it is more difficult to assess how important they were in keeping East German intellectuals tied to the socialist project. Three reservations should be mentioned. First, the fact that West German intellectuals, initially at least, also rejected unification and argued in favor of a reformed socialist GDR, suggests the primacy of the national question, most notably the long-held animus against nation-state and nationalism that had grown out of the experience of Nazism. Otherwise, one would be forced to put forward the questionable argument that the political and cultural Westernization of the Federal Republic had been unable to root out quasi-genetic Germanness. Secondly, the Slavic cultures of Eastern Europe are hardly more inherently democratic than German culture – all suffer from a democratic deficit if compared with the West. If Eastern Europe nevertheless produced genuine "dissidence," while East Germany did not, the essential difference between them seems to be that only Eastern European dissidents had viable nations to fall back on. Finally, no neat distinction between discontinuous "pull" factors and continuous "push" factors can be made, because the cultural continuities suggested here have themselves been involved in producing the aberrant features of German nationhood and nationalism discussed above. Yet the distinction can still be defended in heuristic terms. It allows us to see a striking dissonance between the explicit claims of German intellectuals and the implicit cultural sources that feed these claims; try as they might, German intellectuals could not escape their culture, some of whose more horrible aspects they so emphatically disclaimed.

1989 AND BEYOND

The East German revolution offered a unique historical opportunity to the Germans: to reconcile, for the first time in their history, the principles of nationhood and democracy. The East German democracy movement *could* have delivered the retroactive founding myth that the Bonn republic had lacked.[52] The German division was as artificial and provisional as the Cold War on which it was based. In principle, only the recovery of nationhood reinstated the "historically responsible subject for the catastrophe of Nazism" (Oevermann, 1990:100), and with it the "collective ability to remember" (Bohrer, 1991:81).

The story of this book suggests that the chance has been missed. The inertia of history and culture has led the East

German democracy movement and its intellectual leaders to *misperceive* the end of communism as "revolutionary renewal." Because the democracy movement sees itself as the loser of 1989, the nation-state it inadvertently helped bring about will remain unloved for time to come. Not unlike the socialist movement and its intellectual leaders in the Weimar Republic, this is not *their* republic. The stability of the democratic nation-states in the West rests not least on their consensual founding myths – the Storming of the Bastille and the American Declaration of Independence are unceasing fountains of national cohesion, reinforcing the ties of the national collectivity in an atmosphere of collective happiness and sacred commemoration of the roots of liberty. It is questionable if the 3rd of October, the Day of German Unity, will ever be the unambiguous "Day of Liberty" for the Germans, as Timothy Garton Ash (1990f:12) hopes; to be sure, the quality of "civil, civilian, civilized" that the sympathetic British observer attributes to the grave and understated official founding ceremony in 1990 suits a nation that had brought tragedy to the world and to itself.

While there are good reasons to deplore the rushed and bureaucratic modalities of the unification process, the bitter words "colonization" and "annexation" reveal more about their users than about the reality depicted in these terms. John Torpey (1993a:333) aptly characterized East German dissidents as a "virtuous but ever embattled sect", a "moral minority" that forever failed to transcend its own narrow milieu. "We all knew," admits a former dissident, "that the majority of the populace had quite different goals than to build the true socialism" (Rüddenklau, 1992:12). Against this backdrop, one must see the failure of the dissidents to direct the future of postcommunist eastern Germany with less sentimentality. A case in point is their much-deplored failure to bring about a new constitution, which simply reflects the marginal status of the dissidents in the old society and in the transition process. This is not to diminish the important attempts by the former dissidents, particularly of the parliamentary Alliance 90, to bring their civic legacy to bear on the new Germany, and to correct the ethnic bias of German nationhood by means of liberal laws on immigration, asylum and citizenship. But these attempts still breathe

the old disaffection with the nation. For instance, the constitution drafted by the dissident-influenced "Curatorium for a Democratic Federation of German States" claims to express "not only the fundamental rights of all Germans, but those of all persons."[53] This amounts to the paradoxical attempt at nation-building via bracketing the national component, and entails a vision of global citizenship that is morally irreproachable but politically not viable.

As long as the very meaning of Germanness is not positively associated with the principle of democracy, the new nation-state will remain precarious.[54] As Karl-Heinz Bohrer says sarcastically, Germany's left-liberal intellectuals still mistake the loss of the concept of nation for "advanced political rationality" (Bohrer, 1991:74). The political ramifications of this are obvious. Because the left refuses to reconcile itself with the concept of nation, it is up for grabs by the political right that is being reborn in the turmoils of post-unity Germany. It is precisely the as yet undefined meaning of nationhood in unified Germany that allows the recent neo-Nazi youth movements to smear the discourse of nationhood, with the dreadful tune of racism and xenophobia – there is nothing inevitable about this.[55]

Against this backdrop, the failure of intellectuals to reorient themselves in a world beyond capitalism and socialism is not a small one. After 1989, as Willy Brandt put it aptly, "nothing will be as it was before."[56] The end of socialism is also the end of a view of capitalism as a "closed totality" (A.Heller) that suggested the possibility of a complete alternative. It is the great political insight of Eastern European dissidents that in the modern world there is no alternative to the nation-state and liberal democracy. In this they also pioneered a new understanding of the intellectual as someone who is not committed to the pursuit of the ideal, but to the defense of *existing* democratic institutions against the *concrete* challenges of the day. This change from the "disconnected" to the "connected social critic" (M.Walzer) the German intellectuals still have to make. It will require a more relaxed and positive attitude to the nation – a whole new language has to be learned, a language beyond the antiquated dualisms of *Geist* and *Macht*, capitalism and socialism. The Gulf War episode, which saw most East and

West German intellectuals happily united in a ritualistic "peace" front, and the farcical quarrels about military intervention in Bosnia, suggest that change will be slow. But as Wolf Biermann put it in one of his better songs, "only he who changes remains true to himself."

Notes

1. This essay is reprinted in Michnik (1985).
2. See Judt (1988:199).
3. The best account of the evolution of Eastern European dissidence is still Ash (1990).
4. Here and in the following, the notions of communism and socialism are used mostly interchangeably. This should not conceal the fact that in Marxist doctrine, as set out in the *Critique of the Gotha Programme*, "socialism" meant the transitional stage of the "dictatorship of the proletariat," while "communism" referred to the final utopia of a society without state, politics and conflict. Ironically, in everyday language their meaning has since undergone an implicit conversion, "communism" referring to the real societies organized along Marxist-Leninist principles, the softer "socialism" referring to the unredeemed utopia of a society without coercion. A good example for this conversion is Kagarlitsky's (1989) inside view of Soviet dissent.
5. I am much influenced by Vujacic's (1990) brilliant interpretation of the Eastern European revolution as a "dual revolution of citizenship and nationhood."
6. The notion of Leninist regime is elaborated in Chapter 1.
7. The most important exception is still Touraine (1983).
8. Neil Smelser suggested this interpretation in a letter to the author.

CHAPTER 1: SOCIAL MOVEMENTS IN LENINIST REGIMES

1. Eastern European area specialists were no less surprised (see Bilandzic et al, 1990).
2. The one exception, of course, is the Polish Solidarity movement, which has found widespread scholarly attention. See, among many others, Ash (1983), Touraine (1983), and Staniszkis (1984).
3. Among American social movement scholars, only Neil Smelser (1962) developed a theoretical framework that accounts for the appearance of "value-oriented movements" (of which revolutionary movements are one type) in societies with closed opportunity structures, and of "norm-oriented movements" (i.e., reform movements) in relatively open societies.
4. The totalitarianism approach was developed by Arendt (1951), Neumann (1957), and Friedrich and Brzezinski (1965). Modernization, interest group, and complex organization approaches are represented in Johnson (1970b) and Field (1976). A good overview is Janos (1986:ch.4).
5. Typical examples of the new institutionalism or state socialism approach are Nee and Stark (1989) and Burawoy and Lukacs (1992).

This approach was inspired by internal developments in Eastern European scholarship, such as Konrad and Szelenyi (1979) and Kornai (1980).

6. The Leninist regime approach has been most systematically developed by Jowitt (1992). Jowitt builds on the earlier work of Selznick (1952). The notion of Leninist regime has been criticized for its political top-down conceptualization of communism, and its assumption that the basic continuities in the forms and principles of communist rule outweigh its many discontinuities and historical variations. To the first criticism it may be replied that a politicist bias is justified precisely because communism has been the (futile) attempt to organize modern societies politically from the top (thus violating the structural principle that modern, differentiated societies have neither "top" nor "center" [see Luhmann, 1984; Willke, 1992]). With regard to the assumption of continuity, Cohen (1985:22) has rightly criticized the "Whig" tendency to read history backward, which denies the "lost alternatives," "unintended consequences," and "makeshift measures" out of which the history of communism was also made. But the "lost alternatives" within the communist movement have never questioned the basic principle of communist rule: one-party rule based on charismatic action and a unitary ideology, which precludes the legal existence of competing forces engaged in a secular struggle for popular support (on the useful distinction between monopolistic and multiple party systems, see Aron [1990]). The notion of Leninist regime simply acknowledges Lenin's authorship, as well as the charismatic pretensions, of such one-party rule. *This* notion of Leninism outweighs all historical variations of Bolshevism, Stalinism, Trotskyism and so forth.

7. See Przeworski (1986:56–8), O'Donnell and Schmitter (1986:67), and Bunce (1990:400).

8. To avoid misinterpretations of this crucial point, let me clarify that Leninist rule is "illegitimate" in normative, not necessarily empirical regard. In *normative* regard, Leninist rule shuns legal procedures in the seizure and exercise of power, and fails to subject itself to the test of free elections. This violates our modern, Western conception of legitimate rule for which strong universalist claims can be made (see Habermas, 1992). This does not preclude that in *empirical* regard Leninist regimes may have had "deep popular roots" in certain times and places, such as in the case of mature Stalinism in the Soviet Union (see Cohen, 1985:ch.4). In fact, some of the finest studies of communist regimes have been written from the vantage point of (eventually futile) élite attempts to forge legitimacy while bypassing direct public acclamation (e.g., Verdery, 1991; Meuschel, 1992).

9. In a quantitative content analysis of Lenin's *What Is To Be Done*, Almond (1954:18) found that only six out of 801 references to the traits or actions of militants or the party deal with the ultimate goals of the communist movement, while the rest deal with questions of means and tactics.

10. Before he plunged into the muddy waters of convergence theory, Talcott Parsons (1964) saw very clearly that only liberal democracy can provide and mediate the broad consensus that is a necessary condition of decision-making in a complex society of different interests and values.

11. On the reverse, one could say that the Western option for "freedom", whose darker side consisted of the anarchy of the "self-regulating market," would be counteracted by "organization", i.e., the welfare state (Polanyi, 1944).

12. Offe and Preuss (1990:15) have nicely observed how the Marxist-Leninist suspension of conflict by "truth" becomes expressed in certain political rituals, such as the strange habit of Communist Party leaders of applauding themselves after their speeches.

13. Philip Selznick derived the "combat ethos" of Leninist regimes from the peculiar nature of the Bolshevik party as a paramilitary "cadre" or "leadership" party: "A leadership party must have something to lead, or some group for whose control a struggle can be carried on. This is one of the functions of continuous political combat in the communist movement, wherein targets ... are always available and an opposition must always be destroyed. Hence communist infiltration tactics are valuable not only for the strategic objectives they win, but also for building the party" (Selznick, 1952:19).

14. The military analogy is to be taken quite literally. Lenin praised the modern army as a model for his combat party: "Take the modern army. It is one of the good examples of organization. This organization is good only because it is flexible and is able at the same time to give millions of people a single will" (quoted in Almond, 1954:46). In this regard, the Leninist stress on unity reflects the requirements of successful combat.

15. The following sketch seeks only to spell out the *logic* of communist development. Needless to say, it cannot pay tribute to its full historical complexity and variations across time and places. Similar attempts of reconstructing the logic of communist development can be found in Johnson (1970a), Huntington (1970), and Jowitt (1975). An interesting attempt to conceptualize communist systems not through "stages of development" but through "modes of control" is Verdery (1991:ch.2).

16. See the debate on totalitarianism in Friedrich, Curtis, and Barber (1969).

17. On the other hand, one could say that in the very moment when Leninist regimes *did* assume authoritarian features, as in post-Solidarity Poland, communism was doomed.

18. A better term would be "quasi-groups", which Dahrendorf (1959) defines by their readiness for, but characteristic lack of, formal organization or political mobilization.

19. Following Martin Lipset (1959:333), I define as intellectuals "all those who create, distribute, and apply *culture,* that is, the symbolic world of man, including art, science, and religion." If not specified otherwise, the notions of intellectual and intelligentsia are used interchangeably.

20. See Moore (1951:ch.3), Almond (1954:11f), Malia (1961), Nettl (1970:96), and Bauman (1987:176f).
21. Steven Lukes (1991:314) has caught this important point too: "Communists have promised an end to injustice and oppression. What they promise, however, is not justice and rights, but, rather, emancipation from the enslaving conditions that make them necessary."
22. The notion of revisionism, initially a pejorative term used by orthodox followers of Marxist doctrine against intra-Marxist heretics, was first positively adopted by the German socialist Eduard Bernstein in his attempt to reexamine some tenets of Marxist theory and practice in light of a changed reality (see Labedz, 1962:9–41). In this study, the notion of revisionism refers to the reverse attempt to criticize communist reality in light of the original theory.
23. As Labedz (1962:9) put it, "revisionism is to Marxist movements what heresy is to religious ones."
24. See also Almond (1954:31).
25. See Skilling (1973); Bradley (1982).
26. Quoted in Shrtomas (1979:212).
27. Most notably in the writings of Polish dissident Adam Michnik (1985:91): "A different distinction comes to the fore in the era of totalitarian dictatorships: one between the proponents of an open society and the proponents of a closed society. In the former, social order is based on self-government and collective agreements; in the latter, order is achieved through repression and discipline."
28. A typical celebration of "history-making" from a Western social movement perspective is Flacks (1988).
29. Or put in negative terms, social movements are incited by an elementary sense of "injustice" (see Moore, 1978).
30. Insightful reflections on the role of fear in totalitarian regimes are in Vujacic (1990:29–33).
31. To be sure, already before the Helsinki Accords all socialist constitutions formally guaranteed basic civil liberties such as free expression, assembly and mobility. But, as in the GDR constitution of 1968, the reference to basic rights was always relativized by the "general constitutional principles of the socialist democracy" and the "safeguarding of corresponding duties," which put the interest of the state above the interest of the individual (Sontheimer and Bleek, 1975:44). The novelty of the Helsinki Accords is the *unconditional* recognition of human and civil rights by the signing socialist states. Part VII of the Helsinki Accords stipulates: "The participating states will respect human rights and fundamental freedoms, including the freedom of thought, conscience, religion or belief, for all without distinction as to race, sex, language, or religion. They will promote and encourage the effective exercise of civil, political, economic, social, cultural and other rights and freedoms, all of which derive from the inherent dignity of the human person and are essential for his free and full development" (quoted in Stokes, 1991:161).
32. Good conceptual and historical elaborations of citizenship can be found in Marshall (1977), Bendix (1977:ch.3), Nisbet (1974),

Dahrendorf (1974), and Turner (1990). See also the excellent recent account by Brubaker (1992:21–34).

33. The Hegelian notion of civil society refers to the sphere in which legal citizenship rights are central, notably contract and property rights. Civil society thus defined is identical with the market economy, which Hegel called the "system of needs" (*System der Bedürfnisse*). A characteristic shortcoming of the dissident opposition (with the notable exception of Hungary) is the neglect of the economic underpinnings of civil society, betraying the intellectual origins of dissidence.

34. *This* meaning of civil society is implied in Tocqueville's conception of "political society", Arendt's conception of "public realm", and Habermas's conception of the "public sphere". See the excellent analysis by Weintraub (1990). Marx's tragical error is the confounding of the economic and political aspects of civil society, seeing both as a source of alienation that could be dispensed with in socialism (see Dahrendorf, 1988:ch.1).

35. This corresponds to Ekiert's (1991:300ff) useful distinction between "domestic" and "political society" as the two realms of civil society.

36. Cohen and Arato's (1992) "post-Marxist" perspective on civil society tends to blur this difference. For the concept of new social movements, see Offe (1985).

37. See Rupnik (1988:284–7).

38. Quoted in Rupnik (1989:217).

39. Already during the Prague Spring, the First Republic was reasserted in the public mind as the "most glorious period" of Czech history (Brown and Wightman, 1977:164).

40. See Jowitt (1992:319–26), and more generally Smith (1986).

41. Quoted in Minogue (1967:48).

42. Anthony Smith (1986) stresses that nationhood necessarily includes both civic and ethnic components: "[A]ll nations bear the impress of both territorial and ethnic principles and components, and represent an uneasy confluence of a more recent 'civic' and a more ancient 'genealogical' model of social and cultural organization. No 'nation-to-be' can survive without a homeland or a myth of common origins and descent" (p. 149).

43. I cannot enter here into the complex debate about the precise location and sociocultural features of East-Central Europe or Central Europe. Suffice it to say that the countries of East-Central Europe (which usually include Poland, Czechoslovakia, Hungary, the Baltic States, and sometimes Germany) did have a Western-oriented legacy of a civil society that existed independently from the state, making them ill at ease with the Soviet-Russian model of autocratic rule. Milan Kundera called the "tragedy of Central Europe" the bifurcation between the region's sociocultural allegiance to the West and its political "kidnapping" by the East, i.e., Russia – a country with a "Caesaro-papist" tradition of subservience to an all-powerful state and without a civil society (quoted in Rupnik, 1988:286). A good overview is Graubard (1991).

44. Rupnik (1990:141) makes a similar distinction between the predomi-

nantly civic nationalism of East-Central Europe and the ethnic nationalisms of the Balkans. The latter are not directed against communism *per se*, but reflect the shortcomings of the Wilsonian nation-state solution for Eastern Europe, which forced incompatible ethnic groups into a common state (as in the case of Yugoslavia) or left sizeable ethnic minorities outside their homelands (as, for instance, ethnic Hungarians in Romania). An exceptionally lucid overview of Eastern European nationalism is Hammond (1966).

45. This is the underlying hypothesis of Szporluk's (1988) impressive comparison of nationalism and communism.

46. See, for instance, Brubaker's (1994) study of the unintended consequences of the Leninist nationality policies in the successor-states to the Soviet Union, or Verdery's (1991) study of national ideology in Ceausescu's Romania, which "disrupted the Marxist discourse and thus... was a major element in destroying the party's legitimacy" (p. 4).

47. Quoted in Connor (1984:xiii).

48. More precisely, nationalism "invents" the past for purposes of political integration or mobilization (see Hobsbawm, 1983).

49. Quoted in Dahrendorf, 1990:14.

50. Quoted in Rupnik (1989:217).

51. See Seton Watson (1962). By the same token, human rights dissidence in Russia, actually the first of its kind in the communist world, could not be couched in nationalist terms because of the fusion of Russian and communist hegemony. When a nationalist opposition nevertheless emerged, epitomized by Solzhenitsyn, its advocacy of authoritarian government set it apart from the liberal, Western-oriented dissident opposition. The latter cooperated only with the nationalist movements of the non-Russian republics (see Alexeyeva, 1987:ch.V). We will see that the East German case is diametrically opposed to the Russian case: because communism appeared as the legitimate response to National Socialism, even human rights dissidents had to remain committed to its reform.

CHAPTER 2: REGIME AND OPPOSITION IN EAST GERMANY

1. R.V. Burks's classic study of communism in Eastern Europe also excludes East Germany. Burks defines Eastern Europe as follows: "Eastern Europe is that part of Europe which is sandwiched in between the Germans in the west, the Russians in the east, and the Turks to the south. It is, if you like, the area of the peoples 'in-between', conquered and ruled first by one outside great power, then by another" (Burks, 1961:19).

2. Interestingly, the notion of National Socialism never found entry into the political language of East Germany – presumably because of its treacherous "socialist" component.

3. Austria, the third successor state of the old German Reich, opted for a strategy of "externalization," in which Nazism was seen as a consequence of the country's allegedly forced annexation (*Anschluss*)

by Hitler Germany (Lepsius, 1989:250f).
4. See the vivid autobiography by communist renegade Wolfgang Leonhard (1955), a member of the Ulbricht Group who defected to the West in 1948.
5. Quoted in Mitter and Wolle (1990:120).
6. Quoted in Schnibben, 1991:I, 159.
7. *Interview with Jörg Hildebrandt* (Democracy Now), 19 June 1991, East Berlin.
8. Quoted in Schnibben (1991:I, 161).
9. In Glässner, 1988:121.
10. Many of them were attracted by generous benefits and an initially "liberal" cultural policy by the Soviet military administration, which included immediate mass reprints of books forbidden under Hitler (also by "bourgeois" authors such as Thomas Mann), and an astonishing theatrical repertory that stretched from Jean Anouilh to Thornton Wilder (Childs, 1983:ch.8).
11. Quoted in Leonhard (1955:317).
12. The *locus classicus* of Leninist strategy, of course, is Lenin (1969).
13. At the eve of the October Revolution, Lenin denounced a Blanquist strategy: "We are not Blanquists, we are not in favor of the seizure of power by a minority" (quoted in Moore, 1951:62). To be sure, this was Lenin's claim. Actual similarities between Blanquism and Leninism, both of which amount to a dictatorship of a self-appointed avant-garde that is *indifferent* to the real workers' movement, are stressed by Lichtheim (1961:122–9, 325–51).
14. Jan Gross (1989) captured this crucial characteristic of the emergent Soviet state in his concept of "spoiler state": "[T]he Soviet state is a state unique in modern history, devoted primarily to making sure that no other social force can get things done. It is, so to speak, a spoiler state" (p. 210).
15. Quoted in Weber (1985:24). The affinity between the communist unity rhetoric and the "unpolitical" German political culture is elaborated by Meuschel (1992:15–22).
16. On the part of the KPD, this historical reference is rather ironic. During the Weimar Republic, the KPD had stubbornly refused to enter a coalition with the SPD, dismissing the Social Democrats as "Social Fascists" and "main enemy" (see Brandt 1970:ch.4; Krisch, 1974:ch.1). This faithful execution of the dominant Comintern strategy was a critical factor in Hitler's rise to power.
17. But note the statement by Heinz Brandt, who had sat in various Nazi concentration camps, that "the 'Muscovites', the party-liners, the people around the Ulbricht group, mistrustfully eyed those of us who had remained in Germany" (Brandt 1970:154). That group, however, was not strong enough in number and organization to challenge Stalin's henchmen. This was one reason why East Germany was spared the gruesome show-trials, which accompanied Sovietization in Eastern Europe (see Rothschild 1989:ch.4).
18. Wolfgang Leonhard, who grew up in the Soviet Union, reports his surprise encounter with a Soviet army officer who spoke perfect

German and who turned out to be the son of the later GDR-President Wilhelm Pieck. "I was startled, because I had never seen a German in Soviet uniform before" (Leonhard 1955:251). One-third of the German communists in Soviet exile perished during Stalin's purges from the mid- to late 1930s (Griffith 1989:316). Those who survived, and became the future leaders of East Germany, had to be unyielding Stalinists, such as their prototype Walter Ulbricht (see his good portrait by Stern [1963]).

19. In Weber (1985:193f).
20. Quoted in Henrich (1989:100).
21. From a poem by communist-in-exile Erich Weinert (quoted in Pike, 1982:405).
22. From a communist propaganda leaflet, distributed to German POWs in the Soviet Union (quoted in Pike, 1982:368).
23. These affinities are virtually unexplored, but see Meuschel (1992:70–81; 101–16) and Pike (1992:560–74; 613–56).
24. Quoted in McAdams (1985:31).
25. A typical example is Baylis (1972).
26. Before Bonn's *Ostpolitik*, the so-called Hallstein Doctrine (which considered diplomatic relations with East Berlin an "unfriendly act" toward West Germany) had effectively isolated the GDR on the international scene. By 1976, the GDR was officially recognized as a sovereign state by 121 countries (Ludz, 1977:39).
27. Quoted in Hacker (1987:55). To be sure, the distinction between citizenship and nationality is not unusual – see, for instance, the case of UK citizenship which includes several nationalities. Unusual, however, is the paradoxical attempt to extinguish the "German" component in "GDR" – otherwise the distinction between GDR-citizenship and German nationality makes no sense. The distinction between citizenship and nationality obviously is meaningful only if *several* nations are included in *one* state.
28. Dallin and Breslauer (1970:6) define a "mobilization system" as "the acquisition by the state of control over all societal resources, human and economic, and the commitment of these assets to the attainment of a single, predominant goal."
29. Wolfgang Leonhard describes a typical loss-of-combat-task agony (which followed upon the KPD's successful unity campaign in 1946): "We functionaries, who couldn't imagine a life without permanent political activity and campaigning, were struck by a feeling of emptiness. For the first time, there was nothing left to do except routine work... In the party schools and lower party organizations, there was a visible withering of enthusiasm. *Nothing could be more dangerous to such a party than a few weeks of quiet, the lack of an immediate task which keeps everyone out of breath*" (Leonhard, 1955:394; emphasis added).
30. As Milovan Djilas (1957:87) put it, "Communist regimes are a form of latent civil war between the government and the people."
31. Good accounts of post-mobilization Leninist regimes are Löwenthal (1970, 1976), Dallin and Breslauer (1970:81–144), and Jowitt (1983).
32. Twenty-five per cent of the 2.5 million people who left the GDR

between 1950 and 1962 were members of the technical intelligentsia (Naimark, 1979:571).

33. In 1963, less than one-third of the members and candidates of the
politburo may be defined as technical functionaries and professionals.
In general, this group remained limited to non-voting, candidate
membership. Only one trained technical specialist, the economist
Günther Mittag, ever became a full member of the politburo (Baylis,
1974:211f).

34. Jens Reich, a noted bio-scientist and leading citizen activist in 1989,
characterized the role of the technical intelligentsia as follows: "We
did not belong to the ruling clique in party, Stasi, and military.
These leaders came more from the working-class. But they were 'allied' with us, as the official phrase was. And we were pampered with
privileges such as 'intelligence pensions', paid directly by the state.
We were like useful parasites, fed by the ruling clique. Our life lie
(*Lebenslüge*) was that we deemed ourselves oppressed, while our privileges actually led us to accept the system. We were like the wife of
Buddenbrook, who also had nothing to say, but who nevertheless
belonged to the bourgeoisie" (*Interview with Jens Reich*, 8 Juli 1991,
East Berlin).

35. This was also due to the sobering fact that, by the late 1960s, the
economy had slowed down and the one-sided emphasis on high-
technology industries had led to seriously unbalanced plans and
shortages, thus reinvigorating the apparent virtues of central planning. Nevertheless, the New Economic Policy helped the GDR to
become the second biggest economic power in the Soviet bloc. From
1950 to 1968 industrial production had increased by an impressive
471 per cent (Ludz, 1970:14).

36. Quoted in McAdams (1985:131).

37. A party platform says: "The politics of peaceful coexistence does
not render obsolete the notions of class and class struggle. Peaceful
coexistence is always accompanied by fierce ideological combat.
Peaceful coexistence is class struggle" (in Ludz 1977:244). Of course,
this was a core tenet of Lenin's imperialism theory.

38. By 1971, 40–50 per cent of university students came from non-work-
ing-class backgrounds, raising the ideologically unappealing prospect of a self-recruiting socialist intelligentsia. The tightening of
admission standards also corrected a certain disproportion between
supply and demand on the academic market, which resulted from
Ulbricht's precipitate proclamation of the "scientific-technological
revolution" (Zimmermann, 1978:28–30).

39. Gebhard Schweigler's (1973) provocative thesis of a separate national
consciousness in East Germany has evidently been disproved by history.

40. Since the degree of confidentiality or intimidation during the interview situation has not been specified, these findings must be taken
with caution.

41. *Interview with Wolfgang Apfeld* (Democracy Now), 24 June 1991, East
Berlin.

42. In his study of the Polish Solidarity movement, Michael Kennedy (1991:5) stresses the importance of "cross-class alliance(s)" for an effective challenge to Leninist rule. Indeed, only in Poland could a *lasting* cross-class alliance be achieved.
43. The most comprehensive and detailed overview of East German regime opposition up to this time is Fricke (1984).
44. "Goatie Must Go!" was the most popular slogan of the June revolt ("Goatie" refers to Walter Ulbricht's trademark goatee beard). See Brandt (1970:181).
45. Quoted in Birgit Rätsch, "Nicht die Stunde der Intellektuellen," *Frankfurter Allgemeine Zeitung*, 19 June 1993. Mayer later changed his mind (see Mayer, 1991:ch.5).
46. In fact, Brecht responded to Kuba's infamous "How Ashamed I Feel!" with his sarcastic poem "The Solution":

> After the rising of the 17 June
> The Secretary of the Writers' Union
> Had leaflets distributed on the Stalinallee
> In which one could read that the people
> Had forfeited the confidence of the government
> And could only recover it through redoubled work.
>   Would it not then
> Be simpler, if the government
> Dissolved the people and
> Elected another?
>   (quoted in Ash, 1990e:14)

But Brecht chose not to publish "The Solution" at that time.
47. Between 1954 and 1961, 752 university professors fled to the West – two-thirds of them between 1957 and 1959, the height of the anti-revisionist campaign (Richert, 1967:199). Among them were previous exile-intellectuals who had made the "anti-fascist" GDR the country of their choice. The literary critic Alfred Kantorowicz comments on his escape in 1957: "I believed for too long that these crude, stupid and violent [party] men were still... honest allies in the struggle against Nazism" (Croan, 1962:244).
48. Timothy Garton Ash (1981:16f), in his rather unflattering portrait of East Germany's "honorary dissident," wondered "who was farther removed from everyday life – the party leadership or the dissident."
49. In 1961, Bloch emigrated to the West, accepting a professorship at the University of Tübingen.
50. Harich's "Platform for a Special German Road to Socialism" opens with the demand for a "complete restoration of the Leninist party principles" (Harich, 1993:113).
51. Quoted in Janka (1990:89).
52. In Schnibben (1991:I, 165).
53. In Woods (1986:109). "Truthful [*ehrliche*] books were like nutrition", said a young East German writer (*Interview with Daniela Dahn*, 26 June 1991, East Berlin).
54. Good overviews of literary generations in the GDR are Franke (1971),

Erbe (1987), and Emmerich (1989).

55. Quoted in Mitter and Wolle (1993:353).

56. Ernst-Otto Mätzke, "DDR-Schriftsteller trauern um die Zukunft...," *Frankfurter Allgemeine Zeitung*, 27 March 1990.

57. An overview of the sporadic protest activities during and after the Prague Spring is Burens (1981:68–74). The secret police recorded 2883 cases of individual protest, such as the distribution of leaflets or wall slogans (Mitter and Wolle, 1993:464).

58. A good example is the physicist Gerd Poppe, a leader of the citizen movement of 1989, and who may be considered one of the few authentic dissidents, Eastern European style, in the GDR. Poppe identifies the events in 1968 and his involvement in the Biermann-Havemann circle as his formative experiences (*Interview with Gerd Poppe*, 26 June 1991, East Berlin).

59. A member of the "beat generation" remembers scissors-armed police forces taking action against long-haired beatniks in the early 1960s. By the mid-1970s, this was certainly no longer possible (*Interview with Reiner Flügge*, Democracy Now, 18 June 1991, East Berlin).

60. As stipulated by the conference protocol, even the heretical speeches of Santiago Carrillo (Spain) and Enrico Berlinguer (Italy), the two champions of Euro-Communism, were reprinted in the party newspaper *Neues Deutschland* (see Fricke, 1976).

61. One of the more impressive pieces of prose to be published by an East German writer in the 1970s, *Die wunderbaren Jahre* echoes the traumatic experience of the Czechoslovak invasion of 1968. Kunze was the only communist renegade among the East German writers of rank, making him a much-insulted outsider. Milan Kundera once called him "the most Slavic German I know" (in Ash, 1981:124). In 1977, Kunze emigrated to West Germany.

62. See the documentation of the Biermann case in Roos (1977). A German television commentator said about Biermann's Cologne concert, which became the pretext for his expatriation: "His first song ('So or So, the Earth Will Be Red') was an unequivocal confession for socialism and against cooptation by false friends" (ibid., 7).

63. Rudolf Bahro said in an interview: "In the first hours and days after the intervention something changed in me forever. From that point on I wanted to deliver them a reply against which they would be as helpless as we had been against their tanks" (in Bathrick, 1978:4).

64. The political organization of exit petitioners, such as the 1976 Civil Rights Initiative of Riesa, remained the exception – and its jailed members soon landed in the West (Fricke, 1984:169–72). The trade of political prisoners for hard currency was profitable business for the Honecker regime (see Naimark, 1979:572–5).

65. The writer Siegmar Faust (1980:172) describes how his decision to leave the GDR made him *persona non grata* among his previous friends in the Biermann-Havemann circle.

CHAPTER 3: DETENTE AND THE PEACE MOVEMENT

1. For Charter 77, see Kavan and Tomin (1983); for Solidarity, see Tymowski (1984). A general overview is Asmus (1983a).

2. Among the numerous German-language accounts of the East German peace movement, Kuhrt (1984) stands out. Good English-language assessments are Asmus (1983a) and Tismaneanu (1990b).

3. *Interview with Erhart Neubert*, 15 June 1991, East Berlin. The labeling of the East German peace movement as a "new social movement" was also common in the West (e.g., Knabe, 1988).

4. Günter Gaus (1989:127) writes: "there was a visible parallel between the state's disarmament campaign and the peace movement..." Along these lines, an internal discussion paper of the GDR peace movement distinguishes the "peace intention (*Friedenswille*) of our state" from the "aggressiveness of the US... and NATO military doctrines" ("Zur Friedensbewegung in der DDR," *Die Tageszeitung*, 7 August 1984, p. 10).

5. *Interview with Gerd Poppe* (Initiative for Peace and Human Rights), 26 June 1991, East Berlin.

6. Reliable surveys about the size of the peace movement do not exist. In spring 1982, the number of peace activists in the GDR was estimated to be between 2000 and 5000 (Asmus, 1983b:304). In 1983 and 1984, the peak years of the movement, the number may have been somewhat higher.

7. *Interview with Werner Fischer* (Initiative for Peace and Human Rights), 27 June 1991, East Berlin.

8. Helga Hirsch, "Der falsche Weg: Politik von oben." *Die Zeit*, no. 9, 28 February 1992, p. 3.

9. Egon Bahr, "Indem ich durch diese Hölle gegangen bin." *Die Zeit*, no. 12, 20 March 1992, p. 19.

10. In post-war West Germany, Social Democrats from Kurt Schumacher to Egon Bahr became proponents of the national cause, whereas large sections of the conservative Christian Democrats became staunchly pro-Western Atlanticists. This is a curious reversal of roles with regard to the discourse of nation and nationalism, which had been previously the prerogative of the political right. The older, Schumacherian version of Social-Democratic nationalism differs from the more recent one of Brandt and Bahr in its deep suspicion of the Soviet Union and its non-acceptance of the political division of Germany. The biggest irony of the Bahr-Brandt defense of the national cause is that it was premised on recognizing the legitimate existence of the GDR, and thus helped seal the division of Germany and Europe (see Holmes, 1984:32–7; Gress, 1985:ch.2; Hassner, 1983:307). This outcome should not let one forget the original intention of *Ostpolitik*: to reopen the national question through the envisioned links of communist regime stabilization, reform, and eventual self-determination of the East Germans (see Groh and Brandt, 1992:309–34).

11. Egon Bahr formulated this centrepiece of *Ostpolitik* in a speech at

the Evangelical Academy of Tutzing in July 1963: "The Wall was a sign of the anxiety and survival instinct of the communist regime. The question is: aren't there possibilities to relieve the regime of its justified worries, so that an opening of the borders and of the Wall becomes practicable because the risk is tolerable. This is a policy which one could call 'change through rapprochement'" (Bahr, 1991:17).

12. Arnulf Baring (1989) spoke of "our new megalomania." Not inappropriately so. See, for instance, East German church secretary Manfred Stolpe's entirely un-ironical call upon West Germany to become a "peace super-power" (*Friedensgrossmacht*) (in Rein, 1985:108).

13. See Baring (1989:129–45); Wehler (1983:37–46); Markovitz (1989).

14. The diary of dissident Freya Klier, a fascinating document of East German everyday life at the fringes, shows only a two-line entry for December 1981: "Helmut Schmidt and Erich Honecker exchange candies at the Güstrow train station. We begin to hope" (Klier, 1989:13). No word is spared for the dramatic events in Poland.

15. *Interview with Reiner Flügge* (Democracy Now), 18 June 1991, East Berlin.

16. Short on indigenous resources, the GDR was heavily dependent on foreign oil imports, mostly from the Soviet Union. In 1970, the GDR payed for imported Soviet oil with seven per cent of its total exports to the Soviet Union. By 1985, payments for oil were up to 40 per cent of Soviet exports (Sodaro, 1990:293). In 1982, state subsidization of consumer staples (housing, basic food products, etc.) took almost 12 per cent of the total budget (Baylis, 1986:414).

17. In 1946, 80 per cent of the East German population were members of the Protestant Church (Goeckel, 1989:130).

18. The turn to German history included a positive revaluation of previously shunned Prussian icons such as Bismarck or Friedrich II, whose equestrian statue returned to its old location on Unter den Linden (see Kuhrt and Löwis, 1988).

19. Brian Schuster, "Kreuzgang als Fluchtweg," *Die Tageszeitung* (West Berlin), 11 December 1987.

20. Werner Hülsemann, East Berlin's Protestant church minister for youth affairs (*Stadtjugendpfarrer*) from 1984 to 1991, said: "I became a theologian *in the GDR*; I wouldn't have become one in any other country" (*Interview*, 1 July 1991, East Berlin).

21. *Interview with Reinhardt Schult*, 1 July 1991, East Berlin.

22. In 1991, Reverend Gartenschläger was exposed as a fifteen-year-long collaborator of the security police (Stasi) (*Frankfurter Allgemeine Zeitung*, 27 April 1992, p. 3). This bizarre aspect of East German opposition politics is discussed in Chapter 4.

23. A participant lucidly describes the eery atmosphere of this rare event: "This was the first independent peace rally. No police, nobody intervened. Surprised, even helpless, we stood around in the cold. I think we were hiding behind our silence, because none of us knew how to demonstrate. Suddenly a small van approached us – a West German television team. Not knowing what to do at first, a few seized

hands, and soon everybody joined in to form two big circles. Slowly our thin voices raised a song: 'We shall overcome.' But already during the second verse most of us didn't know the text" (Saab, 1988:36).

24. "We only fulfill our church duties and don't want to be pushed into an oppositional attitude to the state" said Bishop Gienke of Greifswald in 1983 (in Kuhrt, 1984:8).

25. "This is smart; no one can accuse us of imitating the West" said a young peace activist (in Ehring and Dallwitz, 1982:63).

26. Even the Soviet Union seems to have disapproved of the GDR's heavy-handed repression of the "swords to plowshares" symbol. In May 1982, at the height of the clampdown, Radio Moscow praised the odd sculpture as "one of the best works of Soviet art" and a work of "great political importance" (in Asmus, 1983b:340).

27. *Interview with Irena Kukutz*, 24 June 1991, East Berlin.

28. "DDR-Staat verhaftet die eigene Friedensbewegung," *Die Tageszeitung* (West Berlin), 23 December 1983, p. 4.

29. *Interview with Gerd Poppe*, 26 June 1991, East Berlin.

30. The Berlin Appeal is reprinted in Woods (1986:195–7).

31. *Interview with Werner Hülsemann*, 1 July 1991, East Berlin.

32. *Interview with Ulrike Poppe*, 9 July 1991, East Berlin.

33. The "Appeal of the Writers of Europe" is reprinted on the back cover of Engelmann et al. (1982).

34. Only the churches had the resources to issue programmatic statements in the peace debate. Throughout the 1980s, the Theological Study Section (*Theologische Studienabteilung*) of the Evangelical churches produced a number of influential studies on nuclear deterrence, security policy, and related topics.

35. As the dissident theologian Edelbert Richter (1988) outlined, Lutheran protestantism had always been at odds with the liberal human rights tradition, stressing the "duties" rather than the "rights" of the *Christenmensch*. Along these lines, Bishop Hempel made a distinction between the "humanist spirit of the human rights declarations" and the "biblical view of humankind": "The declaration of human rights contains an element of noble illusion. I say this without irony" (in Kuhrt, 1984:82). A Berlin church minister who excelled as one of the most ardent defenders of youthful peace rebels still betrayed the Lutheran heritage: "This stale (*wischi-waschi*) pluralism in Western democracy, where the positions are unclear, is frustrating and boring... Capitalism gives free rein to the blind instincts of individuals, it cannot steer them. Christian-social thinking is closer to the socialist utopia than to the market economy" (*Interview with Hans Simon*, 25 June 1991, East Berlin).

36. On the reverse, Günter Gaus, in a discussion with East German church secretary Manfred Stolpe, deplored that "freedom" had become a "propaganda tool" in the East–West conflict. "Couldn't it be," Gaus asks cunningly, "that the GDR is still [*sic*] lacking something that we no longer have... What good is freedom (*Freizügigkeit*) for someone who is permanently unemployed, who lives on welfare and cannot afford holidays in Mallorca?" (in Rein, 1985:83). This is a good example

of the *détente*-induced "boundary erosion" between liberal democracy and communism.

37. Church secretary Manfred Stolpe put it more bluntly: "Neither East nor West should accuse the other side of human rights violations, because this puts the other side's existence in question, and thus amounts to a threat to peace" (DDR-Komitee für Menschenrechte, 1985:96).

38. *Interview with Peter Eisenfeld,* 1 August 1991, West Berlin.

39. Most notably those dissidents who founded the Initiative for Peace and Human Rights in 1986 (see Chapter 4).

40. The quotes are from a position paper of the East German Peace Movement, which was made public at the 1984 European Nuclear Disarmament Conference in Perugia (Italy). The paper is reprinted in Woods (1986:204–8).

41. Ibid.

42. The 1982 Church Synod in Halle blamed the "spirit of deterrence" for obscuring the "real threats" in the world: the North–South conflict and the ecology question (Zander, 1989:267). Along these lines, the dissident theologian Heino Falcke (1985:150) called "peace" and "ecology" the "two great problems of the 1980s."

CHAPTER 4: THE INCOMPLETE TURN TO HUMAN RIGHTS DISSIDENCE

1. Important in this regard was the "Initiative for an East–West Dialogue," which was sponsored by a faction of the West German Green Party and its Berlin affiliate, the Alternative List. See their "Open Letter" in *Across Frontiers,* vol. 1, no. 1, 1984, pp. s1–s4.

2. Ibid.

3. The East–West rapprochement was ratified by Charter 77's Prague Appeal of 1985, which emphasized the "indivisibility" of the struggles for human rights and peace as well as the importance of the Helsinki process for overcoming the post-war division of Europe. The Prague Appeal is reprinted in *Across Frontiers,* vol. 2, no. 1, 1985, 13–16.

4. The IFM was founded after several attempts to organize a GDR-wide "human rights seminar" under the protective umbrella of the Protestant Church had failed due to the veto of the church leadership. As an internal document of the security police (Stasi) asserts, the "focused intervention" (*gezielte Einflussnahme*) of the Stasi was responsible for this church veto (Stasi, 1986:4).

5. See the interview with IFM leader Werner Fischer, in *East European Reporter* (London), vol. 3, no. 3, 1988, 65–8.

6. In June 1989, the security police estimated that the majority of the leadership of East German opposition groups was between 25 and 40 years old, a "considerable" number of them unemployed (the report mentions 12 per cent, which is indeed "considerable" in a society where work was not only a right but also a state-enforced

duty) (Mitter and Wolle, 1990:48).

7. Of the 160 East German opposition groups counted by the security police in June 1989, 35 considered themselves "peace circles", 39 were ecology groups, 39 groups worked on Third World issues, and only 10 defined themselves as "human rights groups" (Mitter and Wolle, 1990:47). However, the impact of IFM far outweighed its numerical size. The security police, always a reliable source in these matters, attributed a "certain key role" to the IFM (ibid., 68f).

8. As two GDR-sociologists say, the notion of peace "attained an unquestioned, quasi-absolute status" among opposition groups (Elvers and Findeis, 1990:30).

9. The first declaration of Gegenstimmen closes with the demonstrative words: "This paper shall be used within the GDR only" (Vera Wollenberger et al., *Comment on the Preparation of a Seminar "Peace and Human Rights"*, East Berlin, 6 March 1986, pamphlet, p. 4).

10. *Interview with Werner Fischer* (IFM), 27 June 1991, East Berlin.

11. The "Open Letter to the Party" is reprinted in *Across Frontiers*, vol. 3, no. 3, 1987, 16–20.

12. Jiri Wyatt, "Charter 77 After Poland," *Across Frontiers*, vol. 1, no. 1, 1984, p. 7.

13. However, the steady presence of Western media was limited to East Berlin and, partially, Leipzig (because of its biannual trade and industry fairs). Among other factors, this helps explain why regime opposition was concentrated in these two cities.

14. Marcel Reich-Ranicki's characterization of Christa Wolf as a "state laureate" (*Staatsdichterin*) is strikingly accurate. See his "Macht Verfolgung kreativ?" *Frankfurter Allgemeine Zeitung*, 12 November 1987.

15. In June 1979, nine writers, including Stefan Heym, Adolf Endler, and Rolf Schneider, were excluded from the Writers' Union because of alleged "hard currency offences" (*Devisenvergehen*). The tribunal against the writers is documented in Walther et al. (1991).

16. Marlies Menge, "Etwas kommt in Fluss," *Die Zeit*, 4 December 1987, p. 56.

17. A good, if somewhat harmonizing, overview is Dahn (1987).

18. Squatting in East Berlin was in fact easier than in West Berlin or Amsterdam. With the payment of a small fine the use of vacant space could be *de facto* legalized. See Büscher and Wensierski (1984:14).

19. Quoted in Emmerich (1989:423).

20. Ibid., p. 425.

21. One of the few anthologies to appear in the West is Anderson and Erb (1985).

22. Print reproductions of up to 99 copies were legal. See Heller (1988) and Günther (1992).

23. *Interview with Gerd Poppe*, 26 June 1991, East Berlin.

24. B.V. Flow, "The Literary Avantgarde Leaves the GDR," *Radio Free Europe Research* (Munich), 3 September 1986, hectographed.

25. *Interview with Lutz Rathenow*, 2 July 1991, East Berlin.

26. Members of the Bundestag had diplomatic passports, which allowed them to enter the GDR without personal controls. A few Green depu-

ties who frequently visited the GDR transported everything from books and journals to printer's ink and personal computers to support East Berlin opposition groups. In fact, the bulk of the book collection in the Ecology Library consisted of discarded materials from the central office of the Green Party in Bonn.

27. A complete reproduction of all *Grenzfall* issues can be found in Hirsch and Kopelew (1989).

28. The literal meaning of *Grenzfall* consists of a wordplay of "withering border" and "extreme position."

29. A representative collection of articles appearing in the *Umweltblätter* is reprinted in Rüddenklau (1992), the most comprehensive overview of East German opposition politics in the 1980s available today.

30. A 1989 report by the security police counted 25 samizdat journals in the GDR (Mitter and Wolle, 1990:50).

31. "Political" is the notion used in several internal documents of the security police. For instance, a 1986 overview of security police activities says that the "struggle against hostile-negative forces was increasingly led by *political* means" (Stasi, 1986: 17).

32. *Interview with Ralph Hirsch* (IFM), 10 July 1991, East Berlin.

33. By comparison, the former Soviet Union had 17 times the population of the GDR but only 5.4 times as many secret police officers (488 000) (Tyler Marshall, "Secret Files Haunting Eastern Europe," *Los Angeles Times*, 22 January 1992, p. H5).

34. Quoted in Ulrich Greiner, "Die Falle des Entweder-Oder," *Die Zeit*, 31 January 1992, p. 1.

35. The latest Stasi count (June 1989) was 2500 dissidents in 170 local and GDR-wide opposition groups (Mitter and Wolle, 1990:47).

36. *Interview with Ralph Hirsch* (IFM), 10 July 1991, East Berlin.

37. Wolf Biermann, "Tiefer als unter die Haut," *Der Spiegel* 5/1992, p. 181. Biermann's comparison is not far-fetched. Consider yet another Stasi curiosity, its "Library of Suspect Smells," which was discovered in Leipzig. It consists of hundreds of numbered glass jars, which contained the body odours of Leipzig dissidents. This "library" had been assembled by removing unwashed underwear and socks from dissidents' laundry hampers, bits and pieces of which were placed in jars to preserve typical body odours, as one preserves cucumbers. With the help of trained dogs, the distinctive smells would later help identify distributors of illegal leaflets. "The Stasi had a complete smell-collection of the Leipzig opposition," said a former dissident (quoted in Elon, 1992:8).

38. *Interview with Irena Kukutz* (Women for Peace), 24 June 1991, East Berlin.

39. According to a 1989 Stasi report, this hard core of dissidents consisted of only 60 persons. What "permanent observance" meant may become clear with the following excerpt from the Stasi file of dissident writer Lutz Rathenow: "Rathenow then crossed the street and ordered a sausage at the sausage stand... The following conversation took place: Rathenow: 'A sausage please.' Sausage seller: 'With or without roll?' Rathenow: 'With, please.' Sausage seller: 'And mus-

tard?' Rathenow: 'Yes, with mustard.' Further exchange of words did not take place" (quoted in Kinzer, 1992:27).

40. *Interview with Irena Kukutz* (Women for Peace), 24 June 1991, East Berlin.

41. *Interview with Wolfgang Templin* (IFM), 4 July 1991, East Berlin.

42. *Interview with Ralph Hirsch* (IFM), 10 July 1991, East Berlin.

43. A Stasi document claims that an average of "two to three" Stasi informers had been planted into the "core" of each opposition group (Stasi, 1988:41).

44. Some of the following observations are based on original Stasi documents, which I obtained from a private source.

45. The literal translation of *zersetzung* is "decomposition." But the word also conveys the active sense of "smashing."

46. The quotes are from Christian Wernicke, "Vorgang auf," *Die Zeit*, 13 March 1992, pp. 11–12.

47. *Interview with Ralph Hirsch* (IFM), 10 July 1991, East Berlin.

48. The story of Stasi agent Monika H. alias "Karin Lenz" is documented by Kukutz and Havemann (1990).

49. C. Wernicke, "Vorgang auf," *Die Zeit*, 13 March 1992, p. 12.

50. See Jones (1993). The founder of Netzwerk Arche, the clearing-house of independent ecology groups in the GDR, confirms that the ecology issue was "more accepted" than the human rights issue, and that the "Stasi tried hard to integrate us into the official structures" (*Interview with Carlo Jordan*, 16 July 1991, East Berlin). A 1989 Stasi report lauds "many members" of the ecology groups for their "honest participation in the solution of environmental problems" (Mitter and Wolle, 1990:59).

51. Whenever mentioned in internal Stasi documents, the IFM is seen as "most closely connected with antisocialist forces in the West" (quoted in Mitter and Wolle, 1990:69). A typical statement can be found in the party newspaper *Neues Deutschland*, 17 February 1988 ("Wer steuert die sogenannte DDR-Opposition"), which argues that the "so-called inner opposition" in the GDR was the product of "imperialist secret services . . . and antisocialist forces in the FRG and Westberlin."

52. A typical example is Klenner (1977).

53. "The right to live in peace . . . [is] the most important and basic human right" (quoted in Golla and Rodenbach, 1986:492).

54. "Berliner Pfarrer wegen Stasi-Tätigkeit beurlaubt, *Frankfurter Allgemeine Zeitung*, 27 April 1992, p. 3.

55. The quotes are from an undated *Grenzfall* issue, which is reprinted in Hirsch and Kopelew (1989:16).

56. Stasi ordinance 1/79, quoted in *Der Spiegel*, "In wahnsinniger Todesangst," 3/1992, p. 27

57. Lutz Rathenow, "Offenheit als Alternative," *Die Andere* (East Berlin), no. 20, 1990, p. 19.

58. These are ideal types in the Weberian sense, that is, "one-sided accentuations of reality." The typology does not claim to exhaust reality. There were many more motivations to collaborate with the security police, most notably simple coercion and fear.

59. Jürgen Leinemann, "Sie hat nichts merken können," *Der Spiegel* 3/ 1992, pp. 34–8. The following quotes are from this perceptive documentation of the Wollenberger case.
60. A Stasi informer remembers: "With the Stasi, you could risk a lip and complain. They didn't bother" (quoted in Kukutz and Havemann, 1990:47).
61. Quoted in John Tagliabue, "Berlin Journal," *New York Times*, 30 January 1992. In his *Homo Sovieticus*, Alexander Zinoviev (1985:54) argues similarly: "[I]f a man finds himself... beneath the minimum that is indispensable if moral norms are to be considered applicable in real life, then it is senseless to apply moral criteria to his behavior." He then concludes: "A man in such a position is not only freed *ipso facto* from normal norms, he is freed from them by these moral concepts themselves." If that is the case, the dissident ethos of "living in truth" appears all the more heroic.
62. In this mold, a former Stasi collaborator (one of the few who publicly repented) admits that he "was looking for adventure," hoping that "this kind of work might somehow get me out of boring East Germany" (quoted in Kinzer, 1992:52).
63. *Interview with Lutz Rathenow*, 2 July 1991, East Berlin.
64. After moving to West Berlin in 1986, Anderson continued to report to the Stasi about the local exile community. See Iris Radisch, "Die Krankheit der Lüge," *Die Zeit*, 31 January 1992, pp. 16–17.
65. Ibid.
66. Her story is told in Kukutz and Havemann (1991).
67. *Interview with Irena Kukutz* (Women for Peace), 24 June 1991, East Berlin.
68. IFM, *Erklärung der Initiative "Frieden und Menschenrechte"*, 19 January 1988, East Berlin, pamphlet.
69. Rainer Eppelmann et al., "Appeal on the Occasion of the 25th Anniversary of the Berlin Wall," *East European Reporter* 2(3) 1987, p. 50. This was certainly not a plea for the right to emigrate, but for free travel. Note that the appeal contains the (rather odd) suggestion to "[suspend the] right to renounce GDR citizenship for the duration of [the] trip" (ibid.).
70. *Interview with Hans-Jürgen Fischbeck* (Democracy Now), 3 July 1991, East Berlin.
71. A detailed description of the event is Gaus (1989:13–55).
72. B.V. Flow, "Church Synod Debates Increasing Emigration Requests in the GDR," Munich: *Radio Free Europe Research*, 24 September 1986, hectographed.
73. B.V. Flow, "The GDR's Approach to Emigration," Munich: *Radio Free Europe Research*, 30 July 1986, hectographed.
74. Barbara Donovan, "Is the East German Economy Running into Trouble?" Munich: *Radio Free Europe Research*, 13 April 1988, hectographed.
75. An East German expert said that the forgery of economic data became a sort of "social game" played from the shopfloor up to the politburo (Uhlmann, 1989:72). East German economic statistics also failed to disclose vital indicators such as balance of payments, im-

port and export figures, domestic use of national income, not to mention price and unemployment data (Barbara Donovan, "The East German Economy – What is Behind the Success Story?" Munich: *Radio Free Europe Research*, 26 February 1985, hectographed).

76. "In der DDR-Wirtschaft Zeichen einer Überanstrengung," *Frankfurter Allgemeine Zeitung*, 24 December 1987.

77. Quoted in *Deutschland-Archiv* 20(6) 1987, p. 656.

78. "Die Reformabstinenz der SED unter Begründungsdruck," *Neue Züricher Zeitung*, 26 July 1989.

79. Quoted in Barbara Donovan, "Fear of Change: The East German Dilemma," Munich: *Radio Free Europe Research*, 27 June 1988, hectographed. See also Stolpe's own account of this troubled period (Stolpe, 1992:143–74).

80. As Rüddenklau (1992:196) reports, the *Sputnik* ban provoked widespread indignation even outside the usual opposition circles, including local strikes and party defections.

81. In this light, the "baffling mixture of crackdown and backdown" observed by *The Economist* ("Sharing an Uncommon House," 23 April 1988) appears a bit less baffling.

82. The joint SED-SPD paper, entitled "The Struggle of Ideologies and Common Security," is reprinted in *Deutschland-Archiv* 21(1) 1988, 86–91. Apogee of the culture of *détente*, the paper revels in the imagery of "peace" and "security"; the word "freedom" does not appear once. While the paper became the fixpoint for a reformist faction in the SED (see Reissig, 1991:30–5), the party leadership left no doubt that it did not mean to abandon the language of class struggle. A few weeks after the paper was issued, Kurt Hager declared: "Our image of the enemy (*Feindbild*) is clear: we won't cease combat against the aggressive forces of imperialism and to consider them enemies and opponents of peace on earth" (quoted in *Deutschland-Archiv* 21(1) 1988, p. 93).

83. Quoted in V. Kusin, "Honecker on Reform and the German Question," Munich: *Radio Free Europe Research*, 30 September 1987, hectographed.

84. Previously, traveling to the West was restricted to a tiny number of foolproof cadres and GDR citizens above retirement age. The new practice was to grant generous travel permits to average citizens *below* retirement age also.

85. Quoted in *Welt am Sonntag* ("Westreisen führen in der DDR zu Unzufriedenheit", 13 December 1987).

86. It is important to note that the German word for those who wanted to leave was *Ausreiser* (departee), not *Emigrant* – as if to indicate that the move to West Germany occurred within the boundaries of one nation. The English term "would-be emigrant" is used here as a matter of convenience.

87. *Interview with Wolfgang Rüddenklau* (Ecology Library), 20 June 1991, East Berlin.

88. Ibid.

89. As Jens Reich (1991:33) describes the atmosphere of a society where

everybody seemed to be on the way out, "you felt like in a waiting-room of a train station, asking yourself when your own train would depart."

90. Joachim Garstecki, "Leben und bleiben in der DDR," *Die Zeit,* 5 April 1985.
91. "Die Schlaraffenlandbewegung," *Umweltblätter* (East Berlin), 12 February 1988, pp. 7f.
92. Ibid.
93. *Interview with Edgar Dusdahl* (New Forum), 26 July 1991, Leipzig.
94. John Torpey, *Interview with Günter Jeschonnek* (hectographed, Berlin 1991). I thank John Torpey for making this interview available to me.
95. *Interview with Wolfgang Templin* (IFM), 4 July 1991, East Berlin.
96. "In die falsche Republik," *Der Spiegel,* 25 January 1988. Eventually all exit-bound prisoners ended up in the "right" republic.
97. Some, like Bärbel Bohley, Werner Fischer, and Wolfgang Templin, were granted the right to return after a specified period. Bohley and Fischer returned in August 1988, Templin directly after the fall of the Wall in November 1989.
98. *Umweltblätter* (East Berlin), no. 2, 1988.
99. Reinhardt, Schult, "Gewogen und für zu leicht befunden," *Friedrichsfelder Feuermelder* (East Berlin), April 1988, pp. 1–7.

CHAPTER 5: A GERMAN REVOLUTION

1. Quoted in Dahrendorf (1990:27).
2. Echoing Nietzsche, Hannah Arendt (1963:20) argues that the violence in modern revolutions stems from the "problem of beginning" – the one element absent in the Eastern European revolutions.
3. Habermas's notion of catching-up revolution obscures, however, the one important novelty of the Eastern European revolutions: the overcoming of the political left versus right and socialism versus capitalism schema, which had accompanied modern politics since the French revolution and had found its apotheosis in the Bolshevist revolution. Why German intellectuals would not abandon this schema is discussed in Chapter 6.
4. See Bendix's (1977) classic study of nation-building and citizenship, and Dahrendorf's (1990) implicit application of it to the case of Eastern Europe.
5. See, for instance, Flora Lewis, "People Make History," *New York Times,* 29 December 1990, p. 13. For a sociological reflection, see Sztompka (1991).
6. From a Western left-wing perspective, a similar statement is Decker and Held (1989).
7. Albrecht Hinze, "DDR-Bürger demonstrieren für ihre Ausbürgerung," *Süddeutsche Zeitung,* 15 February 1988.
8. Barbara Donovan, "Emigration and Dissent in the GDR," Munich: *Radio Free Europe Research,* 16 February 1988, hectographed.
9. "Volkspolizei duldet in Leipzig Aktion von Ausreisewilligen," *Die Welt*

(Hamburg), 16 March 1988.
10. "Die Sicherheitsorgane in Ost-Berlin stellen sich Gottesdienstbesuchern in den Weg," *Frankfurter Allgemeine Zeitung,* 7 March 1988, p. 1.
11. "SED lässt Ausreisewillige vorladen," *Die Welt,* 7 April 1988.
12. See, for instance, Egon Bahr, "Auf die Sicherung des Friedens konzentrieren," *Vorwärts* (Bonn), 9 February 1985.
13. "Life-lie" is the word used by SPD Bundestag member Freimut Duve (quoted in Marlies Menge, "Wider die Sünde der Ausreise," *Die Zeit,* 21 April 1988). The case against abandoning the all-German citizenship is competently made by Kewenig (1987).
14. An internal party information stated that the new travel and emigration rules should strengthen the image of the GDR as a "cosmopolitan" (*weltoffen*) country. However, the new rules were not meant to install a "right" in the freedom of movement (*Freizügigkeit*); instead, they were seen as "an element in the securing of peace" (quoted in *Deutschland-Archiv,* vol. 22, no. 1, 1989, p. 118).
15. A would-be emigrant remembers: "Once the sanctions lessened, people became more assertive. And with the new travel and emigration rules our claims seemed suddenly justified. This fueled the emigration wave" (quoted in Joachim Nawrocki, "Gemüse ins Regal, Wahrheit in die Zeitung," *Die Zeit,* 18 August 1989, p. 3).
16. "Behutsamkeit Bonns in der DDR-Krise," *Neue Züricher Zeitung,* 9 October 1989.
17. The mass flight left whole sectors of the economy and infrastructure in disarray. By fall 1989, numerous bakeries, restaurants and retail stores had closed, small factories and shops could no longer meet orders, doctors, dentists and nurses were in short supply, and whole hospital departments had to be closed because of staff shortages (see Barbara Donovan, "The GDR's Emigration Problem: A Catalyst for Reform?", Munich: *Radio Free Europe Research,* 13 September 1989, hectographed).
18. An academic replication of this voice cosmology is Philipsen (1993).
19. *Interview with Reiner Flügge* (Democracy Now), 18 June 1991, East Berlin.
20. *Interview with Werner Fischer* (IFM), 27 Juni 1991, East Berlin.
21. *Interview with Erhart Neubert,* 15 June 1991, East Berlin.
22. The last sentence of this quote is taken from Albert Hirschman's translation (1993:195).
23. *Interview with Irena Kukutz,* 24 June 1991, East Berlin.
24. Quoted in "DDR-Opposition: Der lange Weg aus dem Ghetto," *Die Tageszeitung* (West Berlin), 6 September 1989.
25. *Interview with Bärbel Bohley,* 8 July 1992, East Berlin.
26. See Reich (1991:186).
27. Rolf Henrich, a lawyer and former SED-member, who wrote the second part of the founding manifesto, called the New Forum a "political platform" – well knowing that in Leninist parlance this meant "competing faction." The use of this term was certainly ironical, but also revealing. See Reich (1991:187).
28. A good review of the manifold literature on this subject is Jesse

(1990).

29. *Interview with Hans-Jürgen Fischbeck* (Democracy Now), 3 July 1991, East Berlin.
30. *Interview with Lutz Rathenow*, 2 July 1991, East Berlin.
31. *Interview with Pavel Strohner* (New Forum), 20 June 1991, East Berlin.
32. *Interview with Jens Reich*, 8 July 1991, East Berlin.
33. On the eve of the GDR's 40th anniversary celebration, New Forum leaders even urged their fellow citizens *not* to demonstrate, in fear of a violent clash with security forces. Serge Schmemann, "Dissident Movement in Spite of Itself," *New York Times*, 16 October 1989, p. 4.
34. *Interview with Erhart Neubert* (Democratic Awakening), 15 June 1991, East Berlin.
35. The following observations are based on interviews with key members of both Leipzig opposition groups.
36. See the precise observations by dissident Freya Klier: "We still believed in socialism, and gained strength by holding the socialist ideals against a flawed reality. Today's young generation no longer has this illusion" (Interview with Freya Klier and Stephan Krawczyk, *Die Welt*, 10 March 1988).
37. *Interview with Frank Sellentin* (IGL), 26 July 1991, Leipzig.
38. Ibid.
39. Most Leipzig opposition groups were represented in the church-based *Synodalausschuss für Frieden und Gerechtigkeit*. This provided the groups with the necessary church legitimation, but at the same time released them from direct supervision by a parish
40. *Interview with Rainer Müller* (AKG), 24 July 1991, Leipzig.
41. *Interview with Katrin Walter* (AKG), 25 July 1991, Dresden.
42. *Interview with Thomas Rudolph* (AKG), 25 July 1991, Dresden.
43. See Petra Bornhöft, "Ich bin das oberste Organ dieses Staates," *Die Tageszeitung*, 16 September 1989, p. 11.
44. *Ost-West-Diskussionsforum*, no. 4, November 1988, p. 8.
45. See Sievers (1990: 26–8); Feydt, Heinze, Schanz (1990).
46. *Ost-West-Diskussionsforum*, no. 6, 1988, p. 9.
47. Ibid., p. 10.
48. Ibid. In a meeting with Bishop Hempel, opposition groups could witness the orthodox cosmology of Saxony's Lutheran church. A participant remembers: "(Hempel declared) that the slogan 'freedom, equality, solidarity' did not belong into the church, because it was atheistic. In addition, according to Hempel, church visitors were not entitled to call for the self-liberation of the people, because liberation could only come from God" (quoted in Unterberg, 1991:129).
49. *Interview with Rainer Müller* (AKG), 24 July 1992, Leipzig.
50. Before that, would-be emigrants identified themselves by small white shreds of cloth attached to their car antennae. This harmless act was soon punished with heavy fines and licence withdrawal.
51. Dieter Dose, "Erst als der Stasi eingriff, wurde aus dem Leipziger Schweigemarsch lauter Protest," *Die Welt*, 15 March 1989.
52. See the documentation in Arbeitsgruppe Menschenrechte, ed. *Forum*

für Kirche und Menschenrechte (Leipzig), no. 2, 3 November 1989, pp. 52–5 (hectographed).

53. *Interview with Rainer Müller* (AKG), 24 July 1991, Leipzig.
54. See the documentation in *Ost-West-Diskussionsforum*, no. 8/9, October 1989.
55. Writer Christoph Hein coined this notion in his speech at the 4 November rally in East Berlin (see Schüddekopf, 1990:209).
56. Hungary's opening of its border with Austria occurred in two steps. In May, the border fortifications were removed, which greatly facilitated illegal border crossings. Since 10 September, East Germans were legally free to move on from Hungary to Austria.
57. The Reverend Johannes Richter of Leipzig's Thomas Church says: "In retrospect, it appears quite normal that those who stayed now had to articulate themselves, if they did not want to be stamped as dumb mass incapable of thinking" (quoted in Rein, 1989:184).
58. "Reisefreiheit statt Massenflucht," *Süddeutsche Zeitung*, 6 September 1989.
59. Petra Bornhöft, "Ausreiser und Bleiber marschieren getrennt," *Die Tageszeitung*, 6 September 1989; Karl-Heinz Baum, "Nach Giessen reisen oder Leipzig verändern," *Frankfurter Rundschau*, 6 September 1989.
60. Quoted in Bornhöft, see note 57.
61. *Interview with Thomas Rudolph* (AKG), 25 July 1991, Dresden.
62. The short declaration is reprinted in Rein (1989:171).
63. Serge Schmemann, "100,000 Protest in Leipzig in Largest Rally in Decades," *New York Times*, 17 October 1989.
64. *Interview with Ulrike Poppe* (Democracy Now), 9 July 1991, East Berlin.
65. Wolfgang Dore, "Eine halbe Million auf Leipzig's Strassen," *Die Tageszeitung*, 1 November 1989.
66. New Forum leader Sebastian Pflugbeil, quoted in Rein (1989:23). Another typical declaration goes as follows: "[Comrades], you claim to hold the leading role – exercise it!" (New Forum, 1989:8).
67. Pflugbeil, quoted in Rein (1989:23). One must keep in mind, however, that "what one thought and said was conditioned by what was *allowed* to be thought and said" (*Interview with Sebastian Pflugbeil*, 17 June 1991, East Berlin). And the margins of the allowed expanded with breathtaking speed. What may look harmless and polite today, was often daring and risky at the time.
68. Quoted in Baumann et al. (1990:159).
69. Of course, for Leninist Egon Krentz the "dialogue" protestations were camouflage. A secret tape documents how the freshly installed party chief addressed his comrades: "We have to exercise our leading role more skillfully; we are not prepared to give it up" (quoted in *Die Welt*, 28 November 1989).
70. *Demokratie Jetzt* (East Berlin) no. 11, November 1989, hectographed.
71. Quoted in TAZ Journal (1990b:144).
72. Many of these platforms and declarations are reprinted in Schüddekopf (1990).
73. *Interview with Lutz Rathenow*, 2 July 1991, East Berlin.

74. Christa Wolf (1990:12) even invoked the notorious notion of "security partnership."
75. The 4 November rally was also notable for its denial of an Eastern European perspective. Participant Lutz Rathenow remembers that a representative of the Hungarian dissident group FIDES was initially not allowed to speak, obviously because he was suspected of anticommunist intentions: "I noticed then that no one of the organizers was interested in Eastern Europe. Because of the exclusion of Eastern Europe, the plea for the GDR was caught in a German perspective. Indeed, this had to be an unwitting plea for Germany, which gave the event a certain tragicomic note" (*Interview*, 2 July 1992, East Berlin).
76. Klaus Hartung, "Die Wut in Leipzig nimmt zu," *Die Tageszeitung*, 8 November 1989.
77. Quoted in Serge Schmemann, "Emigres are Given Passage to West," *New York Times*, 5 November 1989, p. 1.
78. *Interview with Irena Kukutz*, 24 June 1991, East Berlin.
79. Few saw this as clearly as Ludwig Mehlhorn of Democracy Now: "The opposition did not want to save anything of the old SED regime. But we needed independent statehood in order to pursue the inner democratization" (quoted in TAZ Journal, 1990b:96).
80. Quoted in Gwertzman and Kaufman (1990:178).
81. Heiner Müller, East Germany's foremost playwright, bluntly admits his "leftist illusion": "We were for the Wall, so that we could then start the open debate about everything" (quoted in Ernst-Otto Mätzke, "DDR-Schriftsteller trauern um die Zukunft...," *Frankfurter Allgemeine Zeitung*, 27 March 1990).
82. New Forum leader Sebastian Pflugbeil, quoted in Serge Schmemann, "Opposition Sees Blessing and Threat," *New York Times*, 13 November 1989.
83. The "Four Our Country" appeal is reprinted in Schüddekopf (1990:240f).
84. *Interview with Sebastian Pflugbeil*, 17 June 1991, East Berlin.
85. See Barbara Donovan, "The GDR in 1989," Munich" *Radio Free Europe Research*, 5 December 1989, hectographed.
86. Quoted in "Die Macht liegt auf der Strasse," *Der Spiegel*, 11 December 1989.
87. *Interview with Jens Reich*, 8 July 1991, East Berlin.
88. *Interview with Erhart Neubert*, 15 June 1991, East Berlin.
89. See Matthias Geis, "Neues Forum: Keine Einheit für die Einheit," *Die Tageszeitung*, 29 January 1990.
90. Interview with Edelbert Richter, *Die Tageszeitung*, 16 September 1989.
91. Walter Süss, "Die Wendehälse der Revolution," *Die Tageszeitung*, 8 March 1990.
92. *Interview with Gerd Poppe*, 26 June 1991, East Berlin.
93. *Interview with Ludwig Mehlhorn*, 3 July 1991, East Berlin.
94. Quoted in TAZ Journal (1990b:101).
95. Quoted in Mühler and Wilsdorf (1990:161).
96. Alexander Smoltczyk, "Hoffen auf den grossen Bruder," *Die Tages-

zeitung, 23 November 1989.

97. Western élite involvement was primarily conditioned by the "pull" factor of the GDR's collapse. In addition, there were several "push" factors such as the fact that 1990 was a federal election year, and the need to stop the unabated exit movement, which greatly taxed West Germany's budget and welfare facilities (see McAdams, 1990).

98. Observing the light-handed and playful post-Wall enthusiasm in Berlin, Robert Darnton (1991:118) even found that "the reunification of the two Germanies ... took its tone from the student movements and popular culture of the recent past, not from any deep-seated Teutonic natinalism."

99. The following analysis covers only the *"Central* Round Table" that met 16 times between 7 December and 12 March in East Berlin. Besides the Central Round Table, numerous local and regional round tables were set up between opposition groups and old regime.

100. *Interview with Gerd Poppe*, 26 June 1991, East Berlin.

101. *Interview with Erhart Neubert*, 15 June 1991, East Berlin.

102. A close observer of East German opposition politics rightly argues: "It is the weakness of the opposition that it never built up the SED as its political enemy" (Klaus Hartung, "Auflösung und Demokratisierung," *Die Tageszeitung*, 23 January 1990).

103. *Interview with Reinhardt Schult* (New Forum), 1 July 1991, East Berlin. Another New Forum representative at the Round Table expresses the same attitude: "Our attitude had in many ways been that the ones who got us into this mess should also now be responsible for getting us out of it" (quoted in Philipsen, 1993:325).

104. The best accounts of the history of the Round Table are Thaysen (1990) and Süss (1991). David Binder ("East German Party Proposes Talks with 'Other Forces'," *New York Times*, 23 November 1989, p. A16) erroneously reports that the SED had proposed to set up the Round Table; however, this impression was deliberately engineered by the party to underline its "dialogue" intentions.

105. The idea of a Round Table was first mentioned on October 27 in a church speech by Wolfgang Ullmann, a leader of Democracy Now. The speech is reprinted in Ullmann (1990:147–8).

106. Wolfgang Templin (1990:80) sees the Round Table as "part of a joint SED-government strategy to neutralize (*entschärfen*) the political force of an organized opposition."

107. *Interview with Erhart Neubert*, 15 June 1991, East Berlin.

108. The "new forces" included the New Forum, Democracy Now, Democratic Awakening, and the Initiative for Peace and Human Rights.

109. The aloof yet state-obedient mores of the church moderators at the Round Table reflected the ambiguous role the church had played in the larger society. Thaysen (1990:162), no unfriendly observer he, mocked the "almost courtly (*höfisch*) ceremonies" in which the church moderators "escorted" invited regime representatives in and out of the meeting room, and the obedient manner in which the latter were thanked for even the most trivial statements.

110. See Reinhardt Schult, "Die Ecken des Runden Tisches," *Die Andere*

(East Berlin), no. 1, 25 January 1990.

111. *Interview with Gerd Poppe*, 26 June 1991, East Berlin.

112. The Stasi itself is believed to have engineered the "neofascist smearings" ("Nationalism for a Europe of Free People" being one among them) that became the pretext for the Treptow demonstration (see Knütter, 1991:23). The whole affair was soon exposed as what it was – a last-ditch attempt to save the old regime (see Jürgen Leinemann, "'Verkrüppelt und gezeichnet'," *Der Spiegel*, 22 January 1990).

113. The New Forum obtained a secret document of the Stasi headquarters of Gera ("Call For Action", dated 9 December) that seemed to be a direct call for a putsch. The document is reprinted in Thaysen (1990:60f).

114. The ultimatum was incited by an outrageous Round Table appearance of a regime spokesman on security affairs, who pretended "not to know" where the central data bank of the Stasi was located (Süss, 1991:472).

115. *Interview with Lutz Rathenow*, 2 July 1991, East Berlin.

116. Like so many others in this tumultuous period, Modrow invoked the *détente* notion of "security partnership" (Thaysen, 1990:64).

117. Because the doors of the besieged Stasi building were opened from the inside, it is believed that the Stasi itself, in a last manifestation of its perverse fantasy, had engineered the rampage in order to destroy incriminating materials ("Stürmte die Stasi die eigene Zentrale?" *Frankfurter Allgemeine Zeitung*, 5 August 1991, p. 3).

118. "The new election date was a decision between me and the SPD," admits Hans Modrow (in Thaysen, 1990:91).

119. *Interview with Ludwig Mehlhorn*, 3 July 1991, East Berlin.

120. In April 1990, the first freely elected People's Chamber refused to consider the Round Table's constitution outline, because it justifiably considered constitutional matters its own prerogative.

121. I borrow this nice variation on Brecht's poem "The Solution" from Timothy Garton Ash (1990e).

122. *Interview with Wolfgang Apfeld*, 24 June 1991, East Berlin.

123. Ludwig Mehlhorn, "Unfähigkeit zu politischen Handeln," *Die Tageszeitung*, 21 June 1990.

124. For this reason, I find Mary Fulbrook's (1987, 1992) attempts unconvincing in drawing a kind of parallel history between West Germany and East Germany, where the deficiency of each appears as mirror image of the deficiency of the other. This obscures the fundamental difference between a democratic and a Leninist regime: that only the former stands the test of the "*plebiscite de tous les jours*" (Renan, 1964). From Fulbrook's accounts one would not know why one half-Germany collapsed, but not the other.

125. Quoted in *Bündnis 2000* (East Berlin), 26 July 1991, p. 20.

126. *Interview with Bärbel Bohley*, 8 July 1991, East Berlin.

127. Bärbel Bohley, "Neues Forum – Bürger für Bürger oder Anhängsel der Fraktion?" *Regenbogen* (East Berlin), no. 1, 19 July 1990, p. 2.

128. Konrad Weiss, "Die Bürgerbewegungen als Erinnerungsvereine an

den Deutschen Herbst," *Demokratie Jetzt* (East Berlin), 40, 17 October 1990, p. 5.
129. See, for instance, Joppke (1993:77–89).
130. *Demokratie Jetzt* (East Berlin), no. 36, 5 September 1990.
131. *Demokratie Jetzt* (East Berlin), no. 13, February 1990, p. 2.
132. *Interview with Sebastian Pflugbeil,* 17 June 1991, East Berlin.
133. "Citizens for Citizens" was the major slogan of the Alliance 90 in the federal election campaign of fall 1990.
134. Jens Reich, "Bürgerbewegungen als politischer Faktor der Zukunft?" *Neues Forum Bulletin* (East Berlin), no. 4, 14 January 1991.
135. Gunter Hofmann, "Des Ostens gesammelte Verwunderung," *Die Zeit,* 16 August 1991, p. 3.
136. Stephan Bickhardt, "Revolutionsromantik oder Neuformierung." *Demokratie Jetzt* (East Berlin), no. 37, 19 September 1990, p. 3.
137. *Neues Forum Bulletin* (East Berlin), no. 7, 10 April 1991, p. 8.
138. In a similar way, Gregor Gysi ("Die ungewollten Verwandten," *Der Spiegel* no. 24, 1991, pp. 34–8) depicts the GDR as a (rather idyllic) "personal" society. "In the GDR," the smart PDS leader knows, "we were somehow all important, at least we could perceive ourselves this way" (p. 38).
139. *Interview with Sebastian Pflugbeil,* 17 June 1991, East Berlin.

CHAPTER 6: WHY WAS THERE NO "DISSIDENCE" IN EAST GERMANY

1. Adam Ulam's (1992) magisterial history of communism after World War II comes to the same conclusion.
2. Tocqueville (1955) delivered the prototype of a sociology of intellectuals that does not take the universalistic claims of intellectuals at face value, but grounds them in particular group interests. He was followed, among others, by Max Weber (1977), Schumpeter (1942), Gouldner (1979), and Bourdieu (1984).
3. Edmund Burke, the first modern counter-intellectual, spoke of "geometrical policy" (Burke, 1987:201).
4. In this regard, Francis Fukuyama's (1989) controversial thesis of the "end of History" (with capital "H") is undoubtedly true. In the twentieth century battle between communism, fascism and liberalism, it is liberalism that has emerged as the winner.
5. For instance, Pollack (1990b), Torpey (1992), and Hirschman (1993) himself.
6. "National discourse" is understood here as the invocation of national symbolism and rhetoric to express demands for individual rights and collective self-determination.
7. Quoted in Philipsen (1993:139).
8. The "logic of fields" is elaborated in Bourdieu and Wacquant (1992:94–115).
9. Quoted in Bracher (1971:381).
10. For European nationalism in general, see Hobsbawm (1990). Among

the numerous studies of German nationalism, I found particularly helpful Krockow (1970), Alter (1986), Hughes (1988), and Dann (1992).

11. Lutz Rathenow, quoted in Torpey (1993a:259).

12. The importance of economic success in German national identity is stressed by James (1989).

13. The best study of Weimar nationalism remains Sontheimer (1992), which was originally published in 1962.

14. Interview with Andrzej Szczypiorski, in *Bündnis 2000* (East Berlin), vol. 1, no. 10, 19 April 1991, p. 19.

15. As we will see below, this does not mean that there was no *empirical* continuity of certain (less desirable) patterns of culture and political traditions.

16. Already in May 1951 denazification officially ended with a law that granted an amnesty to all former Nazi Party members (see Borneman, 1992:231).

17. Quoted in Aust (1986:54). The neo-Marxist "new social movement" literature overlooks this generational aspect of West Germany's protest culture. Excellent accounts of West German protest movements from a generational perspective are Elias (1992:300–389) and Borneman (1992:ch.8).

18. A typical historiographical example is Benser (1985).

19. The founding myth is to be seen in the negative light of Renan's remark, because it obscures the dictatorial principles on which the GDR was based from the start. The "anti-fascism" formula also hides obvious inconsistencies in the opposition of communism to fascism, such as the Hitler–Stalin pact, the persecution of many "anti-fascists" who deviated from the party line, or the creation of a pseudo-nationalist party – the NDPD – to tacitly integrate ex-Nazis into the GDR (see Fippel, 1992).

20. Quoted in Emmerich (1989:113).

21. Quoted in Anz (1991:255).

22. Quoted in *TAZ-Journal*, vol. 2, 1990, p. 22 (emphasis added).

23. Quoted in Emmerich (1989:422).

24. Tony Judt (1992:178) observed a similar "anti-anticommunist" orientation among French intellectuals after World War II. Not unlike the German case, the French "anti-anticommunism" pays tribute to the prominent role of communists in the resistance to Hitler.

25. This is also the reason why most West German GDR-research, as pioneered by Peter Christian Ludz, is essentially apologetic. See Jäckel (1990).

26. "Radical break" was premised on Marxist fascism theory, according to which fascism and Nazism were the logical culmination of capitalism. This theory was also widely shared by West German intellectuals (see the popular treatise by Kühnl, 1971).

27. Quoted in Grunenberg (1990:44).

28. Quoted in Dieter Zimmer, "Die Verbitterung," *Die Zeit*, 10 July 1992, p. 14.

29. Quoted in Augstein and Grass (1990:59).

30. This is evident if one looks at the biographies of some of these dissidents, most of whom had privileged backgrounds and initially had set out on promising academic or professional careers. Typical examples are Gerd Poppe, who was unable to take up a position in the prestigious Academy of Sciences because of his protest against the Biermann expatriation, and then worked in various manual jobs; Wolfgang Templin, a trained philosopher, who was forced out of the Academy of Sciences in 1983, and then was unable to find work; Ludwig Mehlhorn, a mathematician, who was driven from his position at the élite Hochschule für Ökonomie in 1985, and then worked in various church-supported jobs, including as a night-watchman (short biographies of these and other dissidents are provided by Torpey, 1993a:419–29). Most of these "blocked ascendents" became closely affiliated with the "Initiative for Peace and Human Rights."

31. Ludwig Mehlhorn, quoted in Philipsen (1993:88).

32. *Interview with Edgar Dusdahl* (New Forum), 26 July 1991, Leipzig.

33. Gerd Poppe, quoted in Rüddenklau (1992:112f).

34. *Interview with Gerd Poppe*, 26 June 1991, East Berlin.

35. An example are the harsh attacks by former dissidents on Manfred Stolpe, the former church secretary and now Minister President of Brandenburg, who has been accused of conspiring with the Stasi. The dissidents had previously considered Stolpe an ally in their fight against hardliners in and outside the church. Now he appears to them as a "representative of a German–German diplomat conglomerate" – which is not intended to be a compliment (Lutz Rathenow, "Alles geht seinen weiteren Gang," *Der Spiegel*, no. 10, 1993, pp. 73–8).

36. "Thesen zur Aufklärung der Vergangenheit", *Deutschland Archiv* 25(4), 1992, pp. 445–7.

37. I owe this reference to John Torpey (1993b:20, fn.12).

38. In the post-communist Czech republic, by contrast, the infamous "lustration laws" originated not from the ex-dissidents, but from those who had "kept quiet" under the old regime. This reflects the greater political role played by the ex-dissidents in the new Czech republic (they simply have better things to do), as well as a tacit need of the opportunistic majority to smirch the more daring dissident élite with the suspicion of collaboration (see Lawrence Weschler, "The Velvet Purge: The Trials of Jan Kavan," *The New Yorker*, 19 October 1992, pp. 66–9).

39. See Klaus Poche, "Die Zeugen leben noch," *Die Zeit*, 17 April 1992, p. 14.

40. Reinhardt Schult, "Gewogen und für zu leicht befunden," *Friedrichsfelder Feuermelder* (East Berlin), April 1988, p. 6, hectographed.

41. Ulrich Greiner, "Der Potsdamer Abgrund," *Die Zeit*, 22 June 1990. The cozy relationship between the West and East German Writers' Unions is illuminated by Noll (1992).

42. Quoted in Le Gloannec (1989:111).

43. See Fuchs (1990:68) and the interview with Biermann ("Die DDR ist ein Erziehungsheim", *Die Tageszeitung*, 21 August 1989).

44. Note, however, that the word "pseudo-left" wants to convey that a

truly "leftist" regime could not be a dictatorship.

45. Among the East German dissidents interviewed by the author in summer 1991, only the exiled dissident responded to the question whether she clonsidered herself a German with an unambiguous "yes" (*Interview with Freya Klier*, 25 June 1991, West Berlin). In a similar way, the young writer Uwe Kolbe, who moved to the West with a special visa in 1987 and then spent some time in the United States, admitted that "the word 'Germany'" existed for him only since he had seen "both parts of the previous unity, and other parts of the world as well" (Kolbe, 1990:69).

46. Ulrich Oevermann (1990) makes this point most forcefully.

47. The historic-analytical concept of *sonderweg* has been sharply criticized by Blackbourn and Eley (1984).

48. Norbert Elias (1969) has shown that the distinction between culture and civilization was originally a domestic one: "It is the polemic of the German educated middle class against the mannerisms of the aristocratic upper class" (p. 9). Because these mannerisms, from dress to language, were unmistakably French, the domestic could be easily transposed into a national distinction.

49. The best short treatment of this topic is Greiffenhagen (1986).

50. See the excellent recent study on the "conservative revolution" by Stefan Breuer (1993).

51. This connection is convincingly elaborated by Meuschel (1992: part I).

52. "It is our fate that our political origin does not lie in the event of a founding (*Gründungsereignis*)," wrote Karl Jaspers (1966:68), shortly before the student movement shook the Federal Republic. Rödel et al. (1989:74–82) then argued that this movement, along with the other "new social movements", accomplished the "retroactive founding" of the Federal Republic in terms of building a democratic civil society. This argument is questionable for two reasons. First, the notion of founding conveys a temporal rupture and conscious collective act of beginning that cannot be replaced by the *gradual* and *implicit* changes produced by these movements. Second, these movements lacked a national orientation, without which the founding of a political collectivity is not even thinkable in the modern world of nation-states.

53. Quoted in Torpey (1993a:325).

54. Peter Graf Kielmansegg's good discussion of the "legitimacy of unification" makes the same point (Kielmansegg, 1993:573).

55. Here I agree with Martin Walser, "Deutsche Sorgen", *Der Spiegel*, no. 26, 1993, pp. 40–7.

56. Quoted in Stürmer (1992:11).

Appendix

METHODS AND DATA

This study follows the canon of Weberian interpretive-historical sociology. As the study of a single case, it tries to give an in-depth account of the origins, trajectory, and impact of the East German dissident movement, although in the comparative light of parallel Eastern European movements. A Weberian approach is committed to the interpretation of meaning as embedded in structural context. This suggests an eclectic research design that mixes interview analysis, archival work, and the use of secondary sources.

Between June and August 1991, I conducted about 35 qualitative interviews with dissidents and opposition leaders in Berlin, Leipzig and Dresden. The interviews (see the following list) are between 60 and 200 minutes long and have been tape-recorded and transcribed with permission of the interviewees. Though the sample was constructed as a snowball sample, several criteria determined the selection of interview partners. First, I tried to cover the entire movement spectrum, which includes long-involved 'veteran' dissidents, only recently mobilized members of the new citizen groups emerging in the fall of 1989 (such as New Forum or Democracy Now), protestant priests and theologians opening their churches to opposition groups, and literary intellectuals who watched the movement from the side-lines, but with sympathy. Second, in order to avoid an overly Berlin-centered point of view, I conducted an additional set of interviews in Leipzig and Dresden. This proved to be an important corrective, because the relationship between "voice" oppositionists and "exit" constituencies (*Ausreisewillige*) differed significantly in the south of the former GDR.

In addition to conducting interviews, I obtained a rich primary data basis from archival and private sources, including classified documents of the secret police that was spying on the dissident movement. The Ecology Library (*Umweltbibliothek*) in East Berlin provided me with an overview of the samizdat publications in the former GDR.

In June 1992, I visited the archives of Radio Free Europe in Munich, which provided me with a large amount of newspaper articles and RFE background information on East Germany and Eastern Europe.

INTERVIEWS

Wolfgang Apfeld, *Democracy Now*, 24 June 1991, East Berlin.
Michael Bartoszek, *Democracy Now*, 19 June 1991, East Berlin.
Bärbel Bohley, founder of the *New Forum*, 8 July 1991, East Berlin.
Daniela Dahn, writer and novelist, 26 June 1991, East Berlin.
Edgar Dusdahl, *Arbeitskreis Solidarische Kirche* and *New Forum*, 26 July 1991,

Leipzig.

Peter Eisenfeld, *Ökumenischer Friedenskreis Dresden*, 1 August 1991, West Berlin.

Ralf Ellsässer, *Arbeitskreis Umweltschutz* and *Eco-Lion*, 24 July 1991, Leipzig.

Hans-Jürgen Fischbeck, *Democracy Now*, 3 July 1991, East Berlin.

Werner Fischer, *Initiative for Peace and Human Rights* (IFM), 27 June 1991, East Berlin.

Reiner Flügge, *Democracy Now*, 18 June 1991, East Berlin.

Jörg Hildebrandt, *Democracy Now*, 19 June 1991, East Berlin.

Ralph Hirsch, co-founder of IFM, 10 July 1991, West Berlin.

Werner Hülsemann, church officer for youth affairs, 1 July 1991, East Berlin.

Carlo Jordan, *Network Arche* and *Green Liga*, 16 July 1991, East Berlin.

Freya Klier, writer and theater director, 25 June 1991, West Berlin.

Irena Kukutz, *Women for Peace* and *New Forum*, 24 June 1991, East Berlin.

Ludwig Mehlhorn, *Democracy Now*, 3 July 1991, East Berlin.

Rainer Müller, *Arbeitskreis Gerechtigkeit* (AKG) and IFM, 24 July 1991, Leipzig.

Ehrhart Neubert, *Democratic Awakening*, 15 June 1991, East Berlin.

Rudi Pahnke, theologian, 24 June 1991, East Berlin.

Sebastian Pflugbeil, *New Forum*, 17 June 1991, East Berlin.

Gerd Poppe, IFM and *Alliance 90* (member of the Bundestag), 26 June 1991, East Berlin.

Ulrike Poppe, *Women for Peace* and *Democracy Now*, 9 July 1991, East Berlin.

Lutz Rathenow, writer and novelist, 2 July 1991, East Berlin.

Jens Reich, *New Forum*, 8 July 1991, East Berlin.

Thomas Rudolph, *Arbeitskreis Gerechtigkeit* (AKG) and *New Forum*, 25 July 1991, Dresden.

Wolfgang Rüddenklau, founder of the Ecology Library, 20 June 1991, East Berlin.

Reinhardt Schult, *Peace Circle Friedrichsfelde* and *New Forum*, 1 July 1991, East Berlin.

Frank Sellentin, *Initiativgruppe Leben* (IGL), 26 July 1991, Leipzig.

Reverend Hans Simon, Zion Church, 25 June 1991, East Berlin.

Pavel Strohner, *New Forum*, 20 June 1991, East Berlin.

Wolfgang Templin, co-founder of IFM, 4 July 1991, East Berlin.

Katrin Walter, *Arbeitskreis Gerechtigkeit* (AKG) and *New Forum*, 25 July 1991, Dresden.

Werner Wiemann, *Democracy Now* and *Free Democratic Party*, 1 July 1991, West Berlin.

ARCHIVES

Die Andere, East Berlin.
Ecology Library, East Berlin.
House of Democracy, East Berlin.
Die Tageszeitung, West Berlin.
Archive of the Initiative for Peace and Human Rights, Leipzig.
Radio Free Europe/Radio Liberty, Munich.

Bibliography

Alexeyeva, Ludmilla. 1987. *Soviet Dissent.* Middletown, Conn.: Wesleyan University Press.

Almond, Gabriel A. 1954. *The Appeals of Communism.* Princeton: Princeton University Press.

Alter, Peter. 1986. "Nationalbewusstsein und Nationalstaat der Deutschen," *Aus Politik und Zeitgeschichte,* 4 January, pp. 17–30.

Alter, Peter. 1992. "Nationalism and German Politics after 1945," in John Breuilly, ed. *The State of Germany.* London: Longman.

Anderson, Benedict. 1983. *Imagined Communities. Reflections on the Origin and Spread of Nationalism.* London: Verso.

Anderson, Sascha and Elke Erb, eds. 1985. *Berührung ist nur eine Randerscheinung. Neue Deutsche Literatur aus der DDR.* Cologne: Kiepenheuer und Witsch.

Anz, Thomas, ed. 1991. *"Es geht nicht um Christa Wolf." Der Literaturstreit im vereinten Deutschland.* Munich: Edition Spangenberg.

Arato, Andrew and Mihaly Vajda. 1980. "The Limits of the Leninist Opposition. Reply to David Bathrick." *New German Critique* 19, pp. 167–175.

Arendt, Hannah. 1951. *The Origins of Totalitarianism.* New York: Harcourt.

Arendt, Hannah. 1958. *The Human Condition.* Chicago: University of Chicago Press.

Arendt, Hannah. 1963. *On Revolution.* New York: Viking Press.

Armstrong, John. 1988. "Toward a Framework for Considering Nationalism in Eastern Europe." *Eastern European Politics and Societies* 2, 280–305.

Aron, Raymond. 1962. *The Opium of the Intellectuals.* New York: Norton.

Aron, Raymond. 1967. *Eighteen Lectures on Industrial Society.* London: Weidenfeld and Nicolson.

Aron, Raymond. 1990. *Democracy and Totalitarianism.* Ann Arbor: University of Michigan Press.

Ash, Timothy Garton. 1981. *"Und willst du nicht mein Bruder sein..." Die DDR heute.* Hamburg: Spiegel Verlag.

Ash, Timothy Garton. 1983. *The Polish Revolution: Solidarity.* New York: Vintage.

Ash, Timothy Garton. 1990. *The Uses of Adversity.* New York: Vintage.

Ash, Timothy Garton. 1990a. "Eastern Europe: The Year of Truth." *New York Review of Books,* 15 February, pp. 17–22.

Ash, Timothy Garton. 1990c. "The German Question." In Ash, *Uses of Adversity,* op. cit.

Ash, Timothy Garton. 1990d. *The Magic Lantern.* New York: Random House.

Ash, Timothy Garton. 1990e. "East Germany: The Solution." *New York Review of Books,* 26 April, pp. 14–20.

Ash, Timothy Garton. 1990f. "Germany Unbound," *New York Review of Books,* 22 November, pp. 11–15.

Asmus, Ronald D. 1983a. "Is there a Peace Movement in Eastern Europe?" *Radio Free Europe Research,* Background Report 213, 2 September.

Asmus, Ronald D. 1983b. "Is there a Peace Movement in the GDR?" *Orbis,* Summer, pp. 301–41.

Asmus, Ronald D. 1983c. "Dresden 1983 and the Peace Movement in the GDR." *Radio Free Europe Research* Background Report 37, 21 February.

Asmus, Ronald D. 1983d. "Jena: An Atypical City in the GDR?" *Radio Free Europe Research,* Background Report 76, 8 April.

Asmus, Ronald D. 1983e. "Further Expulsions of Peace Activists in the GDR." *Radio Free Europe Research,* Background Report 128, 6 June.

Asmus, Ronald D. 1984. "What Future for the 'Peace Movement' in the GDR?" *Radio Free Europe Research,* Background Report 127, 13 July.

Asmus, Ronald D. 1985. "The Dialectics of Detente and Discord: The Moscow–East Berlin–Bonn Triangle." *Orbis,* Winter, pp. 743–74.

Augstein, Rudolf and Günter Grass. 1990. *Deutschland, einig Vaterland?* Göttingen: Steidl.

Aust, Stefan. 1986. *Der Baader Meinhof Komplex.* Hamburg: Hoffmann und Campe.

Bahr, Egon. 1981. "Zehn Thesen über Frieden und Abrüstung." In Hans Apel et al., *Sicherheitspolitik contra Frieden.* Berlin: Dietz.

Bahr, Egon. 1991. *Sicherheit für und vor Deutschland.* Munich: Hanser.

Bahr, Egon. 1992. "Indem ich durch diese Hölle gegangen bin." *Die Zeit,* no. 12, 20 March, p. 19.

Bahro, Rudolf. 1977. *Die Alternative.* Hamburg.

Baring, Arnulf. 1972. *Uprising in East Germany: June 17, 1953.* Ithaca, NY: Cornell University Press.

Baring, Arnulf. 1989. *Unser neuer Grössenwahn. Deutschland zwischen Ost und West.* Stuttgart: Deutsche Verlags-Anstalt.

Bathrick, David. 1978. "The Politics of Culture: Rudolf Bahro and the Opposition in the GDR." *New German Critique* 15, pp. 3–24.

Bauman, Zygmunt. 1987. "Intellectuals in East-Central Europe: Continuity and Change." *Eastern European Politics and Societies* 1, pp. 162–186.

Baumann, Eleonore et al. 1990. *Der Fischer Weltalmanach. Sonderband DDR.* Frankfurt: Fischer.

Baylis, Thomas. 1972. "East Germany. In Quest of Legitimacy." *Problems of Communism* 21, pp. 46–55.

Baylis, Thomas. 1974. *The Technical Intelligentsia and the East German Elite.* Berkeley: University of California Press.

Baylis, Thomas. 1986. "Explaining the GDR's economic strategy." *International Organization* 40(2), pp. 381–420.

Beck, Ulrich. 1991. "Opposition in Deutschland." In: Bernd Giesen and Claus Leggewie, eds. *Experiment Vereinigung.* Berlin: Rotbuch.

Bender, Peter. 1989. *Deutsche Parallelen.* Berlin: Siedler.

Bendix, Reinhard. 1977. *Citizenship and Nation-Building.* Berkeley and Los Angeles: University of California Press.

Benser, Günter. 1985. *Die KPD im Jahre der Befreiung.* East Berlin: Dietz.

Beyme, Klaus von. 1991. "The Legitimation of German Unification between National and Democratic Principles." *German Politics and Society,* no. 22, pp. 1–17.

Bickhardt, Stephan, ed. 1988. *Recht ströme wie Wasser.* Berlin: Wichern Verlag.

Bickhardt, Stephan et al. 1988. *Spuren. Zur Geschichte der Friedensbewegung in der DDR.* East Berlin: hectographed.

Biermann, Wolf. 1992. *Ein deutsch–deutscher Liedermacher.* Los Angeles: Goethe Institute.

Bilandzic, Dusan et al. 1990. "Post-Communist Eastern Europe: A Survey of Opinion." *East European Politics and Societies* 4(2), pp. 153–205.

Blackbourn, David and Geoff Eley. 1984. *The Peculiarities of German History.* Oxford: Oxford University Press.

Blanke, Thomas and Rainer Erd, eds. 1990. *DDR – Ein Staat vergeht.* Frankfurt: Fischer.

Böttger, Uwe-Eckart. 1989. "Stichwort: Reise und Ausreise." *Deutschland Archiv* 22(1), pp. 24f.

Bohrer, Karl-Heinz. 1991. "Why We are Not a Nation – And Why We Should Become One," *New German Critique*, no. 52, pp. 72–83.

Borneman, John. 1992. *Belonging in the Two Berlins. Kin, State, Nation.* New York: Cambridge University Press.

Bourdieu, Pierre. 1984. *Homo Academicus.* Paris: Minuit.

Bourdieu, Pierre and Loic Wacquant. 1992. *An Introduction to Reflexive Sociology.* Chicago: University of Chicago Press.

Bracher, Karl Dietrich. 1971. *Das deutsche Dilemma.* Munich: Piper.

Bradley, James. 1982. "Prague Spring 1968 in Historical Perspective." *East European Quarterly* 16(3), pp. 257–76.

Brandt, Heinz. 1970. *The Search for a Third Way.* Garden City, NY: Doubleday.

Brandt, Peter and Herbert Ammon, eds. 1981. *Die Linke und die nationale Frage.* Reinbek: Rowohlt.

Brown, J.F. 1988. *Eastern Europe and Communist Rule.* Durham, NC: Duke University Press.

Breuer, Stefan. 1993. *Anatomie der Konservativen Revolution.* Darmstadt: Wissenschaftliche Buchgesellschaft.

Breuilly, John, ed. 1992. *The State of Germany.* London: Longman.

Brown, Archie and Jack Gray, eds. 1977. *Political Culture and Political Change in Communist States.* London: Macmillan.

Brown, Archie and Gordon Wightman. 1977. "Czechoslovakia: Revival and Retreat." In: Brown and Gray, op. cit.

Brown, J.F. 1988. *East Europe and Communist Rule.* Durham, NC: Duke University Press.

Brubaker, Rogers. 1992. *Citizenship and Nationhood in France and Germany.* Cambridge, Mass.: Harvard University Press.

Brubaker, Rogers. 1994. "Nationhood and the National Question in the Soviet Union and Post-Soviet Eurasia." *Theory and Society* 23(1), pp. 47–78.

Brückner, Peter. 1978. *Versuch, uns und anderen die Bundesrepublik zu erklären.* Berlin: Wagenbach.

Brzezinski, Zbigniew. 1989. *The Grand Failure.* New York: Scribner's.

Bubner, Rüdiger. 1991. "Brauchen wir einen Begriff der Nation?" In Petra Braitling and Walter Reese-Schäfer, eds. *Universalismus,*

Nationalismus und die neue Einheit der Deutschen. Frankfurt: Fischer.

Büscher, Wolfgang and Peter Wensierski. 1984. *Null Bock auf DDR.* Reinbek: Rowohlt.

Bugajski, Janusz and Maxine Pollack. 1989. *East European Fault Lines.* Boulder, Colo.: Westview Press.

Bunce, Valerie. 1990. "The Struggle for Liberal Democracy in Eastern Europe." *World Policy Journal* 7, pp. 395–430.

Burawoy, Michael and Janos Lukacs. 1992. *The Radiant Past.* Chicago: University of Chicago Press.

Burens, Peter-Claus. 1981. *Die DDR und der 'Prager Frühling'.* Berlin: Duncker und Humblot.

Burke, Edmund. 1987. *Reflections on the Revolution in France.* Buffalo, NY: Prometheus.

Burks, R.V. 1961. *The Dynamics of Communism in Eastern Europe.* Princeton University Press.

Childs, David. 1983. *The GDR: Moscow's German Ally.* London: Unwin Hyman.

Chirot, Daniel. 1991. "What Happened in Eastern Europe in 1989?" in D.Chirot, ed. *The End of Leninism and the Decline of the Left.* Seattle: University of Washington Press.

Cohen, Jean and Andrew Arato. 1992. *Civil Society and Political Theory.* Cambridge, Mass.: MIT Press.

Cohen, Stephen F. 1985. *Rethinking the Soviet Experience.* New York: Oxford University Press.

Connor, Walker. 1984 *The National Question in Marxist-Leninist Theory and Strategy.* Princeton, NJ: Princeton University Press.

Conze, Werner and Dieter Groh. 1966. *Die Arbeiterbewegung in der nationalen Bewegung.* Stuttgart: Klett.

Craig, Gordon A. 1982. *The Germans.* New York: Putnam's Sons.

Croan, Melvin. 1962. "East German Revisionism: The Spectre and the Reality." In: Leopold Labedz, ed. *Revisionism.* New York: Praeger.

Croan, Melvin. 1980. "Eurocommunism and East Germany." In: Vernon V. Aspaturian, Jiri Valenta, and David P.Burke, eds. *Eurocommunism Between East and West.* Bloomington: Indiana University Press.

DDR-Komitee für Menschenrechte, ed. 1985. *Schriften und Informationen.* no. 2.

Dahl, Robert. 1973. "Introduction." In: R. Dahl, ed. *Regimes and Oppositions.* New Haven: Yale University Press.

Dahn, Daniela. 1987. *Kunst und Kohle.* Frankfurt am Main: Luchterhand.

Dahrendorf, Ralf. 1959. *Class and Class Conflict in Industrial Society.* Stanford: Stanford University Press.

Dahrendorf, Ralf. 1971. *Gesellschaft und Demokratie in Deutschland.* München: DTV.

Dahrendorf, Ralf. 1974. "Citizenship and Beyond," *Social Research,* Winter, pp. 673–701.

Dahrendorf, Ralf. 1988. *The Modern Social Conflict.* New York: Weidenfeld and Nicolson.

Dahrendorf, Ralf. 1990. *Reflections on the Revolution in Europe.* New York: Random House.

Dallin, Alexander and George W. Breslauer. 1970. "Political Terror in the Post-Mobilization Stage." In: Chalmers Johnson, ed. *Change in Communist Systems.* Stanford: Stanford University Press.

Dallin, Alexander and George W.Breslauer. 1970a. *Political Terror in Communist Systems.* Stanford: Stanford University Press.

Dann, Otto. 1992. *Nation und Nationalismus in Deutschland 1770–1990.* Munich: Beck.

Darnton, Robert. 1991. *Berlin Journal 1989–1990.* New York: Norton.

Decker, Peter and Karl Held. 1989. *DDR kaputt-Deutschland ganz.* München: Resultate Verlag.

Diedrich, Torsten. 1991. *Der 17. Juni 1953 in der DDR.* Berlin: Dietz Verlag.

Dirks, Walter. 1946. "Die Zweite Republik." *Frankfurter Hefte* 1(1), pp. 12–24.

Dirks, Walter. 1950. "Der restaurative Charakter der Epoche." *Frankfurter Hefte* 5(9), pp. 942–54.

Djilas, Milovan. 1957. *The New Class.* New York: Praeger.

Döhnert, Albrecht and Paulus Rummel. 1990. "Die Leipziger Montagsdemonstrationen." In: W.J. Grabner et al., op. cit.

Domdey, Horst. 1993. "Die DDR als Droge." *Deutschland Archiv* 26(2), pp. 161–9.

Donovan, Barbara. 1988. "Is the East German Economy Running into Trouble?" Munich: *Radio Free Europe Research*, 13 April, hectographed.

Donovan, Barbara. 1989. "Reform and the Existence of the GDR," Munich: *Radio Free Europe Research*, 24 August, hectographed.

Drakulic, Slavenka. 1993. *How We Survived Communism and Even Laughed.* New York: Harper-Collins.

Dubiel, Helmut. 1991. "Deutsche Vergangenheiten." *Frankfurter Rundschau.* 6 July, p. ZB3.

Dubiel, Helmut. 1991b. "Beyond Mourning and Melancholy on the Left." *Praxis International* 10(3/4).

Ehring, Klaus and Martin Dallwitz. 1982. *Schwerter zu Pflugscharen. Friedensbewegung in der DDR.* Reinbek: Rowohlt.

Eisenfeld, Bernd. 1978. *Kriegsdienstverweigerung in der DDR.* Frankfurt: Suhrkamp.

Ekiert, Grzegorz. 1991. "Democratization Processes in East Central Europe. *British Journal of Political Science* 21, pp. 285–313.

Elias, Norbert. 1969. *Über den Prozess der Zivilisation,* vol. 1. Bern and Munich: Francke.

Elias, Norbert. 1992. *Studien über die Deutschen.* Frankfurt: Suhrkamp.

Elon, Amos. 1992. "East Germany: Crime and Punishment," *New York Review of Books,* 14 May, pp. 6–11.

Elvers, Wolfgang and Hagen Findeis. 1990. *Was ist aus den politisch alternativen Gruppen geworden?* Leipzig: Karl-Marx-Universität, hectographed.

Emmerich, Wolfgang. 1989. *Kleine Literaturgeschichte der DDR.* Frankfurt: Luchterhand.

Engelmann, Bernt et al., eds. 1982. *"Es geht, es geht..." Zeitgenössische Schriftsteller und ihr Beitrag zum Frieden.* München: Goldmann.

Erbe, Günter. 1987. "Schriftsteller in der DDR." *Deutschland Archiv* 20(11), pp. 1162–79.

Evans, Sarah. 1980. *The Personal is Political.* New York: Vintage.

Falcke, Heino. 1985. "Unsere Kirche und ihre Gruppen." *Kirche im Sozialismus,* no. 4, pp. 145–52.

Faust, Siegmar. 1980. *In welchem Lande lebt Mephisto?* München: Olzog.

Feher, Ferenc. 1988. "Eastern Europe's Long Revolution Against Yalta." *Eastern European Politics and Societies* 2, pp. 1–34.

Feher, Ferenc and Agnes Heller. 1986. "Eastern Europe Under the Shadow of a New Rapallo." *New German Critique* no. 35, pp. 7–57.

Feidt, Sebastian, Christiane Heinze, and Martin Schanz. 1990. "Die Leipziger Friedensgebete." In: W.J. Grabner, op. cit.

Field, Mark, ed. 1976. *Social Consequences of Modernization in Communist Societies.* Baltimore: Johns Hopkins University Press.

Findeis, Hagen. 1990. "Überblick über die sozialethisch engagierten Gruppen in Leipzig Anfang 1989." In: W.J. Grabner et al., op. cit.

Fippel, Günter. 1992. "Der Missbrauch des Faschismus-Begriffs in der SBZ/DDR." *Deutschland Archiv* 25(10), pp. 1055–65.

Flacks, Richard. 1988. *Making History.* New York: Columbia University Press.

Förster, Peter and Günter Roski. 1990. *DDR zwischen Wende und Wahl.* Berlin: LinksDruck Verlag.

Franke, Konrad. 1971. *Die Literatur der DDR.* Munich: Kindler.

Fricke, Karl Wilhelm. 1976. "Die SED und die europäische KP Konferenz." *Deutschland Archiv* 9(7), pp. 673–7

Fricke, Karl Wilhelm. 1984. *Opposition und Widerstand in der DDR.* Cologne: Verlag Wissenschaft und Politik.

Fricke, Karl Wilhelm. 1987. "Die DDR auf dem Weg zum Rechtsstaat?" *Deutschland Archiv* v. 20 n. 8, pp. 788–91.

Friedrich, Carl F. and Zbigniew K. Brzezinski. 1965. *Totalitarian Dictatorship and Autocracy.* Cambridge, Mass.: Harvard University Press.

Friedrich, C.F., M.Curtis, and B.Barber. 1969. *Totalitarianism in Perspective: Three Views.* New York: Praeger.

Friedrich, Walter. 1990. "Mentalitätswandlungen der Jugend in der DDR." *Aus Politik und Zeitgeschichte* B16/17, pp. 25–37.

Fritze, Lothar. 1990. "Ausreisemotive," *Leviathan* no. 1, pp. 39–54.

Fritze, Lothar. 1991. "Der Traum der Intellektuellen." *Sinn und Form* 43(3).

Fuchs, Jürgen. 1984. *Einmischung in eigene Angelegenheiten.* Reinbek: Rowohlt.

Fuchs, Jürgen. 1990. *". . . und wann kommt der Hammer?".* East Berlin: Basis Druck.

Fukuyama, Francis. 1989. "The End of History?" *The National Interest,* Summer, pp. 3–18.

Fulbrook, Mary. 1987. "The State and the Transformation of Political Legitimacy in East and West Germany since 1945." *Comparative Studies in Society and History* 29(2), pp. 211–44.

Fulbrook, Mary. 1989. "From "Volksgemeinschaft" to Divided Nation: German National Identities and Political Cultures since the Third Reich," *Historical Research* 62(148), pp. 193–213.

Fulbrook, Mary. 1992. "Nation, State and Political Culture in Divided

Germany, 1945–1990." In: John Breuilly, ed. *The State of Germany.* London: Longman.

Furet, François. 1990. "1789–1917, Rückfahrkarte." *Transit* 1, pp. 48–62.

GDR Ministry for State Security. 1986. *Aktuelle Erfahrungen und Erkenntnisse bei der Bekämpfung feindlich-negativer Kräfte und Gruppierungen politischer Untergrundtätigkeit in der Hauptstadt Berlin.* East Berlin, 15 September, hectographed.

GDR Ministry for State Security. 1988. *Erfahrungen bei der Beeinflussung feindlich-negativer Personenzusammenschlüsse* (Diploma thesis by Stasi officer T.Rieger). East Berlin, 1 April, hectographed.

GDR Ministry for State Security. 1989. *Erfahrungen, Möglichkeiten und Grenzen beim Einsatz gesellschaftlicher Kräfte gegen Aktivitäten politischer Untergrundtätigkeit.* East Berlin, 22 February, hectographed.

Gaus, Günter. 1981. *Texte zur deutschen Frage.* Darmstadt: Luchterhand.

Gaus, Günter. 1986. *Wo Deutschland liegt.* München: Deutscher Taschenbuch Verlag.

Gaus, Günter. 1989. *Deutschland im Juni.* München: Deutscher Taschenbuch Verlag.

Gedmin, Jeffrey. 1992. *The Hidden Hand. Gorbachev and the Collapse of East Germany.* Washington: American Enterprise Institute Press.

Geertz, Clifford. 1973. *The Interpretation of Cultures.* New York: Basic Books.

Gellner, Ernest. 1983. *Nations and Nationalism.* Ithaca, NY: Cornell University Press.

Gellner, Ernest. 1990. "The Dramatis Personae of History." *East European Politics and Societies* 4(1), pp. 116–33.

Geremek, Bronislaw. 1991. "Between Hope and Despair." In: Graubard (1991).

Gesamtdeutsches Institut. 1991. *Dokumentation zur politischen Justiz in der ehemaligen DDR* (by Peter Eisenfeld). Berlin: Gesamtdeutsches Institut.

Glässner, Gert-Joachim. 1988. "Politische Kultur und nationales Erbe in der DDR." In: Karl-Ernst Jeismann, ed. *Einheit-Freiheit-Selbstbestimmung.* Frankfurt am Main: Campus.

Glässner, Gert-Joachim. 1991. *Der schwierige Weg zur Demokratie.* Opladen: Westdeutscher Verlag.

Goeckel, Robert F. 1989. "Dissent and the Lutheran Church in Eastern Europe." In David Childs, Thomas A.Baylis, and Marilyn Rueschemeyer, eds. *East Germany in Comparative Perspective.* London: Routledge.

Goeckel, Robert F. 1990. *The Lutheran Church and the East German State.* Ithaca, NY: Cornell University Press.

Golla, Joachim and Hermann Josef Rodenbach. 1986. "Friedenssicherung und Menschenrechte," *Deutschland-Archiv* vol. 19 no. 5, pp. 492–96.

Gouldner, Alvin. 1979. *The Future of Intellectuals and the Rise of the New Class.* New York: Continuum.

Grabner, Wolf-Jürgen et al. 1990. *Leipzig im Oktober.* Berlin: Wichern.

Grass, Günter. 1990. *Deutscher Lastenausgleich.* Frankfurt: Luchterhand.

Grass, Günter. 1991. *Gegen die verstreichende Zeit.* Hamburg: Luchterhand.

Graubard, Stephen R., ed. 1991. *Eastern Europe. Central Europe. Europe.* Boulder, Colo.: Westview Press.

Greenfeld, Liah. 1985. "Nationalism and Class Struggle: Two Forces or

One?" *Survey* 29(3), pp. 153–74.

Greenfeld, Liah. 1992. *Nationalism. Five Roads to Modernity.* Cambridge, Mass.: Harvard University Press.

Greiffenhagen, Martin. 1986. "Intellektuelle in der deutschen Politik." In: M. Greiffenhagen, *Von Potsdam nach Bonn.* Munich: Piper.

Gress, David. 1985. *Peace and Survival.* Stanford, Calif.: Hoover Institution Press.

Griffith, William E. 1962. "The Decline and Fall of Revisionism in Eastern Europe." In: Leopold Labedz, ed. *Revisionism.* New York: Praeger.

Griffith, William E. 1978. *The Ostpolitik of the Federal Republic of Germany.* Cambridge, Mass.: MIT Press.

Griffith, William E. 1989. "The German Democratic Republic." In: W.E. Griffith, ed. *Central and Eastern Europe: The Opening Curtain?* Boulder, Color.: Westview Press.

Groh, Dieter and Peter Brandt. 1992. *"Vaterlandslose Gesellen." Sozialdemokratie und Nation, 1860–1990.* Munich: Beck.

Gross, Jan. 1989. "Social Consequences of War", *Eastern European Politics and Societies* 3(2), 198–214.

Grunenberg, Antonia, 1990. "Das Ende der Macht ist der Anfang der Literatur." *Aus Politik und Zeitgeschichte.* B44, 26 October, 17–26.

Günther, Thomas. 1992. "Die subkulturellen Zeitschriften in der DDR und ihre kulturgeschichtliche Bedeutung." *Aus Politik und Zeitgeschichte* B20, 8 May, pp. 27–36.

Gwertzman, Bernard and Michael T. Kaufman, eds. 1990 *The Collapse of Communism.* New York: Times Books.

Habermas, Jürgen. 1981. *Theorie des kommunikativen Handelns* vol. 2. Frankfurt: Suhrkamp.

Habermas, Jürgen. 1986. "Heinrich Heine und die Rolle des Intellektuellen in Deutschland," *Merkur* 40 (6), pp. 453–68.

Habermas, Jürgen. 1990. *Die nachholende Revolution.* Frankfurt: Suhrkamp.

Habermas, Jürgen. 1992. *Faktizität und Geltung.* Frankfurt: Suhrkamp.

Hacker, Jens. 1987. "SED und nationale Frage." In: Ilse Spittmann, ed. *Die SED in Geschichte und Gegenwart.* Cologne: Edition Deutschland Archiv.

Hammond, Thomas T. 1966. "Nationalism and National Minorities in Eastern Europe." *Journal of International Affairs* 20(1), pp. 9–31.

Hankiss, Elemer. 1990. *East European Alternatives.* Oxford: Clarendon Press.

Haraszti, Miklos. 1987. *The Velvet Prison. Artists Under State Socialism.* New York: Basic Books.

Harich, Wolfgang. 1993. *Keine Schwierigkeiten mit der Wahrheit.* Berlin: Dietz.

Hassner, Pierre. 1982. "Was geht in Deutschland vor?" *Europa Archiv.* no. 17, pp. 517–26.

Hassner, Pierre. 1983. "Zwei deutsche Staaten in Europa." In: Werner Weidenfeld, ed. *Die Identität der Deutschen.* Munich: Hanser.

Hauner, Milan. 1990. "Anti-Militarism and the Independent Peace Movement in Czechoslovakia." In Tismaneanu, *In Search of Civil Society,* op. cit.

Havemann, Robert. 1978. *Ein deutscher Kommunist.* Hamburg.

Havel, Vaclav. 1985. "Peace: The View from Prague." *New York Review of Books,* November 21, pp. 28–30.

Havel, Vaclav. 1988. "Anti-Political Politics." In: Keane (1988).
Havel, Vaclav. 1990. "The Power of the Powerless." In: V. Havel et al., *The Power of the Powerless.* Armonk, NY: Sharpe.
Heller, Agnes. 1990. "The End of Communism," *Thesis Eleven*, no. 27.
Heller, Frithjof. 1988. "Inoffizielle Publizistik in der DDR," *Deutschland-Archiv* vol. 21 no. 11, pp. 1188–96.
Henrich, Rolf. 1989. *Der vormundtschaftliche Staat.* Reinbek: Rowohlt.
Herf, Jeffrey. 1991. *War by Other Means.* New York: Free Press.
Herzinger, Richard and Heinz-Peter Preusser. 1991. "DDR-Literatur in der Tradition deutscher Zivilisationskritik," in Heinz Ludwig Arnold, ed. *Literatur in der DDR.* Munich: Edition Text und Kritik.
Heym, Stefan. 1982. "Memorandum zum Juni-Aufstand." In: Ilse Spittmann and Karl Wilhelm Fricke, eds. *17. Juni 1953.* Cologne: Edition Deutschland Archiv, pp. 149–53.
Heym, Stefan. 1988. *Nachruf.* Munich: Bertelsmann.
Heym, Stefan. 1990. "Aschermittwoch in der DDR." In: Michael Naumann, ed. *Die Geschichte ist offen.* Reinbek: Rowohlt.
Hilmer, Richard and Anne Köhler. 1989. "Der DDR läuft die Zukunft davon." *Deutschland Archiv*, vol. 22.
Hirsch, Ralf and Lew Kopelew, eds. 1989. *Grenzfall.* Berlin: Selbstverlag.
Hirschman, Albert O. 1970. *Exit, Voice, and Loyalty.* Cambridge, Mass.: Harvard University Press.
Hirschman, Albert O. 1993. "Exit, Voice, and the Fate of the German Democratic Republic." *World Politics* 45(2), pp. 173–202.
Hobsbawm, Eric. 1983. "Mass-Producing Traditions: Europe, 1870–1914." In: E.J. Hobsbawm and Terence Ranger, eds. *The Invention of Tradition.* New York: Cambridge University Press.
Hobsbawm, Eric. 1990. *Nations and Nationalism Since 1780.* Cambridge: Cambridge University Press.
Hoffmann, Lutz. 1990. *Die unvollendete Republik.* Cologne: Papy Rossa.
Hofmann, Michael and Dieter Rink. 1990. "Der Leipziger Aufbruch." In: W.J. Grabner et al., op. cit.
Holmes, Kim R. 1984. *The West German Peace Movement and the National Question.* Cambridge, Mass.: Institute for Foreign Policy Analysis.
Hörnigk, Frank. 1990. "Die künstlerische Intelligenz und der Umbruch der DDR." In: Ilse Spittmann, ed. *Die DDR auf dem Weg zur deutschen Einheit.* Cologne: Edition Deutschland Archiv.
Hughes, H.Stuart. 1958. *Consciousness and Society.* New York: Knopf.
Hughes, Michael. 1988. *Nationalism and Society: Germany 1800–1945.* London: Edward Arnold.
Huntington, Samuel P. 1968. *Political Order in Changing Societies.* New Haven: Yale University Press.
Huntington, Samuel P. 1970. "Social and Institutional Dynamics of One-Party Systems." In S.P. Huntington and Clement H. Moore, eds. *Authoritarian Politics in Modern Society.* New York: Basic Books.
Hyssen, Andreas. 1991. "After the Wall: The Failure of German Intellectuals." *New German Critique*, no. 52, pp. 109–43.
IFM. *See* Initiative für Frieden und Menschenrechte.
Initiative für Frieden und Menschenrechte, 1987. *Vorstellung der IFM zum*

Tag der Menschenrechte. East Berlin, 10 December, pamphlet.

Initiative für Frieden und Menschenrechte, 1988. *Fussnote.* East Berlin, July, hectographed.

Jäckel, Hartmut. 1990. "Unser schiefes DDR-Bild," *Deutschland Archiv* 23(10), pp. 1557–65.

Jäger, Manfred. 1976. "Das Ende einer Kulturpolitik. Die Fälle Kunze und Biermann." *Deutschland Archiv* 9(12), pp. 1233–9.

Jäger, Manfred. 1982. *Kultur und Politik in der DDR.* Cologne: Edition Deutschland Archiv.

Jänicke, Martin. 1964. *Der dritte Weg. Die antistalinistische Opposition gegen Ulbricht seit 1953.* Cologne: Neuer Deutscher Verlag.

James, Harold. 1989. *A German Identity, 1770–1990.* London: Weidenfeld and Nicolson.

Janka, Walter. 1990. *Schwierigkeiten mit der Wahrheit.* Reinbek: Rowohlt.

Janos, Andrew C. 1986. *Politics and Paradigms.* Stanford, Calif.: Stanford University Press.

Jansen, Silke. 1989. "Zwei deutsche Staaten-zwei deutsche Nationen?" *Deutschland Archiv* 22(10), pp. 1132–43.

Jaspers, Karl. 1960. *Freiheit und Wiedervereinigung.* Munich: Piper.

Jaspers, Karl. 1966. *Wohin treibt die Bundesrepublik?* Munich: Piper.

Jeschonnek, Günter. 1988a. "Ausreise," in: Kroh (1988).

Jeschonnek, Günter. 1988b. "Der 17. Januar 1988," *Deutschland Archiv* vol. 21 no. 8, pp. 849–54.

Jeschonnek, Günter. 1989. "Ideologischer Sinneswandel in der SED-Führung?" *Deutschland Archiv,* no. 1, pp. 278–83.

Jesse, Eckhard. 1990. "Oppositionelle in der DDR." *Zeitschrift für Parlamentsfragen,* no. 1, pp. 137–46.

Jesse, Eckhard. 1992. "Dritter Weg." In: Werner Weidenfeld and Karl-Rudolf Korte, eds. *Handwörterbuch zur deutschen Einheit.* Frankfurt: Campus.

Johnson, Chalmers. 1970a. "Comparing Communist Nations." In Johnson (1970b).

Johnson, Chalmers, ed. 1970b. *Change in Commmunist Systems.* Stanford, Calif.: Stanford University Press.

Jones, Merrill. 1993. "Origins of the East German Environmental Movement." *German Studies Review* 16(2), pp. 235–64.

Joppke, Christian. 1993. *Mobilizing Against Nuclear Energy. A Comparison of Germany and the United States.* Berkeley: University of California Press.

Jowitt, Ken. 1971. *Revolutionary Breakthroughs and National Development.* Berkeley: University of California Press.

Jowitt, Ken. 1975. "Inclusion and Mobilization in European Leninist Regimes." *World Politics* 28(1), pp. 69–96.

Jowitt, Ken. 1978. *The Leninist Response to National Dependency.* Institute of International Studies: University of California, Berkeley.

Jowitt, Ken. 1983. "Soviet Neotraditionalism: The Political Corruption of a Leninist Regime." *Soviet Studies* 35(3), pp. 275–97.

Jowitt, Ken. 1991. "The Leninist Extinction." In: Daniel Chirot, ed. *The Crisis of Leninism and the Decline of the Left.* Seattle: University of Washington Press.

Jowitt, Ken. 1992. *New World Disorder.* Berkeley: University of California Press.

Judt, Toni. 1988. "The Dilemmas of Dissidence: The Politics of Opposition in East-Central Europe." *Eastern European Politics and Societies* 2, pp. 185–240.

Judt, Toni. 1992. *Past Imperfect.* Berkeley: University of California Press.

Kagarlitsky, Boris. 1989. *The Thinking Reed.* London: Verso.

Kavan, Jan and Zdena Tomin, eds. 1983. *Voices from Prague. Czechoslovakia, Human Rights and the Peace Movement.* London: Palach Press.

Keane, John, ed. 1988. *Civil Society and the State.* London: Verso.

Kennedy. Michael. 1991. *Professionals, Power, and Solidarity in Poland.* New York: Cambridge University Press.

Kennedy, Michael. 1992. "The Intelligentsia in the Constitution of Civil Societies and Post-Communist Regimes in Hungary and Poland," *Theory and Society* 21, pp. 29–76.

Kewenig, Wilhelm A. 1987. "Die deutsche Staatsangehörigkeit – Klammer der Nation?" *Europa-Archiv,* no. 18, pp. 517–22.

Kielmansegg, Peter Graf. 1993. "Vereinigung ohne Legitimität?" *Merkur* 47(7), pp. 561–75.

Kinzer, Stephen. 1992. "East Germans Face Their Accusers," *New York Times Magazine,* April 12, pp. 24ff.

Klenner, Hermann. 1977. "Menschenrechte-Heuchelei und Wahrheit," *Einheit* (East Berlin), no. 9, pp. 1036–44.

Klessmann, Christoph. 1991. "Opposition und Dissidenz in der Geschichte der DDR." *Aus Politik und Zeitgeschichte* B5, 25 January, pp. 52–62.

Klier, Freya. 1989. *Abreisskalender.* München: Knaur.

Knabe, Hubertus. 1988. "Neue soziale Bewegungen im Sozialismus." *Kölner Zeitschrift für Soziologie und Sozialpsychologie,* vol. 40, pp. 551–69.

Knabe, Hubertus, ed. 1989. *Aufbruch in eine andere DDR.* Reinbek: Rowohlt.

Knütter, Hans-Helmuth. 1991. "Antifaschismus und politische Kultur in Deutschland nach der Wiedervereinigung." *Aus Politik und Zeitgeschichte* B9, 22 February, pp. 17–28.

Kocka, Jürgen. 1990. "Revolution und Nation 1989." *Tel Aviver Jahrbuch für deutsche Geschichte* 19, pp. 479–99.

Köhler, Anne and Volker Ronge. 1984. "Die DDR-Ausreisewelle im Frühjahr 1984," *Deutschland-Archiv,* no. 12 v. 17, pp. 1280–6.

Koestler, Arthur. 1941. *Darkness at Noon.* New York: Macmillan.

Kolakowski, Leszek. 1983. "Totalitarianism and the Virtue of the Lie." In: I. Howe, ed. *1984 Revisited.* New York: Harper and Row.

Kolakowski, Leszek. 1992. "Amidst Moving Ruins." *Daedalus* 121(2), pp. 43–56.

Kolbe, Uwe. 1990. "Ich war nicht darauf vorbereitet, ein Deutscher zu sein." In: Françoise Barthelemy and Lutz Winckler, eds. *Mein Deutschland findet sich in keinem Atlas.* Frankfurt: Luchterhand.

Konrad, Gyorgi. 1984. *Antipolitik. Mitteleuropäische Meditationen.* Frankfurt: Suhrkamp.

Konrad, Gyorgi and Ivan Szelenyi. 1979. *Intellectuals on the Road to Class Power.* New York: Harcourt.

Kornai, Janos. 1980. *The Economics of Shortage.* 2 vols. Amsterdam: North

Holland Publishing.

Kosing, Alfred. 1976. *Nation in Geschichte und Gegenwart.* East Berlin: Dietz Verlag.

Krisch, Henry. 1974. *German Politics under Soviet Occupation.* New York: Columbia University Press.

Krockow, Christian Graf von. 1970. *Nationalismus als deutsches Problem.* Munich: Piper.

Kroh, Ferdinand, ed. 1988. *Die Andersdenkenden in der DDR.* Berlin: Ullstein.

Krüger, Horst. 1977. "Fremde Heimat." *Merkur* 31(3), pp. 243–61.

Krüger, Ingrid, ed. 1982. *Berliner Begegnung zur Friedensförderung. Protokolle des Schriftstellertreffens am 13./14. Dezember 1981.* Darmstadt: Luchterhand.

Krüger, Ingrid, ed. 1983. *Zweite Berliner Begegnung "Den Frieden Erklären". Protokolle des zweiten Schriftstellertreffens am 22./23. April 1983.* Darmstadt: Luchterhand.

Kühnl, Reinhard. 1971. *Formen bürgerlicher Herrschaft.* Reinbek: Rowohlt.

Kuhrt, Eberhard. 1984. *Wider die Militarisierung der Gesellschaft: Friedensbewegung und Kirche in der DDR.* Melle: Knoth Verlag.

Kuhrt, Eberhard and Henning von Löwis. 1988. *Griff nach der deutschen Geschichte. Erbaneignung und Traditionspflege in der DDR.* Paderborn: Schöningh.

Kukutz, Irena and Katja Havemann. 1990. *Geschützte Quelle.* Berlin: Basis Druck.

Kundera, Milan. 1981. *The Book of Laughter and Forgetting.* New York. Penguin.

Kunze, Reiner. 1976. *Die wunderbaren Jahre.* Frankfurt am Main: Fischer.

Kuppe, Johannes L. 1989. "Zum 7. Plenum des ZK der SED," *Deutschland-Archiv* vol. 22 no. 1, pp. 1–7.

Kusin, Vladimir V. 1976. "An Overview of East European Reformism." *Soviet Studies* 28(3), pp. 338–61.

Labedz, Leopold, ed. 1962. *Revisionism.* New York: Praeger.

Land, Rainer, ed. 1990. *Das Umbaupapier (DDR).* Berlin: Rotbuch.

Le Gloannec, Anne-Marie. 1989. *La nation orpheline.* Paris: Calmann-Levy.

Lefort, Claude. 1986. *The Political Forms of Modern Society.* Cambridge, Mass.: MIT Press.

Lenin, V.I. 1932 (orig. 1917). *State and Revolution.* New York: International Publishers.

Lenin, V.I. 1969 (orig. 1902). *What is to be Done?.* New York: International Publishers.

Leonhard, Wolfgang. 1955. *Die Revolution entlässt ihre Kinder.* Cologne: Kiepenheuer and Witsch.

Lepenies, Wolf. 1990. "Fall und Aufstieg der Intellektuellen in Europa." *Neue Rundschau* 102(1), pp. 9–22.

Lepsius, M. Rainer. 1982. "Nation und Nationalismus in Deutschland." In: Heinrich A. Winkler, ed. *Nationalismus in der Welt von heute.* Göttingen: Vandenhöck und Ruprecht.

Lepsius, M. Rainer. 1989. "Das Erbe des Nationalsozialismus und die politische Kultur der Nachfolgestaaten des `Grossdeutschen Reiches.'" In: M. Haller, H.J. Hoffmann-Nowottny, and W. Zapf, eds. *Kultur und Gesellschaft.* Frankfurt am Main: Campus.

Lichtheim, George. 1961. *Marxism. An Historical and Critical Study.* New York: Praeger.

Linz, Juan. 1975. "Totalitarian and Authoritarian Regimes." In: Fred I. Greenstein and Nelson W. Polsby, eds. *Handbook of Political Science* Vol. 3. Reading, Mass.: Addison-Wesley.

Lipset, Seymour Martin. 1959. *Political Man.* Baltimore: Johns Hopkins University Press.

Löwenthal, Richard. 1970. "Development vs. Utopia in Communist Policy." In: Chalmers Johnson, ed. *Change in Communist Systems.* Stanford: Stanford University Press.

Löwenthal, Richard. 1976. "The Ruling Party in a Mature Society." In: Mark G. Field, ed. *Social Consequences of Modernization in Communist Societies.* Baltimore: Johns Hopkins University Press.

Ludz, Peter C. 1970. *The German Democratic Republic from the Sixties to the Seventies.* Center for International Affairs, Harvard University, November, Occasional Paper 26.

Ludz, Peter C. 1972. "Continuity and Change Since Ulbricht." *Problems of Communism* 21, pp. 56–67.

Ludz, Peter C. 1972. *The Changing Party Elite in East Germany.* Cambridge, Mass.: MIT Press.

Ludz, Peter C. 1977. *Die DDR zwischen Ost und West.* München: C.H. Beck.

Luhmann, Niklas. 1984. *Soziale Systeme.* Frankfurt: Suhrkamp.

Luhmann, Niklas. 1989. *Ecological Communication.* University of Chicago Press.

Lukes, Steven. 1985. *Marxism and Morality.* New York: Oxford University Press.

Lukes, Steven. 1991. *Moral Conflict and Politics.* Oxford: Clarendon Press.

Maier, Harry. 1989. "Klavierspielen mit Boxhandschuhen," *Die Zeit,* no. 11, pp. 35–6.

Malia, Martin. 1961. "What is the Intelligentsia?", in: Richard Pipes, ed. *The Russian Intelligentsia.* New York: Columbia University Press.

Malia, Martin. 1991. "To the Stalin Mausoleum." In: Graubard (1991).

Mann, Thomas. 1960. *Gesammelte Werke,* vols. 11 and 12. Frankfurt: Fischer.

Mann, Thomas. 1988 (orig. 1918). *Betrachtungen eines Unpolitischen.* Frankfurt: Fischer.

Mannheim, Karl. 1952. "The Problem of Generations." In: K. Mannheim, *Essays on the Sociology of Knowledge.* London: Routledge.

Markovits, Andrei. 1989. "Anti-Americanism and the Struggle for a West German Identity," in Peter H. Merkl, ed. *The Federal Republic of Germany at Forty.* New York: New York University Press.

Markovits, Andrei. 1992. "The West German Left in a Changing Europe." In: Christiane Lemke and Gary Marks, eds. *The Crisis of Socialism in Europe.* Durham, NC: Duke University Press.

Marshall, T.H. 1977. *Class, Citizenship, and Social Development.* New York: Doubleday.

Marx, Gary. 1975. "Thoughts on a Neglected Category of Social Movement Participant: The Agent Provocateur and the Informant," *American Journal of Sociology* 80(2), pp. 402–42.

Mayer, Hans. 1991. *Der Turm von Babel.* Frankfurt: Suhrkamp.

McAdams, A. James. 1985. *East Germany and Detente.* New York: Cambridge University Press.

McAdams, A. James. 1988. "The New Logic in Soviet-GDR Relations." *Problems of Communism* 37(5), pp. 47–60.

McAdams, A. James. 1990. "An Obituary for the Berlin Wall." *World Policy Journal,* vol. VII, no. 2, pp. 357–75.

McAdams, A. James. 1993. *Germany Divided.* Princeton, NJ: Princeton University Press.

McCarthy, John and Mayer Zald. 1977. "Resource Mobilization and Social Movements: A Partial Theory." *American Journal of Sociology* 82, pp. 1212–41.

Meinecke, Friedrich. 1970 (orig.1907). *Cosmopolitanism and the National State.* Berkeley: University of California Press.

Meuschel, Sigrid. 1983. "Neo-Nationalism and the West German Peace Movement's Reaction to the Polish Military Coup." *Telos,* no. 56, pp. 119–30.

Meuschel, Sigrid. 1991. "Wandel durch Auflehnung." In: Rainer Deppe, Helmut Dubiel, and Ulrich Röder, eds. *Demokratischer Umbruch in Osteuropa.* Frankfurt am Main: Suhrkamp.

Meuschel, Sigrid. 1992. *Legitimation und Parteiherrschaft in der DDR.* Frankfurt: Suhrkamp.

Meusel, Georg. 1988. "Königswalde und die Arbeit christlicher Friedensseminare." In Bickhardt, *Spuren,* op. cit.

Michel, Jeffrey H. 1987. "Economic Exchanges Specific to the Two German States." *Studies in Comparative Communism* 20(1), pp. 73–83.

Michnik, Adam. 1985. *Letters from Prison.* Berkeley and Los Angeles: University of California Press.

Michnik, Adam. 1991. "Nationalism," *Social Research* 58(4), pp. 757–63.

Milosz, Czeslaw. 1953. *The Captive Mind.* New York: Vintage.

Milowidow, A.S. and B.W. Safranow. 1978. *Die marxistisch-leninistische Ästhetik und die Erziehung der Soldaten.* East Berlin: Militärverlag der DDR.

Minogue, K.R. 1967. *Nationalism.* London: Batsford.

Mitter, Armin and Stefan Wolle, eds. 1990. *Befehle und Lageberichte des MfS Januar-November 1989.* Berlin: Basis Druck.

Mitter, Armin and Stefan Wolle. 1993. *Untergang auf Raten.* Munich: Bertelsmann.

Mleczkowski, Wolfgang. 1983. "In Search of the Forbidden Nation: Opposition by the Young Generation in the GDR." *Government and Opposition* 18(2), pp. 175–93.

Mohr, Heinrich. 1982. "Der 17. Juni als Thema der Literatur in der DDR." In: Ilse Spittmann and Karl Wilhelm Fricke, eds. *17. Juni 1953. Arbeiteraufstand in der DDR.* Cologne: Edition Deutschland Archiv.

Mommsen, Wolfgang J. 1990. *Nation und Geschichte.* Munich: Piper.

Moore, Barrington Jr. 1951. *Soviet Politics.* Cambridge, Mass.: Harvard University Press.

Moore, Barrington Jr. 1978. *Injustice. The Social Bases of Obedience and Revolt.* White Plains, NY: Sharpe.

Mühler, Kurt and Steffen H. Wilsdorf. 1990. "Meinungstrends in der Leipziger Montagsdemonstration." In: W.J. Grabner, op. cit.

Mühler, Kurt and Steffen H. Wilsdorf. 1991. "Die Leipziger Montagsdemonstration." *Berliner Journal für Soziologie*, special edition, pp. 37–45.
Müller, Heiner. 1990. *Zur Lage der Nation.* Berlin: Rotbuch.
Müller, Heiner. 1992. *Krieg ohne Schlacht.* Cologne: Kiepenheuer und Witsch.
Müller-Enbergs, Helmut. 1990. "DDR-Bürgerbewegung in der Krise." *Links*, no. 10, pp. 22–4.
Müller-Enbergs, H., M. Schulz and J. Wielgohs, eds. 1991. *Von der Illegalität ins Parlament.* East Berlin: Links Druck.
Münkler, Herfried. 1989. "Revolution als Fortschritt oder als Rückkehr?" *Aus Politik und Zeitgeschichte* B22, 26 May, pp. 15–23.
Naimark, Norman. 1979. "Is it True What They're Saying about East Germany?" *Orbis*, Fall, pp. 549–77.
Nee, Victor and David Stark, eds. 1989. *Remaking the Economic Institutions of Socialism.* Stanford, Calif.: Stanford University Press.
Nettl, J.P. 1970. "Ideas, Intellectuals, and Structures of Dissent." In: Philip Rieff, ed. *On Intellectuals.* Garden City, NY: Doubleday.
Neumann, Franz. 1957. "Notes on the Theory of Dictatorship." In: F.Neumann, *The Democratic and the Authoritarian State.* Glencoe, Ill.: Free Press.
New Forum. 1989. *Die ersten Texte des Neuen Forum.* East Berlin: hectographed.
Niethammer, Lutz. 1990. "Das Volk der DDR und die Revolution." In: Schüddekopf, op. cit.
Nisbet, Robert. 1974. "Citizenship: Two Traditions," *Social Research*, Winter, pp.612–37.
Noack, Paul. 1991. *Deutschland, Deine Intellektuellen.* Stuttgart: Bonn Aktuell.
Noll, Chaim. 1991. "Das lächerliche Pathos alter Schwärmer." In: Anz, op. cit.
Noll, Chaim. 1992. "Treue um Treue." In: Cora Stephan, ed. *Wir Kollaborateure.* Reinbek: Rowohlt.
O'Donnell, Guillermo and Philippe Schmitter. 1986. *Transitions from Authoritarian Rule. Tentative Conclusions about Uncertain Democracies.* Baltimore: Johns Hopkins University Press.
Oevermann, Ulrich. 1990. "Zwei Staaten oder Einheit?" *Merkur* 44(2), pp.91–106.
Offe, Claus. 1985. "New Social Movements: Challenging the Boundaries of Institutional Politics," *Social Research* 52, no. 4, pp. 817–68.
Offe, Claus. 1990b. "Vom taktischen Gebrauchswert nationaler Gefühle." *Die Zeit* 21 December, p.19.
Offe, Claus. 1991. "Prosperity, Nation, Republic," *German Politics and Society*, no.22, pp.18–32.
Offe, Claus and Ulrich Preuss. 1990. *Democratic Institutions and Moral Resources.* Zentrum für Sozialpolitik, University of Bremen. Working Paper no.5/90.
Parsons, Talcott. 1964. "Evolutionary Universals in Society," *American Sociological Review* 29, pp.339–57.
Philipsen, Dirk. 1993. *We Were the People.* Durham, NC: Duke University Press.

Pike, David. 1982. *German Writers in Soviet Exile.* Chapel Hill: University of North Carolina Press.

Pike, David. 1992. *The Politics of Culture in Soviet-Occupied Germany, 1945–1949.* Stanford, CA: Stanford University Press.

Piore, Michael and Charles Sabel. 1984. *The Second Industrial Divide.* New York: Basic Books.

Plessner, Helmuth. 1959. *Die verspätete Nation.* Stuttgart: Kohlhammer.

Polanyi, Karl. 1944. *The Great Transformation.* Boston: Beacon.

Pollack, Detlef, ed. 1990. *Die Legitimität der Freiheit. Politisch alternative Gruppen in der DDR unter dem Dach der Kirche.* Frankfurt: Peter Lang.

Pollack, Detlef. 1990b. "Das Ende einer Organisationsgesellschaft." *Zeitschrift für Soziologie* 19(4), 292–307.

Poppe, Gerd. 1988. "Zur Entwicklung des grenzüberschreitenden Dialogs." In: Bickhardt, *Spuren,* op. cit.

Poppe, Gerd. 1991. "Bürgerbewegung im Parlament." *Vorgänge* 110(2), pp.78–85.

Popper, Karl. 1966. *The Open Society and Its Enemies,* vol.1. Princeton, NJ: Princeton University Press.

Prager, Jeffrey. 1985. "Totalitarian and Liberal Democracy." In: Jeffrey C.Alexander, ed. *Neofunctionalism.* Beverly Hills: Sage.

Preuss, Ulrich. 1990. "Auf der Suche nach der Zivilgesellschaft." In: Blanke and Erd, op. cit.

Przeworski, Adam. 1986. "Some Problems in the Study of the Transition to Democracy." In: G,O'Donnell/P.Schmitter/ L.Whitehead, eds. *Transitions from Authoritarian Rule. Comparative Perspectives.* Baltimore: Johns Hopkins University Press.

Ramet, Sabrina P. 1991. *Social Currents in Eastern Europe.* Durham, NC: Duke University Press.

Reese-Schäfer, Walter. 1991. "Universalismus, negativer Nationalismus und die neue Einheit der Deutschen." In: Braitling and Reese-Schäfer, op. cit.

Reich, Jens. 1991. *Rückkehr nach Europa.* Munich: Hanser.

Rein, Gerhard, ed. 1985. *Deutsches Gespräch.* Berlin: Wichern.

Rein, Gerhard, ed. 1989. *Die Opposition in der DDR.* Berlin: Wichern.

Reissig, Rolf. 1991. "Der Umbruch in der DDR und das Scheitern des 'realen Sozialismus'," in: Rolf Reissig and Gert-Joachim Glässner, eds. *Das Ende eines Experiments.* Berlin: Dietz.

Renan, Ernest. 1964. "Qu'est-ce q'une nation" (orig.1882). In: Louis L.Snyder, ed. *The Dynamics of Nationalism.* Princeton, NJ: Van Nostrand.

Richert, Ernst. 1964. *Das zweite Deutschland. Ein Staat, der nicht sein darf.* Gütersloh: Mohn.

Richert, Ernst. 1967. *"Sozialistische Universität." Die Hochschulpolitik der SED.* Berlin: Colloquium.

Richter, Edelbert. 1988. "Fragen an das friedenspolitische Konzept der Sicherheitspartnerschaft." In Bickhardt, *Spuren,* op. cit.

Ringer, Fritz K. 1969. *The Decline of the German Mandarins.* Cambridge, Mass.: Harvard University Press.

Rödel, Ulrich et al. 1989. *Die demokratische Frage.* Frankfurt: Suhrkamp.

Ronge, Volker. 1990. "Die soziale Integration von DDR-Übersiedlern in der Bundesrepublik." *Aus Politik und Zeitgeschichte*, no.1, 5 January.

Roos, Peter, ed. 1977. *Exil. Die Ausbürgerung Wolf Biermanns aus der DDR.* Cologne: Kiepenheuer and Witsch.

Rosenthal, Rüdiger. 1988a. "Publizistische Gegenöffentlichkeit in der DDR." *Kirche im Sozialismus*, no.1, pp.14–16.

Rosenthal, Rüdiger. 1988b. "Gehen oder bleiben," *Ost-West-Diskussionsforum* no.2, pp.5–6.

Rothschild, Joseph. 1989. *Return to Diversity. A Political History of East Central Europe Since World War II.* New York: Oxford University Press.

Rüddenklau, Wolfgang. 1992. *Störenfried. DDR-Opposition 1986–1989.* Berlin: Basisdruck.

Rupnik, Jacques. 1988. "Totalitarianism Revisited." In: *Keane (1988).*

Rupnik, Jacques. 1989. *The Other Europe.* New York: Pantheon.

Rupnik, Jacques. 1990. "Eisschrank oder Fegefeuer," *Transit* 1(1), pp.132–41.

Russell, Bertrand. 1934. *Freedom versus Organization, 1814–1914.* London: Allen and Unwin.

Saab, Karim. 1988. "Fiktiver Brief nach Prag." In Bickhardt, *Spuren*, op. cit.

Schabowski, Günter. 1991. *Das Politbüro.* Reinbek: Rowohlt.

Schapiro, Leonard, ed. 1970. *Political Opposition in One-Party States.* New York: Wiley.

Schneider, Peter. 1993. "Gefangen in der Geschichte." *Der Spiegel*, no.3, pp.156–62.

Schnibben, Cordt. 1991. "Das bessere Deutschland." Part 1. *Der Spiegel* 15, pp.154–67.

Schoepflin, George. 1977. "Hungary: An Uneasy Stability." In: Brown and Gray, op. cit.

Schweigler, Gebhard. 1973. *Nationalbewusstsein in der BRD und der DDR.* Düsseldorf: Bertelsmann.

Schüddekopf, Charles, ed. 1990. *"Wir sind das Volk!".* Reinbek: Rowohlt.

Schulz, Marianne. 1991. "Neues Forum." In: Müller-Enbergs, Schulz, and Wielgohs, op. cit.

Schumpeter, Joseph. 1942. *Capitalism, Socialism and Democracy.* New York: Harper.

Selznick, Philip. 1952. *The Organizational Weapon.* New York: McGraw-Hill.

Serke, Jürgen. 1985. *Das neue Exil.* Frankfurt: Fischer.

Seton Watson, Hugh. 1962. "'Intelligentsia' und Nationalismus in Osteuropa 1848–1918." *Historische Zeitschrift* 195, pp.331–45.

Shils, Edward. 1970. "The Intellectuals and the Powers." In: Philip Rieff, ed. *On Intellectuals.* Garden City, NY: Doubleday.

Shtromas, A.Y. 1979. "Dissent and Political Change in the Soviet Union." *Studies in Comparative Communism* 12(2&3), pp.212–44.

Sievers, Hans-Jürgen. 1990. *Stundenbuch einer deutschen Revolution.* Göttingen: Vandenhöck and Ruprecht.

Skilling, H.Gordon. 1968. "Background to the Study of Opposition in Communist Eastern Europe." *Government and Opposition* 3(3), pp.294–324.

266   *Bibliography*

Skilling, H.Gordon. 1973. "Czechoslovakia's Interrupted Revolution." In: Robert Dahl, ed. *Regimes and Oppositions*. New Haven: Yale University Press.

Sloterdijk, Peter. 1990. *Versprechen auf Deutsch. Rede über das eigene Land*. Frankfurt am Main: Suhrkamp.

Smelser, Neil. 1962. *Theory of Collective Behavior*. New York: Free Press.

Smith, Anthony D. 1986. *The Ethnic Origins of Nations*. Oxford: Basil Blackwell.

Sodaro, Michael J. 1990. *Moscow, Germany, and the West from Khrushchev to Gorbachev*. Ithaca, NY: Cornell University Press.

Sontheimer, Kurt. 1982. "Zwei deutsche Republiken und ihre Intellektuellen," *Merkur* no.11, pp.1062–71.

Sontheimer, Kurt. 1992. *Antidemokratisches Denken in der Weimarer Republik*. Munich: DTV.

Sontheimer, Kurt and Wilhelm Bleek. 1975. *The Government and Politics of East Germany*. New York: St.Martin's Press.

Spittmann, Ilse. 1987. "Die SED und Gorbatschow," *Deutschland-Archiv* v.20 n.3, pp.225–228.

Staniszkis, Jadwiga. 1984. *Poland's Self-Limiting Revolution*. Princeton, NJ: Princeton University Press.

Staritz, Dietrich. 1985. *Geschichte der DDR. 1945–1985*. Frankfurt am Main: Suhrkamp.

Staritz, Dietrich. 1987. "Die SED und die Opposition." In· Ilse Spittmann, ed. *Die SED in Geschichte und Gegenwart*. Cologne: Edition Deutschland Archiv.

Starrels, John and Anita Mallinckrodt. 1975. *Politics in the German Democratic Republic*. New York: Praeger.

Stasi. *See* GDR Ministry for State Security.

Stern, Carola. 1963. *Ulbricht. Eine politische Biographie*. Cologne: Kiepenheuer and Witsch.

Stern, Fritz. 1961. *The Politics of Cultural Despair*. Berkeley: University of California Press.

Stinglwagner, Wolfgang. 1989. "Die wirtschaftliche Lage der DDR," *Deutschland-Archiv* no.2, pp.129–33.

Stolpe, Manfred. 1992. *Schwieriger Aufbruch*. Berlin: Siedler.

Stolz, Rolf, ed. 1985. *Ein anderes Deutschland*. Berlin: Edition Ahrens.

Stokes, Gale, ed. 1991. *From Stalinism to Pluralism*. New York: Oxford University Press.

Stürmer, Michael. 1992. *Die Grenzen der Macht*. Berlin: Siedler.

Süss, Walter. 1991. "Mit Unwillen zur Macht." *Deutschland Archiv* 24(5), pp.470–8.

Szelenyi, Ivan. 1986/7. "The Prospects and Limits of the East European New Class Project." *Politics and Society* 15(2), pp.103–44.

Szczypiorski, A. 1991. "Der verwandelte Staat." *Frankfurter Allgemeine Zeitung*, 10 August.

Szporluk, Roman. 1988. *Communism and Nationalism. Karl Marx versus Friedrich List*. New York: Oxford University Press.

Sztompka, Piotr. 1991. *Society in Action*. University of Chicago Press.

Talmon, J.L. 1961. *The Origins of Totalitarian Democracy*. New York: Praeger.

Tarrow, Sidney. 1989. *Struggle, Politics, and Reform.* Ithaca, NY: Cornell University, Western Societies Program; Occasional Paper 21.

Tarrow, Sidney. 1991. "Social Science and the Recent Rebellions in Eastern Europe." *PS: Political Science & Politics* 24(1), pp.12–20.

TAZ Journal. 1990a. *DDR Journal zur Novemberrevolution.* Berlin: Die Tageszeitung.

TAZ Journal. 1990b. *DDR Journal,* no.2. Berlin: Die Tageszeitung.

Templin, Wolfgang. 1988. "Bemerkungen zur politischen Orientierung in der Friedensbewegung," in: Bickhardt et al. (1988).

Templin, Wolfgang. 1989. "Zivile Gesellschaft," in: I.Spittmann, ed. *Die DDR im 40. Jahr.* Cologne: Edition Deutschland Archiv.

Templin, Wolfgang. 1990. "Die DDR-Opposition am runden Tisch." *Die Neue Gesellschaft/Frankfurter Hefte,* no.1, pp.77–80.

Templin, Wolfgang and Reinhard Weisshuhn. 1991. "Initiative Frieden und Menschenrechte," in: H.Müller-Enbergs, M.Schulz, and J.Wielgohs, eds. *Von der Illegalität ins Parlament.* Berlin: LinksDruck Verlag.

Thaysen, Uwe. 1990. *Der Runde Tisch.* Opladen: Westdeutscher Verlag.

Tilly, Charles. 1978. *From Mobilization to Revolution.* Englewood Cliffs: Prentice Hall.

Tismaneanu, Vladimir, ed. 1990a. *In Search of Civil Society. Independent Peace Movements in the Soviet Bloc.* New York: Routledge.

Tismaneanu, Vladimir. 1990b. "Against Socialist Militarism: The Independent Peace Movement in the GDR." In Tismaneanu, *In Search of Civil Society,* op. cit.

Tocqueville, Alexis de. 1955 (orig.1856). *The Old Regime and the French Revolution.* New York: Doubleday.

Torpey, John. 1992. "Two Movements, Not a Revolution: Exodus and Opposition in the East German Transformation, 1989–1990." *German Politics and Society,* no.26, pp.21–42.

Torpey, John. 1993a. *Intellectuals, Socialism, and Dissent: The East German Opposition and its Legacy.* Unpublished manuscript.

Torpey, John. 1993b. "The Post-Unification Left and the Appropriation of History." *German Politics and Society,* no.30, pp.7–20.

Touraine, Alain et al. 1983. *Solidarity.* Cambridge: Cambridge University Press.

Trommler, Frank. 1991. "Die nachgeholte Resistance." In: Justus Fetscher et al., *Die Gruppe 47 in der Geschichte der Bundesrepublik.* Würzburg: Königshauser and Neumann.

Trotsky, Leon. 1972 (orig.1937). *The Revolution Betrayed.* New York, NY: Pathfinder.

Tschiche, Hans. 1981. "Das Trauma der Bedrohung." *Kirche im Sozialismus,* no.4, pp.11ff.

Tucker, Robert. 1961. "Towards a Comparative Politics of Movement Regimes." *American Political Science Review* 55(2), pp.281–9.

Turner, Bryan S. 1990. "Outline of a Theory of Citizenship," *Sociology* 24(2), pp.189–217.

Tymowski, Andrzej. 1984. "Underground Solidarity and the Western Peace Movement." *Across Frontiers,* vol.1, no.2, 21–32.

Uhlmann, Steffen. 1989. "Missmanagement im SED-Staat," *Der Spiegel* no.25, 19 June, pp.72–9.

268   *Bibliography*

Ullmann, Wolfgang. 1990. *Demokratie–jetzt oder nie.* München: Kyrill and Method.

Unterberg, Peter. 1991. *Vorgeschichte, Entstehung und Wirkung des Neuen Forum in Leipzig.* Unpublished diploma thesis, University of Bochum.

Vajda, Mihaly. 1988. "East-Central European Perspectives." In: Keane (1988).

Verdery, Katherine. 1991. *National Ideology Under Socialism.* Berkeley: University of California Press.

Verdery, Katherine. 1993. "Whither 'Nation' and 'Nationalism'?" *Daedalus* 122(3), pp.37–46.

Voigt, Dieter et al. 1990. "Die innerdeutsche Wanderung und der Vereinigungsprozess." *Deutschland Archiv* 23(5), pp.732–46.

Volkmer, Werner. 1979. "East Germany: Dissenting Views during the Last Decade." In: Rudolf L.Toekes, ed. *Opposition in Eastern Europe.* Baltimore: Johns Hopkins University Press.

Vujacic, Veljko. 1990. *The Dual Revolution of Citizenship and Nationhood in Eastern Europe.* Unpublished manuscript.

Vujacic, Veljko and Victor Zaslavsky. 1992. "The Disintegration of Multinational Communist States: A Comparison of the Soviet and Yugoslav Case." *Telos.*

Walser Smith, Helmut. 1991. "Socialism and Nationalism in the East German Revolution." *East European Politics and Societies* 5(2), pp.234–46.

Walther, Joachim et al., eds. 1991. *Protokoll eines Tribunals.* Reinbek: Rowohlt.

Walzer, Michael. 1970. *Obligations: Essays on Disobedience, War, and Citizenship.* New York: Clarion.

Walzer, Michael. 1988. *The Company of Critics.* New York: Basic Books.

Weber, Hermann. 1978. "Der dritte Weg. Bahro in der Tradition der antistalinistischen Opposition." *Deutschland Archiv* 11(9), pp.921–7.

Weber, Hermann. 1985. *Geschichte der DDR.* München: DTV.

Weber, Max. 1973 (orig.1903). "Die 'Objektivität' sozialwissenschaftlicher und sozialpolitischer Erkenntnis." In Max Weber, *Gesammelte Aufsätze zur Wissenschaftslehre.* Tübingen: Mohr.

Weber, Max. 1977 (orig.1926). *Politik als Beruf.* Berlin: Duncker and Humblot.

Wehler, Hans-Ulrich. 1983. *Preussen ist wieder chic.* Frankfurt: Suhrkamp.

Weintraub, Jeffrey. 1990. *The Theory and Politics of the Public/Private Distinction.* Paper presented at the 1990 Annual Meeting of the American Political Science Association, San Francisco, California.

Wensierski, Peter. 1981. "Thesen zur Rolle der Kirchen in der DDR." *Kirche im Sozialismus*, no.5, p.24.

Wensierski, Peter and Wolfgang Büscher. 1983. "DDR-Jugendszene (III): Die Friedensbewegung." *Der Spiegel* 17 October 1983, no.42, pp.106–32.

Wielepp, Christoph. 1990. "Montags abends in Leipzig." In: Blanke and Erd, op. cit.

Wielgohs, Jan. 1993. "Auflösung und Transformation der ostdeutschen Bürgerbewegung." *Deutschland Archiv* 26(4), pp.426–34.

Willke, Helmut. 1992. *Ironie des Staates.* Frankfurt: Suhrkamp.

Wolf, Christa. 1990. *Reden im Herbst.* East Berlin: Aufbau-Verlag.
Wolschner, Klaus. 1982a. "Was bewegt die Friedensbewegung in der DDR?" In Bücher, Wensierski, Wolschner, *Friedensbewegung in der DDR,* op. cit.
Wolschner, Klaus. 1982b. "Die westliche Friedensbewegung und 'Schwerter zu Pflugscharen.'" *Kirche im Sozialismus,* no.5, 1982, pp.25–32.
Woods, Roger. 1986. *Opposition in the GDR under Honecker, 1971–85.* London: Macmillan.
Worst, Anne. 1991. *Das Ende eines Geheimdienstes.* Berlin: Links Druck.
Wyatt, Jiri. 1984. "Charter 77 after Poland," *Across Frontiers* 1(1), pp.4–7, 12.
Zander, Helmut. 1989. *Die Christen und die Friedensbewegungen in beiden deutschen Staaten.* Berlin: Duncker and Humblot.
Zimmermann, Hartmut. 1978. "The GDR in the 1970's." *Problems of Communism* 27, pp.1–40.
Zinoviev, Alexander. 1985. *Homo Sovieticus.* London: Victor Gollancz.

Index